Andrew Leete Stone

Memorial Discourses

Andrew Leete Stone

Memorial Discourses

ISBN/EAN: 9783337817374

Printed in Europe, USA, Canada, Australia, Japan

Cover: Foto ©Thomas Meinert / pixelio.de

More available books at **www.hansebooks.com**

MEMORIAL DISCOURSES.

BY

REV. A. L. STONE, D. D.,

Late Pastor of the Park Street Church.

BOSTON:
PUBLISHED BY HENRY HOYT,
No. 9 Cornhill.
1866.

Entered, according to Act of Congress, in the year 1866, by
HENRY HOYT,
In the Clerk's Office of the District Court of Massachusetts.

DEDICATION.

To the members of Park Street Church and Society, to whom seventeen years of happy fellowship with them in the service of the gospel have united the author in bonds which no absence or distance can sever, this volume, as an echo of the ministrations to which they have listened so kindly and so long, is most gratefully and affectionately dedicated.

PREFACE.

Not "dead, but absent," it was no thought of mine to be "still speaking" to my former congregation of Park Street, or the larger community on whose patient audience I have so often trespassed. But some of my brethren in the pulpits of Boston and its vicinity, and not a few of the people to whom I have ministered so many years, and hold fast to my heart by so many ties, desired me to leave behind me, as I migrated to a distant part of the country, something which should be to them a memorial of the labors among them which had thus come to an end. There was no reason why I should not comply with this request except my doubt whether these pages would have any other value to them, or others, than that which their partial friendship should attach to them, and this they overruled.

They are selected and grouped by no especial law, but as fitly enough representing and continuing the endeavor of the writer to bring the *profitableness* of "all Scripture" before those with whose spiritual nurture he was charged.

May they yet be tributary to the Christian growth and comfort of all who, for friendship's sake, or Christ's, shall search them for the truth that honors the Master and saves the soul.!'

A. L. STONE.

CONTENTS.

GOD — THE GOVERNOR	1
THE WORK OF NEW ENGLAND IN THE FUTURE OF THE COUNTRY	14
GOD'S DELAY TO PUNISH	46
THE SABBATH IN THE FAMILY	58
KNOWING CHRIST	86
GOD AND THE WORLD RECONCILED	102
WEARING CHRIST'S GARMENTS	115
CHRIST'S CUP	127
WAITING	142
INCOMPLETENESS OF LIFE	154
JOHN'S FAILURE	167
FRIENDSHIP	181
FAITH'S VENTURES	197
PLEA FOR THE MONTHLY CONCERT	212
HUMAN LONELINESS	229
THE MINISTRIES OF TIME	242
SORROWS OF JESUS	258
BALANCE SHEET; OR, TAKING ACCOUNT OF STOCK	266
ALL-SUFFICIENCY OF CHRIST	279

SERMONS.

I.

GOD — THE GOVERNOR.

FOR THE KINGDOM IS THE LORD'S: AND HE IS THE GOVERNOR AMONG THE NATIONS. — Psalm xxii. 28.

THERE are some very special advantages now, in the attitude of the public mind, for considering and appreciating the principles and procedures of the divine government among men. It is to be feared that we are not always in sympathy with God in his estimate of the sacredness of Law, and his measures to preserve or restore its inviolability. That estimate we sometimes look upon as mysterious or extravagant, and those measures as high-handed, sanguinary, and cruel.

It is a grand thing for us, in that great contest of arms in which the nation is engaged, that our stand is on the side of loyalty. There are men as earnest, and perhaps as sincere and conscientious, on the other side. But the whole force of their position and the entire current of their sympathies concur to make not law, but rebellion against it, sacred to them; not the maintenance of government, but its overthrow; not the preservation of Union, but its destruction. The whole educational power of the movement upon them is toward demoralization and lawlessness. It loosens from about their hearts the bands of governmental restraints, all binding sanctities of covenants and compacts and oaths of fealty; makes it right and obligatory in their view to assail, tear down, and subvert the majestic fabric of constitutional authority, and the public order which it guards; changes deceit, treachery, and robbery from crimes to virtues; and presents, on the other side, no countervailing rights and sanctities defended and established, no imperilled liberties fought for and bled for, to offset and neutralize the awful nurture of revolutionary and treasonable violence.

But every outlook of ours upon the great struggle is from the heights of the capitol. We are with the government. We stand for the laws. We sustain the appointed and legitimate administration. We strike at hydra-headed anarchy. For, let this rebellion prevail, and government is impossible. All bands of allegiance are like tow touched by fire. Compacts of confederation are ropes of sand. Disintegration — as between North and South, between State and State, between one portion of a State and another, between cities and towns and neighborhoods, between man and man, — nay, we might say between body and soul in the same man, for there is no final bound to the principle — becomes the supreme law. We see the exigency with the eyes of our rulers. It is a perfectly fundamental and radical issue. It is life or death with all constituted authority. It is the whole question of civil and social order. It is just the problem whether men can dwell together in communities, or whether they shall resolve themselves back into individualism and barbarism, become each an Ishmaelite, his hand against every man and every man's hand against him. And so deep and strong are our convictions that we say, — we all say; no tongue lisps a whisper of dissent, — Government must be maintained AT WHATEVER COST. Constitutional law must be enforced AT ALL HAZARDS. And we suffer no man alive, and no page of history, and no imagination of the thoughts of the heart, to put before us any estimate of the hazard, any computation of the cost, which can make us falter in that stand. Before any possible future, we repeat it with firm lips and steadfast hearts, "AT ALL HAZARDS, AT WHATEVER COST." Here, too, as in the other direction, is an educating power of transcendent force, and the lesson upon us and our children and our children's children will not lose its special vitality for three generations, at least, of human life, and will abide in our history, a voice of wisdom and authority for all times and histories to come.

Now, then, finding us in this attitude of mind, God may speak to us concerning his kingdom. He is a Governor, and he may press us, now, with conclusions affecting his administration, which none of us can gainsay.

If he ask, Shall there be a government at all, set up in his name on earth? we can only now give one answer. Sometimes we speak of God as though he were only a father to our humanity, and should confine himself to that. A father's office we conceive to be to furnish us with a home; to make that home pleasant and safe;

to provide for us there as well as he may; to call us together around the bright hearth and the smoking board; to appoint us a pillow of comfortable rest; to watch at our side with faithful vigils, tender care, and skilful nursing when we are sick, and wipe away our tears when we are sad. We all like to call God, "*Father.*" He appears in such an amiable, smiling aspect when this relation alone is recognized, that we dismiss our fears, and have only grateful sensations as he presents himself thus before us. It is very agreeable to be so cared for and cherished and blessed. So far, we have, none of us, any, quarrel with God. Let him pour his blessed sunshine upon us all the day. Let him soften our fields with his spring showers, and fill our wells with his autumn rains. Let him refresh the arid places of earth with nightly dews. Let him give us the round of the changeful and fruitful seasons. Let him gladden our daily walks with the companionship of kindred and friends, and make our tabernacle musical with household talk. A good father, a kind benefactor. There is not a heart on earth that objects to such a conception of God, or to any such function of his superintending providence. Nay, he may even advise, *in a fatherly way*, as to the temper we ought to cherish and the conduct we ought to exhibit, and chide us gently, if we miss the mark, and seek to persuade us to better purposes and more filial returns.

Our eyes are open a little wider now. We see clearly that such an administration will not do. It is not strong enough. It lacks enforcing and coercive power. It is cruelly weak. In a sense, it tempts to rebellion and defiance. God must be a Governor, as well as a Father. He must enact laws, publish ordinances, set up institutes; come before us not simply with a father's love, but with a ruler's authority. We want to see firmness, as well as kindness, on his face. We want to feel that there is a steadfast will, as truly as a paternal pity; that his throne stands as fast as his promises; and that his control of us and our fellow-men, and of all things around us affecting our interests, is as wide, searching, and absolute as his exploration of our wants, and the generosity with which all need is met. We shall agree in saying, "If God be good, let him give us a government, not shadowy, remote, and ineffective, but near, positive, peremptory, that may be felt, relied upon, and ascertained to be real and solid." The fatherhood of God is a very affecting truth, but it does not of itself go far enough for our confidence and our comfort. Not till we read on his vesture and his thigh, that other title, "King of kings and Lord of lords," are our souls at peace. Here we plant our feet upon a rock.

Again, if God ask, Shall this government be maintained? our answer is equally prompt and hearty. We have not two opinions about it. We want a strong, steady, abiding government. We desire to know how it is bulwarked; what forces wait upon its behests; what executive vigor it possesses. Is omniscience its counsellor? Is omnipotence ready to march at its bidding? Does its control sweep the area of its territory, ubiquitous in every part? Is it prepared for all exigencies? Is it a fair-weather government, on deck in pleasant latitudes, handling the sails, steering the ship, ordering the crew while the winds and currents favor? and does it abdicate if there be gales or lee shores or mutiny? or is it a government for stormy weather overhead and conspiracies on board? What will it do if defied? On that question our chief solicitude hangs. Let God put that question to us. What shall my government do if it encounter combinations and conspiracies against its perpetuity? Shall it give way, retract its edicts, back down, let whoso will renounce allegiance, and throw off the character of subjects, or shall it be maintained? We are ready with our answer. How easy it is to-day to answer! No hesitation! Our response is brief, but emphatic. It repeats the last word of the question with a downright cadence, "maintained!"

Suppose, again, the Great Governor asks us *how far he shall go in the maintenance of his government.* We reply again, without taking time for debate, and without any qualification, As far as is necessary for the object. Shall he proffer, then, the oath of allegiance to every subject? Yes, to every subject. And if this oath be declined, or, having been taken, be broken by falsehood and perjury, shall he insist upon the supremacy of the government there? Yes, he must insist. But if he commit himself to such a demand, how far must he be prepared to back it up? If need be, with the whole power of the government. But it may call for the waters of a universal deluge. Then let the deluge fall. It may necessitate the ten plagues of his wrathful right arm. Then inflict them. It may make our earthly Niles run red with blood. No matter, they must run through loyal dominions. It may call for the extermination of the Amalekites. Then exterminate them. It may compel the administration to keep a standing army of famines, fevers, pestilences, and storms, and an immense police of aches and pains and crosses and disappointments. Very well, then the administration must do it. It may oblige the government to make a terrible example of rebels and traitors, to hold up their tragic end as an awful warning, to show them to all the States of God's empire gibbeted in eternal anguish and infamy, — the shame and condemnation of their great parricide clinging to them forever and ever. Well, if this be needful, it is right. It is therefore good. It is benevolent. The government has no choice. It must be maintained. In the hearts or upon the necks of those who oppose it, its supremacy must be asserted. If it take cycles of probationary centuries, if it cost myriads of subject lives, if it necessitate the laying waste of ten thousand worlds, fortresses of secession and nests of sedition, — if it part brother from brother, cut off unnumbered children of God's loins from their Father's house, cast down from the firmament a third part of the stars set therein by God's hand, — the infinite good of an established government demands and justifies the prodigious outlay. For, government sacrificed, all is lost; no good remains. Better lose a part. The loss *is* partial and temporary. It can be replaced. The good of a sustained administration is universal and eternal. How clearly we see that now! How easy it is to answer these questions here and to-day! The principles of government are one, on earth and in that august court. How fully God vindicates himself in our instinctive and accordant judgments! How absolutely we pronounce, *The cost of maintaining government must not be regarded!* That is sanction enough for any and all of God's procedures.

Again, suppose the divine lips reiterate the question, *What shall be done with rebels?* Possibly we should suggest, especially to a government undeniably strong enough to deal with them, a course of forbearance for a while; time given them for soberer thoughts; attempts to remove their prejudices, to convince them of the benevolent intentions and spirit of the government, to awaken them to penitence and shame, to lead them back, if possible, to their allegiance; but when the question returns, They are obdurate; they will not have God to reign over them; they have set up for themselves; they are determined upon independence of the rightful authority; they are going on under their own flag; what shall be done with them? our answer again is prompt and decisive; the government must proceed against them. It cannot allow their triumph. That dishonors the administration before all worlds, and must disaffect the loyal everywhere and forever. No knee, on earth or in heaven, will continue to pay homage to such a government, which is no government. It must deal with these rebels, if it would not have defection and rebellion general. It must put them down. If need be, it must cut them down, it must mow them down, — it must utterly exterminate them, if it come to that. Rebellion must be crushed out. Admit it in any corner of God's broad kingdom, and allow it to thrive and live and maintain its little rival empire there, and the weakness and incompetency of the administration are confessed, and it is disrobed of royalty from henceforth. Put an end to it. Rebellion itself is responsible for the havoc which it provokes. Bring over it the clouds of heaven, open the magazines of electric fire, hang out the flag set with suns of light and striped with red of dreadful vengeance. March the forces of Almightiness, and let the artillery open its thunders; bring out the reserves of Jehovah, the chariots of God, which are ten thousand times ten thousand, — THE REBELLION MUST BE WIPED OUT! Can we give any other answer? Put the question to twenty millions of people in this our nation to-day, Is God justified in putting down rebellion in his dominions, by whatever pains and penalties needful? and twenty millions of voices answer, with a shout that rises above the choral melodies of heaven, "Ay!" These flags, that have blossomed out, this season past, so suddenly upon all the summer air, symbolize more than the sentiment of loyalty to the great Republic. They float and wave for a more august principle. The mustering and marching among the hills and valleys of our New England homes and across the breadth of prairies and over dividing mountains are in allegiance to a grander call than that of patriotism. All this fervor and self-devotion declare a truth high as the throne of God and eternal as his reign, — Rebellion against good government must be extinguished by utmost power and severity. And more than this, they declare that it must be so extinguished, the treatment be so effectual, the warning so memorable, the crushing so final, that never again, while government endures, shall rebellion lift its head. When before was God's scheme of governing a universe so indorsed by man? Never in the long story of time. But we see exigencies and principles now, as our eyes never beheld them in the past.

If we ask, again, What is the duty of rebels? the same unbroken unanimity replies, To lay down their arms, restore their spoil, and submit unconditionally to the government. No treating with God with arms in our hands. No questioning of his intents, while our traitorous flag is flying. No expectation of his clemency, or demand for his forbearance, while we occupy our fortresses. Submission first. Nothing before that. The government must keep its one aspect, so long as we resist and stand out. It can make no terms with treason. All talk of amnesties and pardon must come in on the basis of absolute surrender.

What is the duty of the loyal? Clear again and unmistakable. They must take side with the government. There must be no question with any mind where they stand. They must not only let it be known, but make it known, with which party they are in sympathy, — whether with the government or with rebellion. There can be no such thing as neutrality. Neutrality is infidelity and disloyalty to the crown. It is aid and comfort to treason. God insists, and we shall say to-day that he has a right to insist, that every man shall run up his flag. We feel like insisting upon the same thing in the earthly issue. God calls, "Come out from among rebels." "Confess Christ before men." "Join the fellowships of my people." "He that is not for me is against me." Oh, how impregnable are these positions! How intelligent is God's earnestness, at the head of his government, in insisting upon being openly acknowledged in a time and in a world of rebellion! · It is not enough for one of us to say, "Why, I mean to be a just and peaceable man; I am going about my business; I am not to be pressed into making demonstrations." That's the mistake. No demonstration is a demonstration. It is disaffection and defection. Men must demonstrate. They must run up their flag, and it must be the right sort of a flag too. We can understand the intense abhorrence with which the lips of God proclaim it to these neutrals,—"So because thou art lukewarm, and art neither cold nor hot, I will spue thee out of my mouth." Are any of us neutral as between God and the great rebellion? Do we leave it in doubt where we are, what colors we secretly prefer? We have not thought of that matter as we ought, have we? See the unutterable meanness and cowardice and wickedness of that attitude. We don't want to fight, do we! We prefer not to arm! we choose not to enlist! When good soldiers are crowned, where shall we be? When traitors are punished, what will become of us?

Again, can the loyal do anything with happier effect than this one thing,—show their confidence in the Supreme administration? God's plans are large; they are slow-moving as we reckon time; they are not submitted to our inspection. Suppose they seem to us too slow; fail of what we call grand chances; give up such capital strategies of our devising; and we, with the king's uniform on, marching under his orders and officers, and enrolled for the war, stop and shake our heads, and vent our criticisms, and propose our emendations, and purse up our lips and shrug our shoulders; what is the effect? The effect is to damage the government; to shake its hold upon other hearts; to interfere with its recruiting; to pour a contagion of faintness and uncertainty through the ranks where we march. That is not for us. It is for us to obey orders; to trust the management of the campaigns to the Great Captain of our salvation; to march when he gives command; to pitch when the word comes; to maintain the post at which he sets us, and keep such a cheerful and trustful air that men shall say, "These soldiers are confident of victory. They trust their leader."

By and by the war will be ended. All rebels will be subdued to penitent allegiance, or punished with final exile and ignominy. The loyal and triumphant forces will gather home to the presence of the King and the glory of the capital. What an ovation will await them as they march in upon the streets of the royal city! All heaven will be moved at their coming. From lip to lip, the tidings will leap, "The warriors of Prince Emmanuel are returned from the fields of earth." And as the long line comes gleaming on, the angelic welcomes will be heard in farthest spheres, on the outer verge of light. There are they that were stoned to death in riotous cities, martyred witnesses of the truth; there are the men, few and alone, that defended some "Sumter" of principle, around which roared aloud the world's hostile scorn; there are they that left houses and lands, and home and kindred behind, to give their lives in the great struggle; and each scar of battle will be a badge of everlasting honor; and the rent banners will be hung out over heaven's battlements, and bathed in living light; and the hand that led the forces on will set upon each brow a crown of glory.

II.

THE WORK OF NEW ENGLAND IN THE FUTURE OF THE COUNTRY.

AND THEY THAT SHALL BE OF THEE SHALL BUILD THE OLD WASTE PLACES; THOU SHALT RAISE UP THE FOUNDATIONS OF MANY GENERATIONS; AND THOU SHALT BE CALLED, THE REPAIRER OF THE BREACH, THE RESTORER OF PATHS TO DWELL IN. — Isaiah lviii. 12.

WE cannot to-day be narrow, and shut our thoughts within the limits of the Commonwealth. THE TIMES are educating us all into views and sympathies broad as the land. We stand in these hours on an eminence, and our horizon is the borders of the Republic. We are lifted to the dome of our nationality, and our field of vision stretches to the water-line that marks either ocean shore, — the blue of the Lakes and the blue of the Gulf.

We cannot name our State, or any State, without thinking at once of our whole country. We are weaned from the idea that a State is complete by itself. It is one component part of a Federal Government, held to its sisters by a deathless bond. It is a branch of a living and fruitful vine, in which alone it has life and fruitfulness. Except it abide in the vine,—we may reverently apply the Scripture,— it " is cast forth as a branch, and is withered;

and men gather them and cast them into the fire, and they are burned."

Let the stars in the heavens break from their constellations, but let not one on our field of blue part the chain of celestial gravitation and attempt to shine alone. It shall soon become a "wandering star," "going out in the blackness of darkness forever."

We belong to a nation — a nation living still — fair and strong and whole, undivided and indivisible, wearing still on its brow, for all the jealous kingdoms to read, the old familiar inscription, "*E pluribus unum,*" and girding itself anew for the race of the future.

And the question which I desire briefly to discuss to-day is this: What is the work of Massachusetts, and of New England, in this near future of the whole country?

We may say, in the first place, that the life of New England cannot be dissevered from the national life. There has been in some quarters certain idle and flippant talk in reference to such a readjustment of the national boundaries as should leave this old Puritan Commonwealth and her five sisters outside the walls of the new confederation. But our connection with the Republic is not a matter of territorial contiguity and geographical lines. Let men run border lines as they please; let them frame ordinances of separation; let them build a Tartar wall between us and the great homestead; neither civil nor material barriers can exile us from the family circle. It were just as possible to separate from the loaf the leaven that made it light and sweet, or from a human life the principles and influences of its early nurture.

New England is not a certain limited portion of the national domain, a sharp eastern angle that can be clipped off. No map of the Union gives to the eye her full and proper extent. No engineering art can explore and project her share of our continental heritage.

Her life is ubiquitous in the nation. From her fountain heart the warm arterial currents have circulated through the whole body and flowed out to the remotest extremities. Her sons have gone forth into every habitable place of the broad land. They have carried with them her enterprise, her intelligence, her art, her ingenuity, the pure and ordered life of her homes, the tranquil securities of her law-abiding communities, her system of common schools, academies, and colleges, her reverence for the Sabbath, the memory and the love of her household altars and public sanctuaries. Their first harvests as they have occupied and opened up virgin soil have been not what the earth yielded to the hand of tillage; they sowed, first of all, Puritan ideas,—the seeds of New England institutions; and that which grew earliest beneath their husbandry has been the transplanted life of their own native hills and valleys. Here are indestructible channels which cannot be closed, and through which the fountained abundance of New England's fulness has flowed out and is flowing still across the prairies, and along the central valley, and through the wilderness, and unto the far Pacific coast. New England can no more be divorced from the Union than the maternity of a mother from her children. That maternity is in their form and features; it gives the coloring to cheek and hair; it looks from their eyes; it speaks from their tongues; it runs in their veins; it beats in their hearts. Not even by miracle could it be separated from them.

Separate New England from the Union! Give us back our sons and daughters, more than half a million of them, from all the homes of the land outside our borders! Give us back our millions of capital that have already changed so much of the western wilderness to a smiling garden, whitened the length of its rivers with the foam of swift steamers, and braided over the land the iron strands of trade and travel; turn back upon us the deep streams of wealth that flow out annually to those granaries of the West for their cereal stores! Give us back the forceful and fruitful words that have gone forth from her press, her pulpit, her rostrum of public oratory, from every platform and every page on which the eloquent lips of her sons have spoken,—words that have quickened and controlled the intellectual life of generations, and guided popular movements in every part of the country; this public speech of New England that has gone forth free and fresh and vital as the air of heaven, gather it up and restore it to its authors; separate it from the popular mind and heart, from the principles and the practice of our homebred millions! Give us back the messengers of a pure gospel that have gone forth at our sending, with large self-sacrifice, to plant the banner of the cross in "western wilds," and bear it on in the very van of our spreading civilization, and with them the churches they have built, and the fair Christian order they have reared amid the outlawry of frontier settlements! Give us back the broad, bright river of our charities, that has branched to so many thresholds of suffering through these four tragic years! Give us back the brave blood that has drenched a hundred battle-fields, and reddened the trail of New England feet wherever the armies of the Union have marched!

When all this can be done, when the nation will consent to this, then may men talk about "leaving New England out in the cold." Till then, her place is in the warm hearts of the people, her life mingled with the life of the nation, "one and inseparable."

We have, we may say, in the second place, to keep New England undegenerate.

The greatness of New England's influence is not so much in what she does as in what she is. The two go together. When she works, when she speaks, it is the background of character that lends to both their weight. Just as when an individual utters his thoughts, — it is not so much what he says as who says it. The chief emphasis of words and of deeds comes from the heart of the doer and the speaker. There is no premium in the sphere of moral power upon idleness, frivolity, and corruption. Both for men and for communities, if we would have the influence pure and strong, these attributes must first be demonstrated in the character. It is when those who speak in the name of New England can say, "Look at her," that their oratory is beyond tongues of flame and words of fire. We have it in charge, then, to guard the purity and nourish the strength of this home-life. The fountain must be full and clear if the streams are to be pure and copious. We must keep the New England ideal rounded and perfect in her actual.

There are some things New England cannot be. She cannot be the granary of the nation, a great agricultural producer. A single prairie lot, where the horses trot at the plough in one straight furrow of miles before they turn, and where, later, the reapers seem struggling like wrecked mariners in the wide, tawny harvest sea,

"Rari nantes in gurgite vasto,"

would swallow as a little morsel all the farming life within our borders. She cannot be a grower of tropical fruits and flowers, breathing from red, ripe lips the fragrance of tropical airs; a tiller of the vine, the orange, and the olive; a nurse of pale invalids hurrying from cold coast winds to seek soft bowers and sunny vales. She cannot show in her granite cliffs and rude ravines the yellow, glittering scales to which the greed of all nations should come rushing and trampling, hewing down her hills, and turning her peaceful wilds back into the bald desolations of old chaos. But she can be the fountain-head of intelligence for the people, kindling in every little vale and hamlet, for the poorest and humblest, the lights of letters and learning, building on favored heights her tall towers of Science, to scatter their rays afar, calling to her classic halls the wisest teachers of the day, shedding upon all the paths of her children, from the untiring enginery of her press, the white leaves of daily knowledge and high research, as orchard trees shed the blossoms of spring, as this January sky sheds its snowflakes to-day. She can be the schoolmistress of the land, teaching the alphabet of all good nurture, leading her pupils up through the great volumes of wisdom, and quarrying out the massive granite of her thoughts for all intellectual builders.

She can be the mother of art and of invention, so that the right hand of all labor, whether of the mind, the shop, or the field, shall stretch itself out to her for the most facile implements of its craft.

She can be the asserter and defender of all humane and noble principles, so that every champion of truth and freedom, every lover of the right and of his fellow-man, shall draw inspiration from her words and strength from her steadfastness.

She can especially be the mother and nurse of men. This is her royal staple. The sands of the Cape are barren and rough, and bleak are the Berkshire hills; but the barren sands and the bleak hills grow men. To train the generations of her sons and daughters is the most peculiar work of New England within her borders. She does not put her infants out to nurse. Her generous breasts suckle all her babes. She is to take each new-born child of every home, and to solve over it this problem: Given a fresh young life, how to conduct it to the noblest manhood, the purest womanhood! From the cradle to the fullest prime, and onward to the chamber of rest, she is to be to this life, in all its physical, mental, and moral culture, the institutions that, from first to last, shall develop, mould, and guard it, the atmosphere that shall fill its lungs, and drape it round about, a wise and faithful foster-parent. Beyond all the newer and more unfurnished portions of our country, she is to provide within her rocky portals a nursery for the children of the Republic.

There is one word which, more than any other, holds before our thought the whole New England ideal. It is not only a descriptive, but an inspiring word. It leads us back to the presence and the heroisms of our dead fathers. There throb in it the stern, strong pulses of martyr life. It is keyed to the music of our early forest temples, in which the Pilgrims worshipped God,

> " And the sounding aisles of the dim woods rang
> To the anthems of the free."

Oh that our New England might be, late and forever, what she was at first, — PURITAN ! Once a word of reproach, veined with sneering irony, — History has written it as our proudest eulogy. To keep it unblotted down the ages is our most sacred trust.

For this there must be a real, practical, public faith in God. We must believe that he is a God nigh at hand, and not afar off. We must not exile him to the seventh heavens, — a cold, remote, hazy spectre. There must be with us a reverent sense of his constant presence and a devout recognition of the mingling of his counsel and his hand in all our private and public affairs. How near he was to our fathers; they walked with him, and talked with him, and questioned his will at every step of life! Their eye sought his, their hand touched his in every strait. We must not be afraid to name him, and avouch him, and appeal to him, in our proclamations and State papers and legislative acts and judicial decisions. We ought to be afraid to leave him out, and to withdraw our public life from the shadow of those tutelar sanctities. If ever we cease to be here a God-fearing people; if we drift away from the faith of a divine, revealed religion, and its rightful control of human affairs; if we give up the Christian Sabbath, as an effete institution; if we discard the Bible as God's code of laws for individuals and for States; if we dissociate politics and religion, breaking up the old Puritan bridal, which wedded them, and pronounced over them this nuptial benediction, "What God hath joined together, let not man put asunder;" if we make our public days of thanksgiving and of humiliation mere festive holidays, in which we seek our own pleasure rather than to please and propitiate God; if we divorce thus the voice of the State, the course of law, the decrees of justice, and the popular life from the word and authority of God, we shall have emptied our old baptismal name of all its significance,—keeping the form, but not the life; the shadow, not the substance,—and in that hour and in that act the sceptre of New England's power will be broken, her crown lost, and her banner that she planted in the wilderness, with its ancient heraldry, "*Christo et ecclesiæ*," trail dishonored in the dust.

Let all of us rather conspire to lift up again the old Puritanic ideal. "It is certain," declares one of the early New England voices, "that civil dominion was but the second motive, religion the primary one, with our ancestors in coming hither. . . . It was not so much their design to establish religion for the benefit of the State, as civil government for the benefit of religion." Another voice, a century earlier, testified that the fathers " came not hither for the world, or for land, or for traffic, but for religion, and for liberty of conscience in the worship of God, which was their only design."

This sacred interest was first everywhere. "As near the law of God as they can be," was the instruction of the General Court of Massachusetts, in old time, to its committee appointed to frame laws for the Commonwealth.

Only in the reproduction and general diffusion of this spirit can we hope to make the New England of the past the New England of the future, a power and a glory in the land.

Looking forward now and beyond our own confines, we may say, in the third place, that it belongs to us to live in and for the future of the whole country.

This, too, is one part of our inheritance from a Puritan ancestry. Our fathers were builders for the future. They lived for all the coming ages. They laid deep foundations whereon they hoped there might rise, after their day, the walls of a Christian empire, to stand until earth's "cloud-capped towers" should fall. We are fond of saying, "They builded more grandly than they knew." Perhaps that is true in respect to the political fabric of which they laid the corner-stone, and the material results that have followed their work. But they had a vision of a spiritual temple that should rise from their humble beginnings, until its dome should span the continent and its arches echo the psalms of meeting and mingling nations.

Foundation-work is congenial to the sons of New England. It runs in our blood to be pioneers of a spreading Christian civilization.

We must look forward, for our past is brief. It is kindling and inspiring, but it is yet fresh and new. We have no calendar of hoary centuries, stocked with events and revolutions that have marked off the eras of history, and rich with the spoils of time. Compared with the life of nations and the courses of history, we began but yesterday. Looking back, a glance reaches the starting-point. More naturally we turn our gaze forward. Not records, but prophecies, hold our eyes. Untempted to live on the glories of a dead ancestry, we are inspired to do something for our posterity to commemorate.

We must look forward, for our ideal is higher than we have reached. We may have been vain and boastful, but none of us can believe that the summit of American greatness has been reached. The magnificent capabilities of the continent, and the adaptation of our forms of life to all possible progress on such a theatre, rebuke our complacency in the past, and hold in prospect a sublime goal for which we have yet to gird up our loins and run.

We must look forward, because revolution leaves us not a finished task, but only a clear track. Give us peace and victory to-morrow, and it brings us only a vacation from fighting, none from work. Revolution does not create a civilization. It opens the door and ushers it in, if it be prepared. If this revolution of ours succeed fully, it will have helped to rid us of some malign forces in the development of American life, — at least, of some incarnations of those forces; it will deliver into our hands a nation saved from crumbling apart; but what this nation shall be and do, what it shall live for and realize, is a problem that will yet remain.

Nations must work, as God works on the earth, for something yet beyond and unmatured. When they pause and say, This is the limit and consummation of our doing, he will say of each of them, " Cut it down, why cumbereth it the ground?" At every stage of progress they must renew their devotion to what is incomplete in the divine scheme for man. Casting off all dead and useless appendages, burning their ships behind them as they touch new shores of discovery and conquest, they must follow hard after the guiding steps that are tracking man's way to the calm heights of a perfect social state.

We may ask, then, in the fourth place, what are the specific tasks to which we are to address ourselves in working for the future of the whole country?

The nearest duty of all is to push this war triumphantly through. Persistent rebellion is alone responsible for all the blood and treasure it shall yet cost to maintain the supremacy of the government. That supremacy can only be maintained by showing its power to be, as well as its right to be, when both are called in question. Let no sign of weariness or impatience in the protracted struggle come from us while a rebel banner taints the air. The length of the war has been absolutely indispensable for the full sense of nationality; the unity and authority of the Federal Government to enter and possess the hearts of the people; for the radical revolutionizing of the old social system of the South; for the education of the masses up to the political and moral issues of the present hour. Let no voice among us call for peace while treason stands erect and defiant. Let no sigh of complaint freight any wind that blows from the North toward the capitol. To every fresh call for men, let us give quick, consenting response. The armies that have been marching through the summer and autumn from victory to victory must needs find their ranks thinner, and the final strokes are yet to be delivered. We have to fill the ranks, to stimulate enlisting, to sound the call for volunteers at all the gateways of our hills and in the streets of our towns, to compensate the forsaken tasks of labor's thrifty hands, to keep a light on the hearth of the absent soldier's home for his wife and babes, and bread on the board and "the wolf from the door." "Fight it through!" Let the press emblazon it morning and evening. Let the ministry of Him who came to send the sword on earth before his reign of peace give it voice. Let legislation in town and State give it all helpful practical indorsement. Let the whole heart of New England give it clear and ringing echo. And here, especially, where the word was first spoken that broke the silent terror of the beginning, let that sound have once more full volume and cheerful tone: "The sons of Massachusetts to the rescue!"

We have, of course, a duty of ceaseless vigilance. The transition periods of a nation's life are perilous crises. They inaugurate the dynasties of moral forces that are to sway the sceptre for a cycle whose diameter no man can calculate. The fortunes of this nation are in transition now. We have reached the line, sailing on in the Ship of State, and are crossing it into seas unploughed before. In respect to opinions, morals, public leaders, society, and institutions, we are leaving the old and entering upon the new. On the other side of this great chasm that separates our past from our future, our national story is to begin afresh, our annals to open a new volume. Public sentiment is to be reformed; new banners are to float in the van of national progress; we are to take down and rebuild many a shattered line of our walls of empire; we are to legislate and to act upon novel questions without precedents.

What shall we carry on with us? What shall we leave behind? What new elements shall come in to leaven the whole lump? What old elements shall be extirpated or neutralized? What things vital and precious, the legacy of the past, shall be studiously garnered up? What dead weights shall be thrown off? Who will watch to see that no divine gift of the old civilization is dropped out, no seed principle of our earlier liberties and evangelisms blown away or smothered, no ancient guarantees of public faith and honor and popular privilege weakened or forgotten? Who will scrutinize as carefully the forces that harness themselves to the onward movement, and make sure that no wanton, profane hand lay hold of the sacred ark of our hopes; that no seed principle of mischief be sown where many hands are scattering grain broadcast; that no insidious attempt to twine around our swelling limbs fetters that shall one day cripple our growth and our free motion, shall prosper?

This is precisely the demand that invokes New England intervention. Her weight in the wavering scales of our public destinies is not the weight of numbers, nor of territorial greatness and promise, nor of political predominance. The centre of political power has forever receded from the East; it will visit no more the Atlantic slope of the Alleghanies; it is crossing meridian after meridian, westward still. Let it pass; our moral sceptre remains. It is open to us still to sway the nation by the force of ideas, to rule through the royalty of principles that can never be discrowned. Let the questions which we have just asked get their clear and authoritative answers in the voice and the attitude of this little sisterhood of commonwealths, and we rule the confederacy still. But we must look well at the foundation of the principles which we attempt to assert and maintain. They must have an unquestionable right of supremacy. They must be royal "*jure divino.*" They must be no temporary policies and expediencies, but everlasting facts and laws. They must take hold of what is imperishable, have their roots in the very nature of God, and be linked to the car of his omnipotent providence. The divineness of government, the supremacy of law, order imperial, human equality, the inalienable rights of man, — intelligence, freedom, law, and religion, — the four immovable pillars of communal peace and perpetuity, — standing by these, holding and teaching this faith, New England will be a power in the Union forever.

For these principles, then, she must be jealous with an infinite jealousy in watching the country through this present crisis. This is the turn of the fever. There must be no negligence nor slumbering now; every change must be noted; every pulse must be felt; the slightest aberration is of moment. We must be Argus-eyed, so that no future disaster shall impeach our vigilance in this critical hour.

Another duty of ours concerns the deliverance of this land from the bondage of the past. That deliverance is not yet complete. For one, I am restless and anxious until that consummation come.

We have been in covenant with a great wrong. We admitted it into partnership with our national life. We awarded it rights and immunities. It proved itself a fraudulent partner from the beginning, but we were held by the bond. We kept it. There was an inherent incompatibility, but the covenant remained. Through all this time our proper national civilization was not born, but only conceived. Jacob and Esau struggled together in this pregenital strife, never dissociated, the one clasping the other's heel.

It was meant that this land should be a home of liberty and justice for all God's creatures to the end of time; that the rights of man should stand and grow here as the old forests of the wilderness had stood and grown, their roots striking deep downward, their tops branching upward to the open, free heaven, their arms intertwining, and the streams of a continent watering their lusty life. There was to be one land on the face of the earth in which political and religious freedom should walk over its length and breadth without let or threat,— one where there should be on the body and on the soul no chain. So our founders builded; so our fathers and mothers suffered and wrought and prayed. And the new temple of promise rose fair and stately, and its light streamed afar, and many feet, weary and wounded, hastened thither to rest within this secure asylum. But, alas, what shrines were built within! Was there one to a pure faith? Was there another to equal law? Was there a third to maiden Liberty? But what other fourth shrine is that, grim and dark, crowding these three? What grisly demon sat within, usurping place in that fair fellowship?

Alas for the new hope and the new nation and the new world! Alas for our bright western star so soon turning wan and dim!

But God had not joined this compact with evil. His hands were not tied if ours were. He has a way of annulling covenants with crime. He found the means to shatter our inviolable bond. He sent the earthquake of revolution to shake down the demon shrined in our sacred temple. It stood strong. It had its foundation deep, and had been buttressed with massive masonry. It was clamped and riveted to the temple walls with many a bolt of iron; but the earthquake was stronger yet. It shook and heaved and wrenched apart till it seemed as though the temple itself would fall. Many said, It will fall. It did, indeed, tremble and rock, and its lights were shivered; but it stands yet, with tower and dome catching the light of earliest and latest day, and the dark shrine is overturned. It lies prostrate and in ruins. Its horrid deity is fallen, like Philistia's Dagon before the ark, maimed and broken, with the stump only remaining. Thus is the bond parted; thus the covenant ceases; and we have to watch now that no hand rebuilds that demolished shrine; that no malign craft sets up Dagon's stump again in our great temple. Surely, we have felt the curse of this corroding bond long enough. Shall we ever bow our necks to it again? Shall we suffer any man among men, or any fiend from below, to press its poisonous links into our flesh once more? We have the shattered materials of that dark altar to sweep out of the consecrated temple, the last vestige of that horrid idolatry to banish and bury forever. This work is not yet done; it needs finishing. There are those who would knit again the ruptured strands of the old, rent covenant. Men of New England, legislators of Massachusetts, suffer this never to be! Here, where the most strenuous voices of the great reformation have been uttered from the beginning, let them still sound forth, full and clear. You will have to watch against cunning, selfishness, and intrigue; against many a nobler sentiment of mistaken generosity and magnanimity and lingering reverence for the Constitution as it was; and against that foul monster, fouler and more misshapen than Satan saw sitting portress at the gate of hell, — PARTY SPIRIT. I do not feel safe or at peace while any legal remnant of this accursed thing clings to us. See to it that this bondage of the past be utterly and forever doomed. Take you care that this incubus of evil never more throne itself upon our national life.

From this last point, we may rise to a higher and more general affirmation. We must see to it that the whole course of this government, both in its constitutional law and in its public administration, shall be determined by strict right and divine principle.

Have we or have we not yet learned the lesson, that evil built into the templed life of a people is an element of weakness and corruption in the structure? It may seem to the builders a necessity. The whole work may pause as though there could be no further progress without allowing the wrong a place. Admitting it, the walls may go swiftly up, as though vindicating the expediency of the measure by a success fair and grand, and not else possible. But God has taught us that this demonstration is a delusion and a terrible mistake. The columns so reared have to be taken down again; that is the divine teaching. It is not real progress to build in with evil, that the work may go swiftly forward; it goes swiftly to decay. All that is built upon it is lost labor. It cannot stand. While God reigns, nothing propped with wrong shall remain firm. That crumbling support will one day fail, and the superincumbent pile lean to its fall. Nothing but truth and right will stand. There is not a trumpet tone so loud in all history as that which proclaims it now, that our national disaster is the fruit of national crime, the issue of mingling evil with the foundations of the republic. Are we not educated yet into the conviction that we must build altogether in righteousness, if we build for posterity and the golden future? Have we not acquired a conscience yet in the heart of this American people? Shall we not walk at length by its light, without swerving?

What is God's idea in a great nation? Merely the better carrying on of commerce and the elaboration of the art of comfortable living? Is it not that it shall stand the noblest representation of the principles of his own supreme government,—nay, the actual vice-regency of his sceptre among men, a temple of concrete justice, in which no right shall suffer harm, and no wrong find a shelter? If in any of its decrees and procedures it contradict his attributes, malign his character, and annul his statutes, will he accept it as his ideal, and write upon its front "*esto perpetua*"? Will he not write that other sentence in the old Hebrew,—"*Mene, mene, tekel, upharsin*"?

We are rebuilding here; we must take better care this time. It should seem enough to say that right is right; but we must add that right is safety, right is perpetuity, right is immortality. Wrong is death and destruction, wrong is treason and disloyalty. We are taking stern measures with rebellion now. But every seeming patriot who consents to any unrighteousness in the reconstructed nation is a more insidious and a more deadly traitor to the Union than any man with arms in his hands in all the rebel hosts.

In this task of rebuilding, only the most resolute steadfastness, only the most sleepless vigilance, will keep evil out. The demand will be incredibly urgent. "Yield here!" "Give way there!" "Consent to this unimportant compromise, and embarrassment will be obviated, and all will go smoothly!" The pinch will be the sorest when rebellion collapses. With the rebels at our feet suing for terms, we shall remember that they were our brothers. All our generous sensibilities will be moved toward them. Our bowels will yearn over them. We shall feel that we cannot be hard with them. We shall be put upon our magnanimity. We shall take them by the hand and lift them tenderly up. We shall be inclined to give them more than they would have the face to ask. We shall desire to show them that the hand that struck down their parricidal weapons was never a hand of hate, but of grieved and reluctant justice. That will be a perilous hour for the constancy of principle. Then, when any voices ask us, in the name and in the spirit of fraternal conciliation, to welcome the erring and the conquered back with their old properties and relations, including some remnant of the ancient wrong or some new vicarious wrong, it will be hard to resist. There is, of course, a place and a sphere for compromise. We may yield our interest, we may forego advantage, we may waive opinion and preference for peace and harmony; but we have it as the most solemn charge of these years of violence and blood, to yield nothing of righteousness and justice to any demand for any gain so long as the world standeth.

It is a part of our work, which ought to have distinct and formal mention, to deepen in the hearts of the people the sentiment of the sacredness of government. There has been in the very nature of our institutions a chronic and growing strain upon this sentiment. Everything in this land tends to the elevation of the individual. We teach that each man, standing erect in the image of his God, is the peer of every other. We provide for the largest training of the individual. He is a graduate of the schools. He is master of tongue and pen. He is a reader of books. He takes at least a daily newspaper; perhaps he posts himself morning and evening upon all the progress of thought and the chronicle of events. He has his opinions. He embraces, it may be, some system of social and political philosophy. More frequently he holds to tenets and prejudices which are his own and unshared. He is the architect of his own fortunes. Every track is free to him. He may aspire hopefully in any direction, and cut for himself steps to any eminence of name and place and power. He has his own religious training and religious creed with no State establishment to coerce him into uniformity. He looks up to no man. He is dependent upon no one. He brooks interference from none.

The nation is bristling all over with these individualities, as isolated and distinct and as sharp as the quills of the "fretful porcupine." How can these millions of independent thinkers be made to see alike, feel alike, and act alike in the matter of the common supremacy of government? The more intelligent and self-reliant they become, the more complete each separate manhood is, the more difficult the problem grows. How can you make any two or more of such constituents take the same yoke and wear it peacefully together? What but anarchy can come of such diverse and resolute elements?

Now if government were something that existed here independently of these self-poised minds, framed for them, laid upon them, with an inherent power to be and to constrain subordination, the conditions of the problem were instantly changed. But with all this independence of thought and opinion, each man is himself clothed with political power. He is a sovereign. There is none above him. He is himself a maker and administrator of laws. Of these millions of sovereigns how will you make one harmonious, self-consistent, and authoritative sovereignty?

Government is their creature, not their monarch. How will you teach them to revere what their hands have made? They will the government into being. If it doesn't please them, they can take it down and set up another. Is it natural that they should fall before it and do it homage? All public officials are their servants, whom they have invested with liveries, and to whom they pay wages. Is it to be expected that they should kiss the feet of their servants? They feel that it is their right and their duty to watch, to criticise, and to rebuke these public servants; and in this duty they cheerfully abound. Is this the way to cultivate reverence and submission?

How obvious is it that the maintenance of government, and especially the hallowing of its authority over such a constituency of free, intelligent, independent, and sovereign minds, is one of those problems concerning which there is always the hazard of an ill-omened issue. Disloyalty and treason, and sympathy with both, are the logical inference of this inflated sense of the popular relation to the government of the land.

We need to insist upon the divineness of human government. Our children must be taught it from the cradle, that, however constituted, "the powers that be are ordained of God." If men elect, God crowns. If we lead our rulers to the chair of state, God puts the sceptre into their hands. They become then, not our officials, but his. They are the servants, not of popular caprice, nor the will of majorities, they are the servants of the throned Justice, the supreme Right.

The natural philosophy of government ought to have clearer, more impressive, and more constant explication in all the literature that trains the American mind. Our schoolbooks, the press, the rostrum, the pulpit, should discuss with more earnestness and more simplicity the fundamental principles of that philosophy.

If men are to dwell together in communities there must, of course, be social order. The opposite of this is anarchy, chaos. For order there must be law, — equal, impartial, universal law.

For the supremacy of law there must be administrative authority, — the right and the power to institute and enforce law.

For the ground of this right, the charter of this authority, we come back again to the will of God, who accepts earthly magistracies as his vicegerents, and clothes them with his own delegated sanctity.

There is no land under heaven that so needs the popular demonstration and the constant iteration of these truths as ours. And it is but the nearest inference to add that there is none where the righteousness of the statute and the purity of the magistrate are more closely connected with the sacredness of the government in the popular heart. Civil enactments, whose inspiration is partisan intrigue, or mercenary favoritism, — an unjust ruler, setting up the dynasty of his own passions, prejudices, and partialities, — a corrupt legislator, writing in the statute-book with unclean hands, — a magistrate swayed by self-interest, and purchasable with gold, — these give public contradiction to their divine paternity, and make contempt of government and revolt against law the instinct of all noble natures. So far as the popular faith goes, the legitimacy of civil government, as an ordinance of Heaven, runs in the channel of purity and equity. For public impression, the proof of divine authorship halts when the divine likeness fails. If we would keep men's hearts among us loyal to civil authority, and help to make the supremacy of law inviolable through the land, we have it in solemn charge to guard the avenues to power from all profane approach, and to exercise the functions of office, legislative and executive, in all honesty and good conscience.

I think it is worthy, also, of a moment's separate plea, that we utter the sentiments and beliefs of New England in full, clear, unequivocal speech. We must hold fast here to our birthright of free thought and free speech. There is nothing that concerns the honor and progress of the nation, or the rights of humanity, in reference to which it is not our privilege to inquire, to form our conclusions, and to declare them in the hearing of our fellow-men. Every principle, every measure that seeks ascendency in this land, every ancient, every fresh-founded institution, we have a right to discuss. Whatever subtle leaven would insinuate itself into the life of the nation, whatever comes to us with the imposing front of precedent and authority, and assumes the prerogative to control our history, we may use our sharpest faculties to search out, and to show forth their nature and their claim. The honest thoughts, the deep convictions, the intense sympathies of our New England hearts, frankly and boldly uttered, have been no mean power in the nation in rectifying public sentiment, undermining the security of wrong, and preparing the national mind for generous and radical progress. There have been those who would have laid a finger of iron on New England's lips, and silenced her faithful witness. But she keeps her birthright yet. Let her guard it well for the future. Let her maintain her right to question, to investigate, to form her opinion upon the wisdom and the morality of all that courts the popular suffrage, not as one ambitious to hold a barren sceptre, but earnest to pour her own copious life into the public veins for the health and vigor of the nation's being. This is one imperial prerogative of New England, one most sacred obligation,—to overstep her own boundaries with the forceful moral influence of her public testimony against all civil and social wrong, her strong protective plea for every imperilled right. Our numbers are few and our territory small; we have no Valley Stream flowing from our hills through the length of the northern continent. But from the pure, cool fountains of these moral and intellectual heights we may send forth a ceaseless utterance for truth, right, and liberty, — a deep, broad river, watering all the land.

There will come upon us soon a call to help repeople

and resettle a desolate South. There is one symbol of prophecy upon the brow of which we might write as its most fitting interpretation this word, — WAR. It is that "fourth beast," that Daniel saw in his night vision, rising out of the "great sea," — "dreadful, and terrible, and strong, exceedingly; and it had great iron teeth; it devoured and brake in pieces, and stamped the residue with the feet of it." Under these horrid hoofs, many parts of the South have become a waste more dreary than any untamed wilderness. In the wilderness of savage nature there is nothing suggestive of violence and destruction. But in following the track of an invading army, we walk amid the wreck of what was once fair and blooming order.

The fences are gone from the fields once bearing up thrifty tillage and rich harvests. Granaries and barns have sunk into black heaps of coal and cinder. The lone chimney tells where the peaceful cottage rose. A ranker growth of tangled weeds betrays the site of the garden. Rows of stumps recall the once fruitful orchard. The level fields of the farm have been ridged up with earthworks, and ditched with rifle-pits. In the once companionable hamlet not a dweller remains. A house or two may yet be standing above the blackened ruins of its fellows, but without doors or window lights, and with wind and storm sweeping through its dismal chambers. Fragments of household furniture lie scattered around, half embedded in the earth. A schoolhouse or a church at the fork of confluent roads shows, in its pierced and shattered walls, how the meeting tides of battle surged around that salient angle. Within, the floor has been rudely cleared; for what purpose many a dull stain on the boards gives testimony. The public roads lead you to the bank of bridgeless rivers. There are no vehicles of travel remaining, no implements of husbandry, no tools of art. No flocks nor herds wander in the pastures, no beasts of draft or burden wait for the harness. The narrow, curving level keeps the memorial of the railway; but the sleepers are burned, and the iron twisted into rusty contortions. Civilization must begin again with all her tasks repeated, and these melancholy ghosts haunting the scenes of her old triumphs. Immense regions at the South are thus blighted. The obduracy of rebellion — and rebellion is still obdurate — has brought upon itself this unsparing scourge.

It seems to me that this tenacity of purpose with the Southern leaders and ruling classes is of God. It wears the aspect of a judicial decree. It is like the hardening of Pharaoh's heart, that the whole Southern system of life, labor, and society may be drowned together in this red sea, and not a vestige of the old malign civilization of that portion of our country survive these bloody years.

Upon such a radical devastation there will come in our new duties, to explore these wastes, to map out the vast territories over which the ploughshare of extermination has been driven, to open up the promise of these fertile and masterless estates to the keen eyes of Northern thrift and the hurrying tread of emigrant feet, to Americanize the new busy marches that will soon press, with mightier armies, and with more peaceful weapons, those silent fields, and to send thither the seeds of New England life and institutions, to be scattered broadcast and first of all to occupy the ground.

There will be also a work, worthy our best endeavors, to bring up, ennoble, and save a degraded remnant of Southern population. Here all that is generous and charitable, all that is magnanimous and forgiving in the heart of New England, will have free scope. We shall have to show our former enemies how sincerely and truly we can be and are their friends. We shall have to bless them in spite of their prejudices and all the depressing weight of their old habits. We shall have to show them how much better we can do for them than they have ever done for themselves. We shall need to parcel out for them new estates, to organize for them home industries, to put into their hands the implements of various work, to help them lift a roof-tree over their heads, to inspire them with hope, diligence, economy, and the ambition for self-improvement, to set before them on their own soil the models of our own sweet and comfortable domestic life, to build schoolhouses and churches and send them teachers and preachers, and sift into all their brightening consciousness the light of letters, the issues of the daily press, and a fresh, healthful, evangelical literature. This grand charity will tax our faith and our self-denial to the utmost for years to come. How many voices will call mournfully to us throughout this bereaved and desolate South! What fragments of broken homes will appeal to us! How many wandering fugitives, not knowing on which side the grave their kindred are, houseless, friendless, penniless, with tragic memories behind them and no light of hope before, will wait our coming to bless them with a shelter, and renew for them some faint interest in life.

Of course the future of the African race in this land is a problem that will press us as it will press the whole country with its urgent and difficult conditions. This land that has held them in bondage will have to give them a home. This nation that has been to them a taskmaster will have to be a foster-parent and a protector. With their restored manhood, they must have such a start in respect to their material interest and their social prospects, as well as in all that relates to their intellectual, moral, and religious nurture, that the future shall, if possible, if they enter its open door, grandly overpay their sorrowful past. For this full redemption of the emancipated slave, New England must by wise and unstinted charities, by generous legislation, and by all social magnanimities, do her royal share.

This is a glance only at the tasks crowding in upon us in the days that now are and the days that are to come. It covers but a small part of the whole field of our duty to our age and our race. But there is enough in these few specifications to invoke our most strenuous diligence, our loftiest consecration. It rests with us, and those who shall succeed us, to make this New England of ours — by her pure life and steadfast principle, her just laws, beneficent institutions, and stainless morals, her clear and commanding utterance for immortal right, her public and private charities, her sense of the grandeur of the ordeal through which this nation and all it involves of hope and promise for man is passing now, and, above all, her faithful adherence to the original ideal of a Puritan commonwealth, walking and talking with God, and holding his will everywhere supreme — an angel of mercy and guidance to our whole land, for this and for all after-times.

We congratulate the State rather than His Excellency that this occasion signals no retirement from the chair of her chief magistracy. It was not needed for him, for any completeness of personal or official honor, for the very summit of a just and wide fame, that the people of Massachusetts should once more with such large consent put the reins of her public affairs into those tried and skilful hands. She honors herself most by so placing this high trust. She knows, and beyond her borders the central government and the nation know, with what prescient forecast, what timely providence, what hopeful courage, what unquenchable loyalty, what indefatigable diligence, and what thoughtful tenderness her administration at home and abroad has been conducted through these dark days of revolution and conflict. Her internal order and prosperity, her renown in the high places of the field, both the spirit and the comfort of her sons doing brave battle for the sacred flag, her weight in the scale of right on the grave questions of the hour, are the bright record which justifies the inference that she is governed well.

If we could spare you, sir, we would give you release from these solemn cares, and follow you with our commemorative gratitude into the peaceful retirement of private life. But in these stern days of work, when our whole New England has so much to do to inaugurate the elect and waiting future, we pile our public burdens upon you once more, and beseech the God of our fathers to give you strength to bear them as worthily in the year to come as in these historic years that have gone.

And may the gentlemen of the Senate, the Council, and the House of Representatives, called of their fellow-citizens to the discharge of duties which would at any time have invoked their best wisdom and highest fidelity, be quickened to discern at what a point they stand in the history and fortunes of the republic, and the lengthening scroll of human progress; and forgetting their own ease and emolument, and rising above every personal and private interest, give to the care of the State, and the honor and safety of the nation in these troubled times, all their heart and all their soul and all their mind and all their strength!

And before the term of official duty which opens for you to-day shall have run out, may we be called to join, with all the people of the land, in keeping such a day of public thanksgiving to Almighty God as has never gathered our joy and praise in the past, — over a nation saved, united, free, at peace with itself, with all the world, and with the throne of Infinite Justice and Goodness!

III.

GOD'S DELAY TO PUNISH.

AND THEY CRIED WITH A LOUD VOICE, SAYING, HOW LONG, O LORD, HOLY AND TRUE, DOST THOU NOT JUDGE AND AVENGE OUR BLOOD ON THEM THAT DWELL ON THE EARTH?—Rev. vi. 10.

AMONG the scenes that rose before the eyes of John of Patmos out of the vast dark future, tracked only by these prophetic lines of light, was one that disclosed to him a company of earthly sufferers gone home to heaven. There, under the shadow of the sacrificial altar, beneath the refuge of the atonement, they were grouped together, resting and waiting. They were resting, for earthly pain and woe were past. They were waiting, for their earthly indication yet lingered. It appears that they were martyrs whom the fierce hand of persecution had done to death for their fidelity to truth and Christ. They seem to be aware of the procedures of the divine Providence in the world they have left behind. They know that the cause for which they died is not yet triumphant. They see the proud crests of bigotry and oppression yet unhumbled. Have they given life in vain, suffered and bled for nought? God is holy and hates evil. Why does he not smile down the crowned wrong? God is true and will redeem his promises. Why does he not show himself the friend of the righteous? And their voices, not fretful and querulous, but earnest for the final victory of the right, address the Highest, "How long, O Lord, holy and true, dost thou not judge and avenge our blood on them that dwell on the earth?"

There are many souls yet dwelling in the flesh, who echo that cry, "How long?" God reigns, we believe, we know; but evil also reigns. God is against it; he has declared that it shall not prosper; but, despite his holiness and his truth, the throne of iniquity stands. Power oppresses, rapacity robs, lust deceives and betrays, detraction stabs in secret, armed injustice defies law human and divine. "How long?" Men join together in earnest league against some specific form of evil, as of tyranny in government, or oppression in political institutions, or intemperance in morals, with God on their side and "the good time coming" before them. But what a dubious warfare! How often are they baffled and defeated! How deep the roots of evil have struck! How securely it lifts its towering growth! They make slow progress. Sometimes it seems as though they did not gain at all. Is God on their side! Is there to dawn a bright, millennial day? The good despond, the bad grow bold. "Because sentence against an evil work is not executed speedily; therefore, the heart of the sons of men is fully set in them to do evil." Why not? The evil-doer is unpunished; he walks at large; no judgments make him afraid; God doesn't silence his proud boasting. Is it so certain that virtue has an infinite ally? How these delays of the Supreme Justice lend heart to the wicked! What do they care for some distant, shadowy terror? Here are the prizes of their corrupt desires right at their feet. Before the crash comes, before the hour of reckoning chimes, they will have enjoyed the lawless sweets to the full, and have escaped into some refuge yet to open. And still God is silent; his hand is motionless; the heavens are serene. The righteous wait for a sign; but earth and sky are mute. "How long, O Lord?" Oh, if evil might be at once put down, and wrong righted now, treason to law, liberty, humanity, and all good brained at a stroke, the almighty thunders flashing instant wrath upon guilt and crime, then might the lowly lift up their heads, and the days of darkness would be numbered! Must we, then, chide these divine delays? Shall we not rather ask if they are not in God's sight both wise and good?

We must remember for one thing that this world is not a world of retribution. The great harvest law is, indeed, established in nature, Providence, and morals, that "whatsoever a man soweth that shall he also reap." But when and where the full harvest shall be garnered are still open questions. The supreme administration takes position in regard to good and evil, and declares it will visit for all wrong; but the times and seasons for such judicial visitation are not disclosed; whether the avenging judgments shall fall sooner or later God gives no pledges. Here and there he drops the bolts of doom visibly and suddenly upon the head of guilt, that men may not forget that there is a God, and that he rules in righteousness. And then again for long, silent intervals, he reserves all his wrath, and the path of crime seems heaped about with impregnable securities. Often the good pass away under a cloud; the wicked carry their bad ventures through with a high hand, and depart amid the blaze of success. God does not undertake to make things equal here and now. No earthly history writes out the whole of his procedures, or balances the accounts he keeps. All human records of his administrative policies must be fragmentary, if not distorted; for the processes of his government pass beyond the ken and the pen of mortal historians, taking in time and eternity. If God wait, therefore, he does not forget. If retribution delay, it is not, therefore, set aside; it only shifts the scene and defers the hour. If some great offender step into the grave before pursuing vengeance overtake him, and they who have watched his course say above the turf that hides him, "Here's a bold, bad man, that came to the end unchecked and unscathed," we may reflect that he has not yet come to the end. The grave is not a refuge from the power of God; it is only a passage from one state to another. Beneath its portal the criminal has gone forward to meet his Judge.

Instead of being a world of retribution, this is a world of probation. Trial with human character is progressive and continuous. It takes in successive incidents, influences, and occasions. It has its stages of advance, its ebb and flood tides. Its grand crises often come late. Its preparatory processes are often veiled and unsuspected, and can only be learned on some great consummation day. Principles, whether right or wrong, grow by slow increments, like oaks on the hill-tops, and by many a wrestle with wind and storm. Were God to rebuke evil with his instant judgments, these deliberate courses of human development would all be cut short. The gradual ripening and strengthening of the soul's moral life would be made impossible; the fair blue sky above would be shrouded from human sight; the thunder cloud of wrath would bow low, and black our daily life; incessantly its fires would gleam and its artillery roll, and underfoot the green earth would be an aceldama of blood; for sinful man's appeal to the justice of a holy God is without intermission.

Again God delays his primitive stroke, that his own character may be more clearly revealed. He has all power; how will he use it? He hates sin with an infinite abhorrence; how will he treat it? When we are injured or affronted, having the power to right ourselves, we make haste to get satisfaction. How will God bear wrong? There is no sublimer spectacle in the universe than the patience with which that Supreme One endures man's trespasses. Wave after wave the tossing sea of human guilt breaks at his feet, and dashes its insulting spray upon his robes of majesty; his name is defiled, his attributes denied, his power defied, his purposes contravened; and to all this the sensibilities of his nature must be exquisitely sensitive; yet there he sits in the bonds of an infinite self-restraint, calm, patient, and forbearing, looking upon the endless succession of the mad waves of human rebellion, and withholding his hand. He was strong when he lifted up the heights of the everlasting mountains and curbed the lawless seas, — strong when he subdued and hauled from heaven the rebel angels, and when he built the worlds and tossed them out like bubbles upon the flood of ether; but is he in any act or work so strong as in this awful self-control? All the voices of human blasphemy cannot ruffle it; all the tragedies of human crime cannot break it down. The day rises and sets on sorrow and guilt; years of sharp wrong fill out their successive revolutions; centuries, ages, lapse slowly away under lusty and jubilant evil, and yet God waits, observant of all, feeling all, remembering all, but passing it by without a reckoning. Is this the way to bear wrong? Would he teach us by his own marvellous example to take patiently the spoiling of our goods, the bitter assaults of malice and all personal injury, and to look also with patient forbearance upon the evils that waste at large in the commonwealth of human happiness. If He to whom vengeance belongeth defers its infliction, shall not we? If that silent endurance of his so move us, shall we not make it an inspiration and a law for our own life?

And how this long-suffering calmness heightens the impressiveness of wrath when wrath comes forth! It is not impulse then; it is not sudden passion; it is not the rash outbreak of a vehement and ungoverned temper. It is slow-moving, deliberate, resolved justice proceeding unto execution because it can no longer delay, — proceeding now inevitably and inexorably because its hour has struck. Nothing is lost from the terror of punishment by this delay, but rather the dreadful tranquillity out of which it takes its way lends it a fearfulness more overawing than the wildest rage.

Again, God's delays often respect the measures and agencies by which the guilty are to suffer. Reprisal in kind and manner is one and a favorite law of the divine retribution. This may take time. A son dishonors and outrages the gray hairs of his father. How shall he be punished? Shall God chastise at once? Will the turbulent boy see and feel his guilt now, or the keenness of the requital, as he would if he live on till his own locks are gray and his age beginning to be solitary, and then the son of his own loins rise up to take him by the beard? Ah, when that late anguish rises in his heart, he will know how he once wounded a heart that cherished him, what a pang he inflicted; and as this answering pang stabs his spirit, he will have it to say in bitter remorse, "It is just." Young Jacob drove a dart to his father's soul when, covering his smooth skin with the hair of the kid, he swore to Isaac, "I am thy very son Esau." How shall he be punished for this deceit? Wait. Come again into his presence when, bowed with years, he leans upon his staff, and his sons, cheating him in turn, ruthlessly lay before him Joseph's coat of many colors stained with blood, saying, "This have we found. Know now whether it be thy son's coat or no." Oftentimes the very prize which the guilty hand seized becomes the instrument of torture. Not all at once of course. Gradually its character changes. It is long perhaps before it ceases to attract. Slowly the leaven of a new virus enters into it, and at last it is worn, like the coat of Hercules, as a poisoned robe, filling the frame with anguish and corruption.

God would have also human help in overcoming evil. He keeps back the thunders of his power and calls in loyal volunteers. He permits them to fight many a strenuous battle, to become heroes on great field days; he drills and musters them in all the manly discipline of a soldier's life and matches them against the stubborn wrongs he would subdue. Their feeble arms take up, instead of his omnipotent arm, the championship of virtue, lift the gage of evil, and measure themselves against the powers hostile to God's reign. This delays the victory, but it exalts and ennobles humanity, tutors and educates the servants of God, and lends an intenser interest in our hearts to the long protracted struggle.

It is not always that the nature of an evil thing is seen at the outset. God understands it. But if he smite as it deserves, men may wonder at his severity. They cannot enter at once into his estimate of what he has scourged, because the evil was yet seminal and unexpressed. Let it live and flourish and blossom by and by and bear its ripe fruits before their eyes, and as those baleful apples fall, men will understand better why the lightnings of heaven should scathe and blacken such a growth. Unless the evil came up thus to its full stature, and put on all its deformity before it were dealt with, if it were choked and checked in its young greenness, there were danger of its repetition when the next hour of temptation should chime. Let it stand and grow yet a while, let its swelling proportions crowd out all healthful growth, let men look upon its kingly coronal of Upas leaves, and mark the death that spreads beneath its fatal dews; let them look upon some vice of character, at first thought well-nigh harmless, as later it pushes its rank leprosy over the whole soul; let some political wrong, at first only a hidden ferment, break out into rancorous, pestilent eruption, where foul and fast the life itself runs away; let men see, let history record, let generations feel, what desperate wickedness lies in the purpose to maintain political ascendency for a sectional end; let wasted treasuries bear their witness, and crimsoned fields and desolated homes and broken hearts; let the punishment linger till the fell spirit, the horrid rapacity, the death-griping wilfulness of this evil thing is stamped upon its brow, the mark of Cain branded in so deep that not all the gloss of the Father of lies can ever efface it; then let the heel of Omnipotence tread it down, and one such demonstration will be enough.

Good and evil are often so mingled in this life that one cannot be dislodged without uprooting the other. The wheat and tares grow together. For the sake of the wheat, it is often better that the tares remain undisturbed. There are bad men whose crimes demand signal rebuke, but there are certain precious interests partly resting upon them which would suffer if they were rudely struck away. They are men of foul hearts and profane lips, but they are husbands and fathers, and dependent lives wait upon their industry, and nestle under their care. They have fields to till and harvests to raise and products of skill and labor to produce for the adornment and comfort of other lives. They do not fear God, nor regard man; but God can make them useful nevertheless. Their muscles are strong, and their wits are sharp for him, and their very wrath shall praise him. They shall serve, though unwittingly, as helpers to human advancement, subduing earth's briers and thorns, — they are good enough for that, — increasing, for selfish ends, useful inventions, sailing the ships of commerce, and manning the ships of war, legislating, ruling, fighting in great battles that set forward the progress of nations.

Shall God make no use of them? If all that he accomplishes by the hands of wicked men were left out of the sum-total of human working, it would greatly change the footing up. Let him delay wrath and subsidize these malign activities for his own beneficent ends.

Meanwhile look in upon the interior experience of these respited lives. The final sentence which they have provoked holds off; but are they therefore exempt from the penal consequences of ill-doing? Are there no sharp returns for wrong which they find they cannot escape? They live; so did Prometheus chained to his rock on the bald Caucasus, with the vulture tearing at his liver every day. Is there no cruel beak that is fleshed perpetually in their tortured heart? Are there not bitter dregs in every cup of sinful pleasure they drink? Are they not taunted with fears and forebodings? Can they lay the pale ghosts of accusing memories? Does not conscience pierce them with her barbed sting? Does not their soul sit in the shadow when it sits alone? Are these criminals really quite at large? If they walk abroad, are they not attended by their jailer who leads them chained, and makes them every now and then to feel the corroding iron?

But there is another side of the divine character that comes into radiant vision often in such delays. To show mercy is the infinite delight of God's heart. To recover the erring, to save the lost, to make the dead live again, to bring enemies to his feet in penitent allegiance, — these are his most illustrious triumphs. There is an intercessor standing between the axe and every barren fig-tree pleading, "Let it alone this year also!" Spared men may become changed men. They are spared often on this peradventure. They may awake from delusion and folly; they may see how their feet are snared; they may meet yet some benign influence that shall prevail over all the solicitation of passion and appetite; afflictions may bring them to their sober selves, and the lips that wantoned with the divine sanctities may call tremblingly out of the dust, "God be merciful to me a sinner." Were not this better than instant and hopeless wrath? Whatever voice asks, "How long?" should we not all answer, "Oh, so long as there is hope; so long as Mercy, sweet angel, can yet smile; so long as the golden sceptre of forgiveness and reconciliation can still be stretched out"?

Reviewing, then, these possible reasons for the delay of God's just punishment of the wicked, we may say, Let no man presume on such respite! Delay is not forgetfulness on God's part. It is not escape on man's part. It may indeed keep the way of return open, but all the while it is but preparing, if such forbearance fail of this end, a more certain and crushing doom. God is silent, is he? while we grow bold in sin. We look and listen; there is no sight or sound to alarm us. Ah, that very silence is appalling. Unseen agencies are at work somewhere. Below the horizon's rim the storm is gathering; the air is breathless; but this hush of the elements precedes the bursting of the tempest. You discern no enemy. Look out, then, for an ambush. Nothing approaches. Be sure, then, you will be surprised. If God delays in mercy, let not our presumption necessitate his wrath; not presumption, but repentance, is the right practical inference from such gracious forbearance.

And, on the other side, let no man's heart doubt or faint because evil seems to have present impunity. God will prove himself an avenger of all violated rights. Wait. The tide will turn, will rise. Wait. The little cloud like a man's hand will cover the face of the sky, and make it black with fury. Wait. Distant the slow-grinding wheels of doom move on. The vast iron rim turns as though it scarce moved at all. The ponderous arc comes down almost imperceptibly; but it crushes where it rolls. Have patience; even a heathen could write, "The mills of the gods grind slow, but they grind fine." The sure, inexorable processes of the heavenly Justice are on their way. Hold on with faith, hope, and good courage. In the end, God and right and truth and virtue will triumph, and wrong will take its hopeless sentence. Endure for a little while, maintain the conflict a little longer, keep a good heart above reverses. God delays, but he will come. To some despairing voice asking for the hundredth time, "How long?" will leap forth his answer, "NOW."

IV.

THE SABBATH IN THE FAMILY.

FOR I KNOW HIM, THAT HE WILL COMMAND HIS CHILDREN AND HIS HOUSEHOLD AFTER HIM, AND THEY SHALL KEEP THE WAY OF THE LORD, TO DO JUSTICE AND JUDGMENT; THAT THE LORD MAY BRING UPON ABRAHAM THAT WHICH HE HATH SPOKEN OF HIM. — Gen. xviii. 19.

THE gifts of the promise made to him who was "called the friend of God" were yet suspended on the conditions of parental faithfulness and a household ordered in "the way of the Lord." The divine purpose of mercy and goodness to a pious line takes up, as indispensable links in the golden chain, the right training of each generation in the long succession. If God's favor is to be transmitted from sire to son, the statutes of God are also to be handed down, and a spirit of obedience and conformity to be, by all strenuous nurture, fostered and secured. The family is God's first and fundamental institution for reproducing and continuing, as the fathers die and their sons succeed them, a people to know and serve him. He ordained it before the Church and the State; or rather it was the earliest Church, the original and germinal commonwealth. He builds States by building families, attaching their members thus to the soil of their nativity, making patriotism an instinct, and the subject's relation a habit from the cradle. He builds in the same way his spiritual kingdom, spiritual knowledge and faith becoming hereditary through the ministry of the Christian home. For these issues he clothes the head of the family with dignity and authority, confirms his sceptre by strong and positive decrees, and makes his name and person venerable and sacred by the offices he fulfils, and the corresponding instincts of dependence and natural affection. If we lose the family as a school of virtue and piety, we lose the heritage of all covenanted blessings, — we displace a unit from the series of God's stepping-stones along our line, breaking off the succession, — we sink a chasm between the deep-freighted divine hand and the future it would have endowed with riches.

The family and the Sabbath — God's first institutions for man — were put in significant proximity when he ordained them both. If God's six days' work includes, as some think, the creation of woman, and we repeat concerning the day that followed the formula that announced the other completed days, "the evening and the morning were the seventh day," then the first bridal eve was the Sabbath eve, the first day of family life in Eden was the Sabbath-day. If this be so, the Sabbath brings to each wedded pair the fragrant memorial of those first nuptials, on which

> "All heaven
> And happy constellations . . . . .
> Shed their selectest influence,"

and pleads that the union thus formed between itself and the family remain perpetual. Over those bands we may hear the great officiating Priest saying, "What God hath joined together let not man put asunder!"

Our home itself suggests the Sabbath. All days of the week it is our rest. Wandering amid strangers, rasped by the sharp and hard contacts of life's jealousies and competitions, lonely in solitude, we turn how gladly to the one threshold on which unfeigned welcomes, companionable voices, the gentle ministries of love, will greet us and fill our spirits with tranquillity and repose. The weary laborer in the field looks up to the declining sun, marks his shadow lengthening toward the east, and bends with fresh vigor to his task, as his thought glides away a swift herald to his own cottage-door. Outside that door, life to him is labor; within it is rest. The implements of toil he lays down before he enters. He goes in to be refreshed and cheered; to sit, not stand; to have a place of ease at the bright hearth and pleasant board; to lay his length upon his couch, and let the soft tide of sleep rise over him, and drown his consciousness. Home is his peaceful evening port after the day's rough voyaging for his body and spirit, — a perpetual Sabbath. One to whom God has given such a daily Sabbath, so pleasant and beneficent a reminder of the weekly rest, ought to hear with most welcoming thankfulness, as though it spoke with a voice of music, the command, "Six days shalt thou labor, and do all thy work; but the seventh day is the Sabbath of the Lord thy God; in it thou shalt not do any work, thou, nor thy son, nor thy daughter, thy man-servant, nor thy maid-servant, nor thy cattle, nor thy stranger that is within thy gates."

The first thing, then, for the parent who asks the question which we have here to answer, "How is the Sabbath to be kept in the family?" is to feel that his own spirit and example will settle the reverence paid to the day and the manner of its keeping in that little community of which he is the head. He must look to himself first. Before he consider methods and measures, and tax his invention, and put his contrivances in operation, let him question his own soul. What is the Sabbath to him? Does he call it "a delight, the holy of the Lord, honorable"? Is it the festival of the week to his heart? For his whole nature, body and mind and spirit, does he esteem it a most gracious boon of God? Is he looking upon it as a severe intermeddling ordinance, breaking off his most fascinating pursuits, taking so much from what he calls, with all the eager relishes of his soul, in one intense word, — "LIFE," dooming him to a dull, pulseless pause of existence? Or is this the culmination, the crown, the zest of desire and hope, the welcome release from worldly care, the banquet-day for a soul hungry and thirsty and denied, amid earthly planning and toiling, fit and full refreshment? There's a compensative beneficence in the Sabbath for the body's need. The weary frame sits at high noon to gather breath and strength before it renews the chase, but the pause is ever too brief. The call afield sounds again before the brow is dry and the swell of the bosom gone down into quiet. The night comes with its anointing dews of sleep, and imparts fresh increments of vigor. But the night is too short. It doesn't impart as much as was expended. The balance is against us still when the morning blows its clarion. The stock on hand, through all the fluctuations, diminishes till the week be spent. Speedy bankruptcy were inevitable, did not the Sabbath come in with compensative relief to supplement the pause at noon and the ministration of the night with one solid day, insisting, kindly, from sun to sun, "in it thou shalt not do any work," and joining two reposeful nights by this pleasant isthmus of restful light. Is there in like manner a compensative element in the Sabbath for the soul's need? How do we think of it? We run to the fountains of spiritual refreshing morning and evening of our toiling days; we moisten our lips as we kneel down at the springs of comfort in our closet and at the family altar; we fill a cup from the precepts and promises of the word; we gather a little manna thus daily as the dew rises and before the sun is hot, — a taste of the bread of heaven; but the soul is kept on short allowance. It expends amid worldly cares and draughts more than it thus receives. It will become lean and famished if a special and more bountiful table be not spread for its need. What is it that supplements for the soul's spiritual compensation the closet, the household worship, the daily Scripture reading? Is the Sabbath welcomed as such a feast-day to our hungry spirits, — a day in which we can lie at the fountains of refreshment through all the bright hours, hear the governing provider urge his large hospitality, — "Eat, O friends; drink, yea, drink abundantly, O beloved"?

No strictness of ruling, no stern administration of Sabbath law, will commend the Sabbath to the fit hallowing of the domestic circle, if the day is not, with the family headship, a loved and choice gift of God's goodness. This little society mirrors the character set over it for guidance and control. Looking into the clear depths of some Alpine lake, you see all the snowy peaks around leaning against that nether sky as in the upper. There below, as above, the torrents foam and the avalanches leap. There float the clouds as overhead, and the lonely and lordly vulture poises in slow flight his broad wings.

Scarce more accurate is this mirrored repetition of the surroundings and overhangings of the lake than the reproduction in the home of the pattern life and character of the family head. Line after line the pattern is worked into their own life by young copyists until the same lines and figures faithfully reappear. With the most youthful members of the circle, long before they can respond to our voices in articulate speech, our words and signals are intelligible, and answering signals give back perfect counterpart of the correspondence. Then it is that what they see and hear in the home, the tones that are uttered, the scenes that are acted, voices of passion and mirth, the hushed and solemn accents of prayer, the quietness around them on the Sabbath-day, or the rude clamor that fills its hours, the postures of kneeling or of revelling households, occupy their mind with images thenceforward vivid, influential, and imperishable. I have thought this ought to be said here, for if the sense of this be not on our hearts as parents, if the question of our personal spirit and example be not our first point of solicitude, and the necessity of honestly being and doing for ourselves all that we propose for the household do not press us, it is of little use to inquire further.

I. There must, of course, be for the hallowing of the Sabbath in the family, as well as out of the family, a refraining from work. It must be seen there that all the workers, so far as possible, rest from labor, cease from their ordinary occupation. This must not be a transfer of the business from the office and the field to the privacy of the home. It is not ceasing from labor to stay in the house, instead of going to the counting-room or the shop, and push forward our business enterprises by letter-writing, posting books, and sifting estimates and calculations. This is to bring the world into the very scene of which we are asking, How shall we keep the Sabbath then? It is invading the sanctuary of the home with what doesn't belong there on any day of the week. A business man ought to leave his knit brow and corrugated face behind him in the workshop, if he can, whenever he comes in across the doorstep of his house; let him go to his wareroom and on 'Change a business man, with all his problems working in the lines about his eyes and lips, but let him come into the family a domestic man, his pack of worldly care and harness of worldly toil depart at the door or further off, and the sunshine of love and joy shining on his countenance. He wants his hands now, not to strike a strong stroke in the earth, or on the anvil, or at trade, but to meet soft and warm palms, to catch and toss aloft his babe. His grim lips may relax for smiles and kisses and gentle words. He comes in to cheer and be cheered as a man who has not only a brain to contrive, a skill to execute, a will to hold his own in the world's competitions, but a heart with which to cherish dear ones, affections to come forth into refreshing play. It is a mistake and an impertinence on any day of the six to transfer the shop to the fireside. It is all this, and a crime beside, to make the transfer on the Lord's day.

As it isn't quite respectable on Sunday to strip the arm for downright work, there are not a few who give up the outward activities of their daily industry and keep on planning. There are plans enough laid on the Sabbath for myriads of fortunes, if God did not cross them, or give them a malign success, — plans for business, plans for travel, plans for pleasure, plans for every pursuit and hope of heart and life. The Sabbath is of all days, with multitudes, the day for planning. And this planning fills the walls of many a home with its busy talk, through almost all the hours of the family intercourse. It makes the changeful interest of conversation whenever the silence is broken. It leads out all the listeners and all the partakers into the dust and heat and glare of life again. They sit together at the family board; the light in the room is perhaps subdued from yesterday's; to the neighbors they seem to be within keeping Sabbath. But they are not within. They are out, going to and fro on free excursion trains, loading and unloading ships, ransacking foreign markets, buying, fashioning, and making up the costume for the season, and settling mercantile and social accounts. I believe it is a great and unceasing desecration of the Sabbath in many a family, this gabbling about what shall be done on the morrow. There can be no household Sabbath where this profanation is admitted.

It has been well remarked that to rest from work in hallowing the Sabbath is for each worker to cease from that which is his own employment; that is, each worker is to cease to be a worker in that matter. But wherein is he a worker? What constitutes him the man he is in that department of human industry? Is he a worker only with his two hands, or with the loins of his back? Does he not bring thought and purpose and arrangement and design into his tasks? Is he not a worker with his invention, his experience, his judgment, his sagacity? But he is to cease to be a worker in his work. Then, in that calling, he must cease from brain work as well as from hand work,— cease from planning as well as achieving, and rest his mind as well as his loins from that use of his faculties with which he fills other days.

The housework itself, that which cannot altogether pause on any day of the year, for any call, human or divine, ought to be restricted and simplified. Every housekeeper knows how to prepare for days of special preoccupancy that interdicts careful attention to the domestic management. Such days occur not unfrequently in the progress of secular time, and are arranged for, without much embarrassment. This precast may be exercised as well for the Sabbath, that, as toiling manhood from without comes in to rest, toiling womanhood within may sit down in the same domestic quiet, with few calls to break in upon the calm, and plead for time and thought and strength in household tasks.

I know that the wives and daughters of many homes are unvisited by any such disturbing summons. Are there not the servants? If the table is to be graced with the presence of Sabbath guests, and a sumptuous banquet is desired, or if we choose ourselves to fare more luxuriously than yesterday because we have more leisure to sit and enjoy the dainties, or because the family circle is more full, or because we shall not be driven forth when the repast is ended to intercourse in which all our keenness and alertness will be in demand, but may drowse our dulness away, if we so please, in extension chairs, or on pillowed couches, the special provision need not greatly tax our personal attention or activity. All that we have to do is to give our orders. The cook will serve up at the appointed time our favorite dishes; the parlor girl and butler will see that the family style suffers no discredit. All will go well. We pay good salaries, and can rely upon having our directions faithfully and gracefully complied with. We need not stay to superintend; we can sit through the morning in our pew, cool and untroubled, our thoughts drifting away occasionally to the entertainment in progress, but not in distressing anxiety, rather in pleasant anticipation; and in decorous observance we and our favored children keep Sabbath ordinances. Meanwhile at home the work goes bravely on. The kitchen is a laboratory of art. The converging processes that are to meet in the issue are put in motion, each in its time and at its proportioned rate of advance. Fires glow, meats steam, savory clouds thicken, and the grand success looms clearly up through all the apparent disorder.

But who are these creatures on whom the heat and the

burden are rolled? Are they machines, automatons? Ah, no. They are men and women, beings with souls, — souls as deathless as those that gave out the order for the dinner, and then rolled at leisure to the house of God, — with the same large capacities, the same immortal destinies pending.

Oh, the unutterable meanness of these family entertainments! The board is covered with generous cheer; but they are not generous souls that preside. They have been somewhat thoughtful, they fancy, for their own spiritual health; they have robbed the cheaper soul, which they have kept grinding in the prison-house of toil, of its Sabbath sunshine, God's house, Jesus' gospel. They themselves must be edified by the formulas of worship, — prayers, music, preaching, — and they must dine well. As for the Irish help, why, it wont make much difference with them, and they are well paid, and like the place too well to leave, and really it is somewhat of a pity, but the thing can't be managed in any other way, and this is the day when these friends can best of all favor them, and so there is nothing to be said. No, "nothing to be said" just now; but there will be something to be said by and by. This is an honorable family, — by courtesy a Christian family, — but I know that the servants' wages there are paid, if not in uncurrent money, in money which the banks wont receive on deposit! This family would insist on being taken to heaven, when the time can't be postponed, in the family coach, though drivers and footmen had to take back the carriage, and thus be themselves shut out!

The Sabbath in the family should breathe its benediction of rest from work along all the levels of the family mansion, and upon every avoidable secular task of hand or thought.

Another thing in the hallowing of the family Sabbath is to secure for the household an atmosphere of order, serenity, and quietness. Some of us can remember the Sabbaths of our childhood in country homes. There was something in the very aspect of the homestead, without and within, that helped the sanctity of the day. The morning broke in unvexed stillness. The plough paused, arrested in mid-furrow. Unyoked, the oxen cropped the dewy grass, or, as the sun rose higher, lay ruminating in the shade. No musical chime from the mower's arm giving edge to his scythe disturbed the halcyon calm. The brooks ran with fuller music, as though they struck a richer melody of praise, and the bees' hum came in with deeper and clearer resonance. A mellower light, as though mingled of chastened elements, mantled the dwelling and brooded over the sacred solitudes of the unwrought fields. The columned vapor from the solid stone-built masonry of the chimney-top rose like morning incense from an altar. Through the east windows, the golden rays streamed in upon a scene of quietness and order. The household furniture was in its place, — for even chairs and footstools were not suffered to be irregular on that day, — the incitements and accompaniments of childish sports were set aside as not to be handled in those hours, the nameless litter of childhood's treasures, strewn as by fairy hands through the "living room," was cleared away, making strange and staid vacancy, and the family clock ticked with a more suggestive and impressive stroke. A spirit of cleanliness reigned, and draped the forms that moved slowly about the mansion, as "with fine linen, clean and white," which "is the righteousness of saints." All rude and harsh noises were hushed, and to our young hearts it was made to seem that the permitted boisterousness of other days would wound the tender sensitiveness of this. It was impossible not to discern that this was a day that differed from other days. We felt as though some most reverent presence came nearer than amid the clash of our implements of toil and instruments of mirth, and that we must walk and talk softly beneath that sacred shadow.

We cannot bring in, in every scene of household life, this witness and echo of Nature to the statute of her Lord. But the tranquil and orderly serenity of the family apartments we may strive to secure. The eve of preparation, diligently improved, may anticipate and save the hurry and bustle of Sabbath morning. A studious carefulness may make our movements more quiet, the tones of our voices more gentle. Our children may be taught that some of the shriller stops of their wondrously-varied organ are not to be drawn on Sabbath-days. The loud, ringing laugh and gleeful shout may be hushed into music more subdued; the sonorous footfall, clattering through entries and up and down stairways, taught a softer tread, and passion and petulance chided as jarring on the pleasant Sabbath harmony. You are thinking how difficult a thing it is to tone down this sharp-chorded spirit, to key lower the spontaneous symphonies of those lips, to find any Sabbath opiate for those restless and tireless nerves. Yes, do the best you can; the *head* of life and energy within the young frame is so high and full that it will force unwitting expression. The school-boy's self-vindication for startling the hum of school life by sending out his breath round and musical from his mouth was almost philosophically correct. "He hadn't whistled," he said; "it whistled itself." This exuberance of strong pulsing vitality is not to be harshly repressed, — frozen silent and stiff by frigid frowns, — but softly hushed down as a gentle sky calms a tossing sea, when all its waves are gambolling at play. What we want is to inspire from earliest life in these young hearts a tender reverence for Sabbath hours, a growing sense that the day differs in sacredness from other days, has other uses, and must have another keeping. Still the problem remains, you say, "How to manage these mercurial spirits, under unwonted restrictions, and deprived of the diversions of other days." Shall we keep from them their toys, deny them the games, the blocks, the picture-books, that amuse so many hours on other days? Then what shall those little empty hands take hold of? What objects shall those restless, roving eyes fasten upon? Daytime is long for these small people when unrestricted fertility invents and caters for their entertainment. How can either they or their guardians bear the burden of unoccupied Sabbaths?

I am not wise enough to answer. Blessed would be the art that could devise and frame for the nursery a set of Sabbath diversions! How many benedictions of mothers, ready to faint by the way, would come upon the head of that fortunate artist! And that word "diversion" is the key to the problem, after all. These young spirits must be diverted from preying upon themselves and upon the rest of the household, in ways that shall come to help the power of Sabbath associations. Occupation is indispensable through some medium of eye or ear or hand for the mind.

I found a group of children one Sabbath-day, with all their secular blocks and cards in the midst of the parlor floor, and engaged in busiest architecture. "But do you play with your blocks on Sunday?" I asked. "Oh, papa!" protested one eager voice, "we are building a church, and there is the pulpit, and we are going to put a preacher in it, and then we shall have meeting." I did not upset their steepled fabric, but I offered my services as preacher, and was somewhat enthusiastically received. A very extensive and elaborate arrangement of chairs and sofas, harnessed with cords and mounted with footstools and cushions, was introduced to me, at another time, as a family coach, the driver in his place, with whip in hand, ready to take the household to the meeting-house for Sabbath worship. A more modest equipage was suggested, occupying less room and attention, with more quiet progress, as better suited to the Sabbath expedition, and the apartment was restored to order, while the incident furnished a good text from which to speak of Christ's meek entry into Jerusalem, and of Elijah's chariot and horses of fire.

If only there could be a rattle for the babe with the mimic chime of Sabbath bells, a trumpet that would blow a Sabbath tune, a soldier's array that would help the little heroes to fight the battles that already summon them to be valiant, what a relief it were! Yes, and what a loss perhaps to the discipline of the parental spirit!

After all our wit and self-devotion, it will be needful full often to issue decrees and interdicts that rest on authority alone. The Sabbath must say to childhood as it says to manhood, as all divine law says to the subject, "Thou shalt," and "Thou shalt not." It is feared, I know, that by such strictness we may make the Sabbath repelling to young hearts, bring over them a chill when it returns, as though a gloomy and cold shadow had fallen upon them, and settle the memory of the day in their hearts as something hostile and unfriendly to their joy. I believe this danger is overrated. I have no doubt that there are homes that are invested with almost funeral gloom on the Sabbath-day, blots in the smiling landscape of good and glad nature, out of which oppressed spirits, feeling as though buried alive, would rush into any avenue for the sake of escaping into light and air. These are superstitious rather than Christian homes. They are not homes where the parental heart retains the sympathy of its own youth, or gives itself in sacrificing love to the comfort and improvement of the young. They are selfish homes, most likely, where sternness prevails because it is cheaper than kindness, and peremptory statutes save indolence from self-reproach. But no home is so truly joyful as a well-governed home, — a home where wise laws are firmly administered, and wholesome restraints imposed. No home is so miserable to all the inmates as one where childhood and youth have the mastery over parental authority, and freely follow out the prompting of their own lawless inclination. Liberty, guarded by law, restrained by law, and obedient to law, is a happier state than full and wild license. Religion itself is a binding of the heart and God and duty; but it is through all its exercises of penitence and submission, faith and hope, a tenderer joy than the roving freedom on which it casts its bonds. The child-heart is steadied and guided by restraining statutes; it touches sure and firm certainties; the sweet sense of right and of its inward approval gathers upon it, and its young feet find themselves, if not in the paths of self-gratification, at least and even more consciously, in "the way of peace." Abraham was to command his children and his household after him. It will be often needful that the parent should exercise his rightful authority during the passing of the Sabbath-day. It is the method by which God teaches the young heart the great and precious lesson of obedience and submission. We need not be afraid as parents, tenderly and firmly in the last issue, to insist upon reverence to the Sabbath in our home, to legislate for quietness and order, sure that in this we are legislating for serenity of spirit and a wealth of happy young thoughts, as well as for many a precious thing in character beside. I can remember a home so guarded by Sabbath-law and the supplemental authority of the family head. I can remember that the whole household group went regularly and reverently to the house of God. No light excuse passed current with that firm arbitration. Any convenient Sabbath sickness, that was sick enough to detain one of us from the sacred porch, was sick enough to be treated with the bitterest remedy the house afforded, not welcome a second time. In pauses of worship, or in the mellow hours softening toward the evening twilight, the whole household were gathered together, and the good old catechism, each question, with its "variations," "what is enjoined," "what is forbidden," etc., was recited from beginning to ending. I think I can remember that childhood then was a little restive at times under this strict constraint, that keen eyes watched the sun's disappearing behind the western hills, — the hour for relaxing the vigilance that had stood on guard till then; but I can remember and do testify that it was not an unhappy home, the Sabbath was not a gloomy day. Either these eyes cannot see clearly through the mist of tender memories, or there was never a happier, more genial, more loving home. The atmosphere of law and love was one. Law was only another name for love, and love administered law. And the Sabbaths thus spent in such regulated observances were then and are now all bright in the review, because gilded with the smile of approving Heaven. It was such a Sabbath as I am pleading for, through which order, quietness, and serenity reigned together.

It follows here naturally to say that it is one office of the family Sabbath to cultivate the domestic affections. The life of the week leads out the members of the family and joins them to various outside fellowships. The master of the home enters the circle of his fellow-craftsmen and exchanges with them greetings and pledges. The mistress looks after the ties that bind her to the social sphere in which she moves. The sons and daughters go to meet their school-day acquaintances or their chosen companions of their age. They are these outside bonds which are strengthened through the six days' contacts and intercourse. Often those that dwell beneath the same roof see but little of one another through the days of toil. They exchange morning salutations, and snatch a hasty meal in company, then drift about till evening brings them together wearied and worn, or thronged still with care, and the night hides them within her curtains. Many a busy man is almost a stranger to his own household; but the Sabbath brings these parted ones together and holds them together. They are for a few hours, at least, members of no fellowship but that of the home; they are all there, and all at rest; they sit side by side, with no hurrying call to bid them "rise and depart;" they can give question and answer in long and intimate communion; the pent-up confidences of their hearts may have utterance now; fond inquiries bring out the troubling or the joyful secret, and heart opens to heart. Then they go to the house of God still in company. They sit again side by side in the same family pew. The great truths of God's word, however absorbing the meditation upon them, do not tend to divide them in thought and feeling from one another, but rather to endear them and draw the tie closer in the anticipation of sharing together an eternal home in heaven. The close of the day and the evening has especial dews of blessing for the life and fragrance of this domestic union. The calm of the day has taken possession of their spirits. Its influences and associations have rebuked littleness and meanness and envy and jealousy, and they are nearer together than when the day began. They look now more closely upon one another's faces and forms. They seem comelier and lovelier to the eye than on other days. All their attractiveness is freshened up. They are in newer and fairer costume than yesterday's; they scarce knew that each wore the family features so becomingly, and that each could be so gracious and winning in figure and manner. "It is not unlawful," says Baxter, discoursing on the "divine appointment of the Lord's day," "to be at the labor of dressing ourselves somewhat more ornately or comely than on another day, because it is suitable to the rejoicing of a festival," nor is it unworthy of us to remember, we may say, that thus the eyes in which we desire to appear and to be our best may look upon us more fondly and pleasantly.

It is well that the evening meal be served invitingly, not sumptuously and at the cost of the Sabbath's leisurely calm to any member of the household, but with such festal and relishing appliances as nimble skill can easily furnish within this unoccupied hour, or generous forethought provide as the old week goes out. We agree with Ephraim, the Syrian, who exhorts against "gluttony and drunkenness" on the Lord's day. "Thou, my brother, shouldst not annul the work of God for meat and dainties, nor to favor an insatiable appetite shouldst thou, occupied and distracted with culinary cares, hinder the sacred purpose of the day. All these things we leave to those whose god is their belly and whose glory is their shame." I am not pleading in the interest of appetite, but in the name of a reunited household keeping the Lord's festival, that their evening meal of itself contribute something to the happy and genial intercourse around the family board. The poet Grahame sings well, —

> " Hail, Sabbath ! thee I hail, the poor man's day;
> On other days the man of toil is doomed
> To eat his joyless bread, lonely, — the ground
> Both seat and board. . . .
> But on this day, embosomed in his home,
> He shares the frugal meal with those he loves."

That is the place and hour for thankful reminiscences, for speaking of God's good hand upon them in their household story, for calling up Sabbaths gone and fellow-worshippers departed, and drawing the bonds of kindred love and union closer about their hearts. The morrow will strike the golden chain that holds them in one to-day and jar them apart. Let them have their light feast as a grateful celebration of the gladness and goodness of such an hour, a help to its joyfulness and a seal upon its memory. In staid and rigid Scotland the "Sabbath-night supper" has been an immemorial institution, a household sacrament, a sunbeam falling across a sombre cloud. It was seasoned with pious talk, and, as Tertullian wrote of the same charmed hour, "prayer concludes the feast." So witnesses the bard of Ayrshire, —

> "The cheerful supper done, wi' serious face,
> They round the ingle form a circle wide;
> The sire turns o'er in patriarchal grace
> The big ha' Bible, and his father's pride."   BURNS.

Add to this chastened festivity music. Most afflicted is that home where there is neither voice, nor art, nor heart for the strains of sacred song. The family harmony culminates in that pleasant concert. All that has kept any spirit there from any other melts away as the varied notes mingle and blend. They all aim at concord. They produce concord. They have come together in agreement and unison. They cannot, after singing in the same strains, soaring in company on wings of praise toward the divine presence, remember differences and cherish alienations. There is a charm in this hour of song for all the members of the household. Fretful childhood and querulous age are alike soothed and spellbound. "I am persuaded," writes Legh Richmond to his daughter, "that music is designed to prepare for heaven, to educate for the choral enjoyment of paradise, to form the mind to virtue and devotion, and to charm away evil, and sanctify the heart to God. A Christian musician is one who has a harp in his affections, which he daily tunes to the notes of the angelic host, and with which he makes melody in his heart to the Lord."

A Sabbath thus spent cannot fail to endear the members of the home to one another. This is an issue it were well to have distinctly in view. Whatever can forward it, by pleasantness of mien and of speech, by using more freely the language of love, for which, perhaps, there are ears and hearts in our dwelling that are aching, — a language that flies our lips in the sternness of our interchanges with a selfish world, — by entering tenderly into the sharp passages of one another's daily experience, rehearsed on this day, by making the rooms of the house bright with firelight and lamplight, or bringing in flowers to shed both beauty and fragrance around, and helping the festal aspect of the home, we ought to call into service. We should so keep the Sabbath within this domestic retreat as to secure by it the full realization of the highest ideal of Christian domestic life.

Finally, the Sabbath should be improved in the family as a day for special religious teaching. The great object of the day is to take off our thoughts from things material, earthly, and temporal, and bring them into communion with things invisible, heavenly, and eternal. This object must be pursued as steadily, and can be secured at least as successfully, with the children of the household as in wider and older circles. The responsibility for this home nurture comes upon the parent or guardian. If he act the part of a faithful and tender provider for these dependent ones in all but this, and carelessly or indolently or timidly omit this, he is yet chargeable with the most unkind neglect. To have denied them daily bread would have been less cruel.

He may think himself unequal to so grave a task. But why is he a parent? The relation is upon him. He cannot flee from the duty.

If he heartily and prayerfully undertake it, he will find himself wonderfully helped. He must, of course, be willing to summon his best energies to the work. The Sabbath will be to him, not a day of self-indulgent sloth, but of great intellectual activity. Nor will he leave all the burdens of the day for the day itself. He may make large preparation for it before it arrive.

It will be his duty to see that his family know the public ordinances of the day. If he teach otherwise by his own example, in whole or in part, if he prefer for himself an easy and undisturbed attendance upon preaching, with no restless elements in his pew, he can, in no way, redeem for those young hearts the proper influence of the day. He is teaching error, though he mean it not, by a fearfully-convincing demonstration.

He may do much by interesting himself in their attendance upon the Sabbath-school, aiding them in the preparation of their lessons, looking with them into the library-books which they bring in, inviting their teacher to meet them under their roof and to become acquainted with them in their domestic development, and lending his whole personal sanction to the influence of this beneficent institution in their religious training.

But this is not the whole, though it is where many parents stop. He may lay up through the week special questions and topics for Sabbath consideration, — questions that have arisen in the progress of family discipline, — topics suggested by peculiarities of disposition and faults or virtues of character which he has observed from day to day, but could not take thoroughly in hand. He may gather night after night a store of touching and impressive incidents from his nightly reading of the press; remember his little school, his small home parish, in all his reading and all his seeing and all his hearing, and have more instructive and suggestive matter accumulated in his Sabbath drawer than he can exhaust.

He must not forget that these young pupils receive

their most vivid and memorable lessons through the senses. It is worth his own while to make himself as carefully and fully acquainted as his circumstances will permit with the wonders of the earth and the air and the sea, and lead out the exploring and eager young thought to those exhibitions of the divine power and skill and goodness, with which the visible creation is filled. The pages of nature are all pictorially illustrated to his hand. Stars and dewdrops, rainbows and violets, clouds and their shadows, thunder-storms, the round and the products of the seasons, their own frame fearfully and wonderfully made, animal and insect life, light, heat, frost, — let him make these sensible things ministers and revealers of God and his character and his truth. He will find no lack of interest, or of stimulating questioning with his young audience.

Following the hint of teaching by the senses, let him be sure to furnish the nursery with a pictorial Bible. This emblazoned typology will draw curious eyes between the leaves, and let in the marvellous histories there upon the mind, and they will never be forgotten. Let him seek to make this book of books a charm and a fascination to the circle of little ones. My own father was a fine reader of Scripture narratives. He took pains to read well in his house to the youngest ears that could listen with any intelligence. It was as good as play to hear him give out some of the stirring scenes of the Scripture record. He used to indulge us often in that way on the Sabbath. He was magnificent upon the duel of David and Goliath. The first verse of that grand chapter, as he began, always thrilled our hearts like the blast of a trumpet. The echoes come back yet, as I read it again, from that part of childhood's Sabbath hour, and all ringing with heroic tones, "Now the Philistines gathered together their armies to battle, and were gathered together at Shochoh, which belongeth to Judah, and pitched between Shochoh and Azekah, in Ephes-dammim."

By whatsoever volumes and helps, we must teach our households religiously on the Sabbath. Not in set forms, not in systematic lessons, not in dry and hard details. We must be men of parables. It is surprising how rich and fertile one may become in this style of teaching, even the humblest and least-favored mind, by making it an object of a little thought and study. Our children's minds and hearts are ours on the Sabbath. On other days they are school-children, they are apprentices, they are clerks; they are studying, with other teachers and masters, the knowledge of this world. On this day they are with us. They are sons and daughters only, while the Sabbath sun lingers. They are heirs with us of immortality. We may join hands with them, draw their arms within ours, and walk on with them toward the gate of heaven.

I feel still that the practical difficulties remain as before. Childhood is restless, volatile, impatient of restraint, and naturally averse to religious truth. With us both brain and heart are often weary. All our devices fail at times to bring the peace of a Sabbath benediction upon the troubled waters of household unrest. We are often, as parents, straitened, ashamed, and desponding. I hope I have not added to this feeling of discouragement, or if we despair over the ideal which so often rises before us, it may serve to lead us down into the valley of humiliation and prayer. God will help us, when, feeling weak, we cast ourselves upon his strength. He will make some of the failures over which we mourn so bitterly — those unsatisfying, weary Sabbath-days — blessed successes.

Some wedded heart here is saying, with a great sorrowfulness, "I stand alone in this formidable effort; the help I most need of all human giving is withheld; it is not help, but hindrance. What I say and do for Sabbath hallowing in my home is unsaid and undone, I fear, by one at my side. How strong, how comforted, I should feel, if this interrupted union could only fill itself out by a harmony offering and example in this sacred observance!"

Oh, lonely wife, I know thee who thou art! Thou canst not bid thy children dishonor their father; thou thyself honorest and lovest him. Thou canst not suffer them to approve; thou art in perpetual dread lest their feet follow after the ways that so grieve thee and that have to them such persuasive sanction. Beseech the merciful One that, through the kindness of thine heart and the weakness of love, thine own feet go not astray. And thou redouble the mother's faithfulness, prayerfulness, and constancy, and doubt not that the strong and living child thus trained will yet conduct down the divine blessing.

Oh, husband, father, who takest thine own pleasure on the Lord's day, shall the seeds of that example grow up in young hearts into hardness and crime, and on some tragic day the child, whose eye follows now your thoughtless Sabbath step, look back out of a stained and blasted manhood to this light pleasuring of yours, as the germ of his awful doom? Do you know how you try the heart, every throb of whose womanly tenderness is yours, and which, keeping reproaches and remonstrances silent, smiles, perhaps, upon you because it cannot grieve you, in that over which it mourns? Are there not gentleness and manliness enough in your soul — if we speak not of the fear of God and the voice of solemn duty — to keep you from such a trampling at once upon God's law, a woman's heart, and a child's fate?

V.

KNOWING CHRIST.

" . . . FOR I KNOW WHOM I HAVE BELIEVED." — 2 Tim. i. part 12.

HOW it is that one who walks with Christ, and whose soul is joined to him in a vital and conscious union knows this Saviour as no other soul knows him, it will be difficult so to explain by any language or imagery which can be employed as to make it intelligible to those who have no experience of it. And yet this is just what many an inquiring spirit desires and waits to comprehend. They stand at a distance and look upon him whom the gospel sets forth as the way of life. They walk round about him without seeing how to approach him, and having no confidence in any addresses they may offer to him. He is to them remote, indistinct, almost mythical. Perhaps they have not yet settled it in their thoughts who and what he is. If they attempt communication with him, it is all on their side; they have only their own voices; there are no returning accents; all is silent, motionless, and unresponsive.

"Does he reveal himself to those that believe in him? Does he come to meet them out of this vague and hazy distance? Does he break his silence so that they hear and recognize his voice? Do they know him as their Friend and Redeemer, and know that they know him, and come into relations of intimacy with him, and exchange with him reciprocities of love, confidence, and sympathy?" So they question.

If now as those to whom Christ is precious, and to whom he has made himself known, we could open to them all the journal of our hearts, introduce them to scenes of an inward personal experience which never can be thrown upon canvas, tell them how it is that we are sure we have seen and felt and touched and embraced him, what it is we know of him, by what process this acquaintance was made and has ripened, and wherein is the daily consciousness of his presence with us, and his power upon us, it would meet perhaps better than any other demonstration the state of mind in which so many now are. True we might answer in the words of Philip to Nathaniel, "Come and see." But they want to be helped to come, and have their eyes guided to that which is to be seen. We might say, "Here's the guide-book; read and follow the directions." But it is not strange that they should feel that it is one thing to look upon a map of an unknown region, or to study a guide-book, and another thing to hear from one who has been a traveller that way what his own lips can say about it.

So they say to us, "Tell us how you know Jesus, and know that he is such a Saviour." It may be that if we attempt to tell, we shall often break down through poverty of words; that we shall often seem to them as speaking without meaning, because the meaning is beyond them;

that when we lead them out into our experiences, we shall get them presently beyond their depth.

Just as when one listens to two artisans conversing upon the subject of their craft, or a circle of professional men discussing the matters of their profession, he may understand much of what is signified, but every now and then is made to feel that he is off soundings where they easily touch bottom. Still something surely can be said, and said intelligibly, though it be said out of an experience to which the listener is a stranger, of that experimental knowledge of Christ possessed by a renewed heart.

1. We know whom we have believed not simply as an historic personage, — just as we know Washington or Columbus or William Tell. It is not simply that we can say where he was born, and of what parentage, and trace, without the omission of one incident, all the story of his life. This you know as well as we.

2. It is not that we have opinions about him which we entertain with entire confidence. Mere opinions might be shaken by some style of argument, some show of evidence, which we have not yet met. But absolute knowledge, of course, nothing can overturn. We have opinions concerning Napoleon Bonaparte and Oliver Cromwell, but not the sort of intimate, experimental knowledge of which we are now speaking. We have opinions concerning our neighbors and acquaintances, the men whom we have seen and mixed with for years, and yet none of these men do we know as we know the Lord Jesus Christ.

3. It is not that we know him through the works of his hand as Creator, and can speak thus of the power that heaved up the mountains and hollowed the oceans and arched the starry skies; of the wisdom that has executed such masterpieces of contrivance, and flows in the countless channels of design; of the taste that has tinted the air, painted the sunset clouds, shaped the forest tree, carpeted the meadow with emerald velvet, and starred it with flowers; of the goodness that shines in the sun, marches in the seasons, lisps down in summer rains, and rolls its great waves in harvest-time. The mere sentimentalist knows all this.

4. It is not that we know him as a Teacher in that record of his short life. Many another eye than ours has perused that Sermon on the Mount, and many another tongue pronounced it sublime, unequalled. The touching and tender beauty of the parables, their simplicity, aptness, force, and naturalness have been appreciated by other minds, who have written them "exquisite, inimitable." The faultless and lofty maxims of his morality, the gentleness of his charity, his purely Christian lessons of forgiveness, have had other admirers than those who know him as we know.

5. It is not that we know him just as an example, have seen how he fulfilled all the relations of life, how patient he was under contradiction, how, when he was reviled, he reviled not again, how diligent and earnest in the work he had to do, how meek, how mild, how long-suffering, how compassionate, how forbearing toward great offenders, how spotless and irreproachable everywhere. All this record is public property, and this example has

even had its eulogies as the crowning purpose of his mission and life.

6. The knowledge we have of him is a present and current knowledge. We know him now and to-day. We do not in this peculiar apprehension of him go back up the centuries. It is not that we have made his acquaintance here in these pages of long ago. Or if we were here introduced to him, we have had another and a later acquaintance with him. We know him in the present, — not as the prophet that trod the shores of Galilee, and the streets of Jerusalem, but as to-day and every day with us and showing himself unto us.

7. We know him thus personally, for ourselves, not as through the testimony of the evangelists, who walked with him and talked with him. We, too, have walked with him and talked with him. It is not of him that we know from those that have been nearer to him than we. We know himself by an intimacy existing directly between his heart and ours. We have had experience of what he is, and have come into personal relations and conscious union to him.

8. We know him as our sacrifice and peace. When we could not but consent to the law of God that it was holy and good; when we could not but confess that we had broken it, and deserved its condemnation; when a sharper sentence was passed against us by our own consciences within, and we carried about this burden, Judas-like, "I have sinned," ourselves our accusers, and knew no way to silence this remorseful accusation, or to escape that condemnation, our peace slain, and a

fearful looking-for of judgment, half slumbering, half wakeful, but always a dull, deep pain, an abiding gloom, in our consciousness, we came one day upon this Jesus as though he had just descended alive from the cross after his agony. He was bleeding in head and hands and feet and side. He looked upon us with ineffable love in his face, and as he fastened thus our wondering eye, he said, "Burdened one, I have brought you a pardon for your sin. Look up and smile; you are acquitted, you are free." Our first thought is one of rapturous amazement; with the second a chill questioning comes back upon our heart, and falteringly we ask, "But did not God then care much about our sinning? Was it but a slight injury done to him and his government? Can he overlook it so easily? Did our consciences make too much of it, and were we burdened more than we need to have been?"

And still that look of love beams upon us, and that wounded hand holds out the pardon, and, with a strangely meaning smile, the voice says, "It is free, it is yours." But our question falters forth again, "The penalty, then, as an expression of God's estimates of holiness and sin, was it too severe? Is it set aside? By simply returning to our allegiance, can we make up all the injury done, and are the interests of a moral government cared for?" And the lips sweetly reply, "The penalty is set aside. I have come in God's name, and bringing God's love, to tell you this good news." It is not clear to us yet; something is evidently held back; the significance of that smile is not interpreted; we are still troubled in our joy about the way the thing is managed, our conscience still shy of resting in it, and we look up again, and another question flashes across us, "Because we have not yet seen the ill-desert of sin recognized and met. There is no expiation. We cannot have peace even by an act of forgiveness at the expense of our conscience. But why do you bleed? The pardon is all stained with crimson. What is this that you have suffered?" And the loving smile half answers as we begin to feel that we are somehow connected with that tragedy, and the voice briefly explains, "The penalty was set aside, and another sanction for the law was substituted." "Yes," we reply, eagerly, for we are on the track now, "and that substitute was this great suffering of one so august and sacred," and our eyes fill with starting tears. "Why," it is answered, "I could not show pity to a sinner, and be suspected of sympathizing with his sin; that were still more to dishonor the law and affront the Lawgiver; that were treason against the crown. So it was arranged that I should give this testimony for the law and against sin, showing that I am on God's side and the law's side as to sin, while still after this sacrificial testimony I could bless and save you." "Then it is you that have made this pardon so free, and oh, at such a price! it is for me you bleed, and God's love has found a channel through that mangled flesh!" "It was a true burden which I felt," says conscience. "We were not mistaken about the desert of sin; but who could have dreamed of such a way?" And we fall at those feet and take the pardon, and wash away the flowing blood with faster flowing tears, and pour out our heart there and say, "Lord, thou hast bought me, thou hast bought me." In this scene we have known Jesus. It could not have been more real to us if it had been between man and man. We have held such an interview with him, and entered into such relations with him. Always when the thoughts of the past trouble us, we see him standing between our sin and our punishment with his bleeding form. Always when we are betrayed afresh into sin, with shame and agony in our hearts, struggling with penitence and love, we see him standing thus our shield from justice. So do we know him ever as our sacrifice and our peace. We do not dream this, we experience it. There is no more positive experience of our life. If you have confidence in our sanity and our veracity, you must receive this testimony.

9. We know again that we have communion with him. Our knowledge is that we are admitted to personal intercourse with him. It is not that we believe in his omniscience and omnipresence, and are persuaded that he hears us and understands us and knows our desires; it is that he makes us feel that his personal presence comes upon us and around us. We are no more sure, without sight, of the presence of a flower by its fragrance, of fire by its warmth, of the open air by its freshness, than we are of his nearness by what he breathes upon us. There comes before him, as he visits our place of kneeling, an influence that heralds his approach. That influence fastens upon our heart and draws it unto him. The influence of the magnet upon steel is not more positive. Love glows, faith clings, hope soars, weakness and want plead, and the whole nature goes to him as his presence draws. It is not imagination that stirs the soul

so deeply and lifts all its passionate waves of trust and desire toward this invisible presence, any'more than it is imagination that raises the tide wave out of the ocean level, and keeps it rolling round the earth. It is not imagination that paints before our inner eye the portraiture of that face in whose speaking lineaments we behold all the heart of God. It is not fancy that calls up to our thought just the promises we most need to cheer us, and the precepts indispensable to guide, and makes us hear his gracious whispers of acceptance and benediction. Imagination is a waking dream; but all this is the most conscious reality, and abides with us in solid results of spiritual comfort and life. Were they fancies, they would evaporate in bright sentimentalisms, brief and unsubstantial as the roseate morning vapors. Imagination could not renew her magic for us thus every day. But communion is, with more or less vividness, our daily experience, and its influence remains a power upon our heart continually. It is not the effect of place and posture with us. We do not go to the closet to meet our Saviour there; he goes with us, as though he said, drawing our arm through his, "Come, let us be alone together for a while." It is not only in the closet that we have this intercourse. As we do not meet there for the first, so we do not part as we recross the threshold with outward step. This consciousness of communion with Christ attends us, so that a glance will look into his friendly eye, a low-voiced call will bring an answering voice, a hand stretched out will meet his clasping hand.

10. We know thus that we have him to lean upon.

The greeting of a new morning wakes us, and we have the day's pilgrimage to set out upon. Whither the way will lead to-day, and how the path will open, we know not. In ourselves we are weak and dismayed before all the uncertainties clustering along the hidden caves our feet are to explore. Then we ask him to join company with us, that we may not go alone; and straightway our sense of solitude and loneliness departs. We know this. Our spirit feels the fellowship and becomes brave and hopeful in this consciousness. Presently the way becomes steep; the climbing steps of arduous duty are to lead us up the acclivities; our panting breath and faltering limbs appeal to him, and he bids us lean upon his supporting hold, and we take him at his word, and find that we are resting upon solid strength. The path becomes obscure and weary; we turn in perplexity to him, and he goes before us to show the right. Our doubts dissolve. Guiding footprints lead us on without wandering. The heat of the noontide becomes oppressive; we are wearied and ready to faint; the day is but half gone and we are spent. "Cast thy care here," is the soothing whisper that glides into our soul, — "Lay off thy burden upon the Lord," "Lean more heavily; I will sustain you." We do lean; we make over our weariness to him, and we feel, we know, that we are rested, refreshed, and recruited. We next see clouds gathering; the sun withdraws his light; we plunge down some dark defile; we are afraid; it is the shadow of an inscrutable Providence that falls upon us, and our heart fails us. But he makes us know that he is near; he ever presses closer to our side, and gives us the comforting assurance, "I will never leave thee nor forsake thee." And so, whatever the experience of the day, when our spirits droop, when we are hard beset, when we know not whither to turn, when our weakness is like the giving up of the ghost, we find this one presence always about us. We cannot be deceived. Every effect must have its cause. We feel the blessed effects of this divine nearness; we are rallied and reinforced in all wavering and despondency; we are breathed upon with a freshening vigor, anointed with healing and strengthening oil, and come through the day, because of this help, with a progress to which we know our own feet to be totally inadequate.

11. We know thus, not only that we lean upon him, but that he strengthens us. This actual reception of strength, when we are altogether void of it, is a wonderful experience. Some old propensity girds itself against us; some habit seen in increasing light to be a hindrance to our spirituality and usefulness is to be thrown off; some sin against which we have forgotten to watch surprises us; some cunningly arranged and mightily enticing temptation gathers before us; some great cross lies at our door to be taken up; some difficult, delicate, intricate duty summons us; some challenge of our powers of endurance or of action, by God or man, or spirit of evil, confronts us. At first, perhaps, we do not feel our weakness. We adventure in our own sufficiency. We try to stand, and cannot; we try to do, and fail; we match ourselves with our adversary, and the contest goes against us; we lift at our cross, and our loins

give way. Our best resolution avails us nothing but to show the absoluteness of our infirmity; our sharpest endeavors only reveal how disproportionate they are to our great need. Empty of resources, we turn to Christ; we confess our emptiness and extremity. We beseech him to make his strength perfect in our weakness. Now, what we have to testify is this, — that with this resort to Jesus the whole aspect of the case changes. We stand, we overcome, we endure, we break the bands of sin, we put to rout the powers of evil, we are more than conquerors through him. We shout aloud our triumph, "I can do all things through Christ that strengtheneth me." We were fainting and sinking; our powers were overborne; there was no help in us. We look to him; we touch his hand, and as fabled Antæus, the son of earth, in his wrestling with Hercules, received new strength every time he touched the ground, so fresh forces of divine aid come to our succor at every look upon Christ, every contact with his sacred form. We cannot be mistaken in this. It is the result of the thousand experiments, all governed by the same law, and all issuing adversely or prosperously as we trust ourselves on him. It is the daily and hourly witness of our lives.

12. So we know him as our *light*. We are blind and ignorant, and turning to him for illumination. Not more surely does the day come with the rising sun than guiding beams stream down to our bewildered thoughts as we invoke his shining. We know it by as many historic scenes in our past as there are days in the years we have lived.

13. So is he our *life*. If the branch of a vine had consciousness, it could not more distinctly testify that its life is in the vine than we can that our spiritual life is in Christ. We look within for it, or without, upon all other helps, and no pulse beats. We look to him, and the vital currents are in motion and the heart throbs with strong and lusty vigor. Our souls feel the living supplies as truly as Nature in all her veins the reviving of spring. We cannot say how this life cuts its channel from his heart to ours; but we know we receive it, and we know we derive it; it is not native, it is imparted, and it flows to us, or flows within us, when, and only when, we turn to him.

14. So he is in sympathy with us. It is not fancy that he comforts us in sadness, for we are really comforted; our tears are dried up; the smile returns to our face and the peace to our hearts; and this transition from mourning to joy is when we ask him to suffer our head to droop upon his breast.

15. So we see his unchanged face in all trying events. "It is I," he says, through the darkness and over the wild heaving billows, "be not afraid." "I am Lord of providence, I am head over all things to my beloved; I am purging my branches, that they may bear more fruit."

My hearers, there is no end to this testimony. I have striven only to produce specimens of it. To those whom I chiefly wish to affect, I shall have failed, after all, to make the apprehension clear how distinct all this consciousness is with a believer, how separate it is from all that is natural and self-originated within him, how certainly and unerringly he knows it.

II. You ask now, Did you know all this at first? Had you this clear perception of a present Christ and his various agency at the outset? I answer, *No.* We only trusted him for it, at the very start. We put our hand in his, but we had no *experience* of his help along the road, for we were not as yet travellers in it. We had the confidence that he could and would carry us through, — a confidence inspired by nothing that we had known, but only by his word of promise.

III. You ask again, perhaps, how this knowledge has grown upon us. I answer, By two kinds of experience. Our experience of weakness, helplessness, and peril in the great work of escaping from the bondage of sin, and our experience of the actual fruits of resorting to Christ. If I could take a single instance of such a twofold experience, it might make the matter clearer. Suppose, then, that there grows upon me the conviction that a certain trait in my character greatly hinders my piety, obstructs my progress, grieves my brethren, stumbles sinners, and clouds my own soul. I resolve to put it down. I grapple with it. The struggle is long and severe. Sometimes I think I have got the better of it. But I find soon that it is as vital as ever. It needs to be plucked up by the roots. Its tyranny becomes so galling that I cannot endure it. I carry it to this Saviour and ask him to undertake my deliverance, and he begins upon it with a process of his own. His treatment is deep and thorough, though trying, his surgery sharp, but final. I am delivered and healed. Can I doubt who has done it? And as these experiences multiply, shall I not more and more come to *know* him as a personal Saviour, and with increasing confidence carry all my needs to him?

IV. Do you ask again, How did this knowledge begin, how can it be entered upon? This is the way. The burden of wanting such a help was upon our hearts, the burden of sin, of captivity to it, and of condemnation for it, of helplessness in ourselves either to escape the latter or break from the former. We heard him set forth as such a complete and glorious Deliverer, as willing and ready to undertake for every soul that would confide its case to him. We said, If this Helper is what he is represented, he is what our great want requires. Tremblingly we approached him and retired again, then drew near shyly and once more retreated. Some single word of his caught our ear,—"Come," "Come unto me," and we went in the dark, and said there as we stood, alone, in the dark, "Is the Deliverer near? Let us know this great deliverance. Here we are, Lord, undertake for us." And we ventured to leave our case with him, as a faint echo stole out of the silence and seemed to whisper, "Him that cometh unto me I will in no wise cast out." And we now know what we did not so certainly know then, at once, that he began with us that hour.

V. Do you ask, Can *we* begin so? Yes, you can. Speak up to him now in the depths of your soul,— "Saviour, Master, Guide, whom as yet we know not, we have heard of thee as a Deliverer from the bondage of wrath and sin. We are in captivity to both. Thou art, we believe, the way of escape. We see not a step of the way. We see not even thee. But we stretch out our hands to thee; we empty them of all our idols; we lift them for thy clasping and guidance. Only lead, we will follow thee. We trust thee, make us know thee." Remember this, — "It is not know and then believe, but believe and you shall see the salvation of God."

VI.

GOD AND THE WORLD RECONCILED.

. . . . . GOD WAS IN CHRIST RECONCILING THE WORLD UNTO HIMSELF.— 2 Cor. v. part 19.

THERE is condensed here into a single line the whole breadth of the gospel. Every word is compact and weighty with the force of this great pressure upon it. The story of the incarnation, its necessity, and its purpose, the historic life and work of Jesus in the flesh, man's apostasy and alienation from God, and the sublime and touching spectacle of the infinite Father coming forth in the sacrifice of his Son and the energy of the new-creating Spirit to accomplish the marvels of redemption, — all these are here.

We have nothing that so rounds and completes the description of the gospel as this word, — it is a RECONCILING gospel. It is not merely a refining and educating system, bringing out the occult virtues and graces darkly sphered in human nature, or training to athletic vigor moral forces already vital within us, though feeble and torpid. Its great work is not to polish the roughnesses of a spirit that only needs discipline and culture to put on the beauty of holiness, just as a lapidary cuts a new-found diamond, that its imprisoned lustres may shine forth.

Its chief travail is to reconcile man to God. No other conception of it discerns its true glory, or enters into the purpose of its divine author. If it come to us merely as a code of higher morals, a stimulant to a more self-sacrificing charity of living, to open to us the inspiring example of that sinless Messenger from Heaven, to spiritualize by teachings of heavenly wisdom and beauty our life of sense, to lift us by its elevating truths above meannesses and vulgarities and dishonesties, — if this be all, it is no gospel for our deepest and most helpless need. The angels might have hushed those choral chants that broke the silence and lit the darkness of midnight above the hills of Bethlehem.

It is an atoning gospel we want, — not one in the first instance to excite and cheer us in our struggles after human perfection, but first of all to restore us to the favor of God, to slay our enmity to him, and propitiate him towards us, bringing us near to him in harmony and friendship forever.

And so it announces itself in our Scripture, "God in Christ RECONCILING the world unto himself."

I. If now this work of reconciliation, proposed as the chief function of the gospel, be a reality in the full significance of the language expressing it, then there is assumed here the essential fact of the GUILT and RUIN of MAN. We cannot advance a step in the explication of the text, without conceding that God and man are at variance. The holy inhabitants of heaven need no reconciling unto

God. He is forever at peace with them. They have never harbored a rebel thought against him. To reconcile is to reunite in love and confidence those who have been estranged, to reinstate in forfeited favor and friendship one who has offended, to make up and put away existing hostilities and alienations. To reconcile man to God is to bring them back to his favor, to appease his wrath against them, to do away the division that has rived them asunder. If such a work needs to be done, how absolutely it argues man an apostate and alien from God. Our first business, therefore, must be to set forth this breach.

God sustains to this creature man, apart from the work of redemption, relations of an infinite force and tenderness. He is the Maker of his frame, the Father of his spirit, the Builder of his home, the Provider of his bounties, the Preserver of his life, the Benefactor of his days, the Giver of every good and every perfect gift. All the offices involved in these relations God has fulfilled with spotless honor to himself, with immeasurable goodness to the creature. He has moreover made himself known to man, disclosed his character, published his will, and furnished him in his law a perfect rule of living. Now the breach is this. There is not one of those relations which man on his part has not violated and outraged. The workmanship of God's power, he has "worshipped and served the creature more than the Creator, who is blessed forever." The child of such a Parent, he has withheld all filial love and reverence; a dweller in God's earth, he has cursed and defiled it with sin; a receiver of God's bounties, he has hardened his heart against all the claims of gratitude; a subject of God's law, he has set at nought its infinite authority, and lifted the banner of rebellion against his sovereign. This is a weighty accusation, but amply and sadly sustained by the testimonies of Omniscience itself and witnessed to in all the rounds of the current human life. Here, then, is sunk a gulf of separation between God and man. God is of purer eyes than to behold iniquity. He hates sin with a perfect hatred. He is jealous of his honor and right as throned king. He has enacted and sanctioned the law, "The soul that sinneth it shall die." How can he remain in friendly communion with such rebels? Is it any wonder he has withdrawn himself from a race in arms against him, and hung over them the fulminations of his eternal wrath? And on the other side man has rejected God. He has trampled on his laws. He has given his honor unto idols. His affections have gone after other gods. His will has hardened itself against his Maker and Monarch. He is sold under sin, a willing captive to Satan, at enmity with God. How deep and awful this chasm! Man cannot cross it in the face of the sentinel thunders that guard the divine justice. God cannot cross it, leaving his broken law and shattered sceptre behind, trophies of successful insurrection. No human prayer can span it, for the condemned cannot plead against this Judge. No divine mercy can overleap it, fettered by the stern necessities of a moral government as yet defied and dishonored. So they stand on either side,—God insulted and offended, men filling up the measure of their guilt, and the yawning gulf between. So they stand, God lifting his dreadful right hand with his glittering sword, man stiffening his puny arm of rebellion. No voice of mercy, no voice of penitence, calls across from brink to brink. If God pass over, it must be to take vengeance, to execute wrath. If man pass, it must be to his trial and doom. Thus is a world divorced from God. The great malign one has wrought fearfully. The Eden intercourse is ended.

> "No more of talk where God or angel guest
> With man, as with his friend familiar, used
> To sit indulgent."

Earth is estranged from God. God has gone up from earth.

> "Foul distrust and breach
> Disloyal, on the part of man, revolt
> And disobedience. On the part of Heaven,
> Now alienated, distance and distaste,
> Anger and just rebuke and judgment given."

Can this gulf be bridged? Can this wandering orb be made to gravitate back toward the central sun? Can the great breach be repaired and God and man commune again in protecting love and filial trust as in the early Paradise? And our Scripture answers, "God is in Christ reconciling the world unto himself." And this is our next point.

II. God first moves in the effort for reconciliation. From his side of the dividing gulf, he looks across upon his rebel subjects. They are the children of his loins. Something of the Father's image is on them still. They have lost their inheritance of immortality. Without God, without hope. Striving to cheat themselves into spasms of fitful mirth, but carrying within them an upbraiding conscience and a heavy heart, and looking out portionless into the dark night of eternity. With all his feelings as a moral Governor, whose authority has been trampled on; with all his care as Sovereign of the universe, whose word and will must be inviolable; with all his hatred of sin, and his unalterable determination to punish it, he yet loves these wretched transgressors. He cannot see them perish. He yearns over his prodigal, riotous children. He longs to gather them to their Father's house, and kill the fatted calf. "How shall I give thee up?" breaks forth his compassionate sorrow. Oh, he will not give them up. Man shall see, and Heaven shall see, and the old Tempter glorying in his triumph shall see, and all the universe shall see what God can do to relight this darkened orb and set it again amid the shining spheres that wheel about his throne. The cloud-veiled heights of mercy, which no angel wing has scaled, no creature eye looked upon as yet, shall be unveiled to the wonder and praise of all loyal intelligences. Oh, what new brightness poured its floods over creation when the cloud moved! Who before could have fathomed this mighty secret of God's heart? God was holy and just and good; this they knew. Who could have hit the amazing truth that he could forgive sin, and advance the sinner to crowns and thrones in heaven? The rebel angels were hurled from their happy seats. God moved to reconcile man unto himself. They who looked to behold another stroke of infinite justice, another province of revolt lopped off from the holy and happy kingdom of Jehovah, saw another sight that held them mute with surprise and awe. Man is helpless and hopeless. He cannot rise to God. He can do nothing to bridge the gulf. He can make no overture to God. He is under sentence. His doom calls for him. But God rises in his place. A voice from the midst of the throne pierces the heavens, rends the skies, and rallies the despairing heart of earth, — "Lo, I come."

III. And he who spake was himself the assurance and type of reconciliation. While yet the gulf is impassable it disappears in the symbol of the incarnation. Look upon the person of Jesus. The lost humanity, the offended Deity, are one again. They are seen united there, blended. God in Christ, ere yet the cross is reared, has taken the rebel nature back to his bosom. He has traversed the distance that separated the two; he has thrown down the barriers between; he has bridged the chasm; the restored humanity is wedded in indissoluble bonds with the pitying Divinity, in and by the reconciling Christ. Though the law be broken, though the creature be fallen, though justice must be satisfied, though the sinner have no offering he can bring, still God and man are met. The outraged Lawgiver, the daring rebel, are joined together, and that mysterious alliance for whatever purposes assumed is clear in this, — pledges entire reconciliation, eternal fellowship. It is a promise for the creature reaching beyond all the privilege and felicity of his former estate in the garden. Adam and his Creator but communed then. They were not one. But this reconciliation after the fall is to elevate and glorify the rescued humanity to heights attainable by no other rank of created mind. "He took not on him the nature of angels." "Know ye not that we shall judge angels?" "Thou hast made us kings and priests unto God." I love to linger here, to dwell upon this living prophecy of the incarnation, to interpret its exceeding great and precious promise, to welcome it as God's bond of so perfect a reconciliation, so consummate a union, so glorious a destiny, for sinful, outlawed man.

IV. And now we must inquire as to the actual method of this reconciliation, whose transcendent issue is given us in such a type. What is needful to be done before such a result can be realized? Clearly the order and supremacy of the divine government must be sustained on the one hand, and the corrupt and alienated heart of man must be rectified and won on the other. A reconciliation must affect both parties. The bridge that spans the gulf must have its double pier to rest upon, — one on God's side, the other on ours. God cannot reconcile us just by coming over to us. He must draw us to him. He cannot come to us leaving the demands of justice clamoring for satisfaction. He cannot draw us to him without overcoming and slaying the enmity of our hearts and renovating our nature. No part of this work is possible to man. Let him seek to build up a righteousness of his own, and pile his good deeds, his laborious virtues, and costly charities one above another, and raise himself on these mole-hill eminences to match the altitudes of the perfect law. Oh, how those towering Alps, from their pure and far heights, look down upon him! Never can his sliding feet and his frail strength of climbing reach the sun-white summit. He cannot blot out one sin of the past. His former guilt nothing but his death can expiate, and his actual and current life, however loftily he aim, wins not one smile from approving law, but darkens forever under its awful frowns. Equally fruitless are his best efforts to catch his truant affections and desires, to bring them chastened and loving to his abused and injured Father, to pacify his reproachful conscience, to bend his disloyal will, to kindle within the life and power of an earnest, practical, persistent godliness. Nor could created wisdom have devised a plan by which God himself could achieve this marvel, could wed these opposites. What a problem it was to solve! Given a law of infinite value, with an infinite penalty and a world of transgressors, to make reparation to law, let the transgressors go free, and restore them to their allegiance! If the sinner be cut off in his guilt, the law is vindicated, justice is satisfied, government sustained, but there is not salvation for the lost. If the sinner be justified and forgiven, while yet there is no expiation for his guilt, it may be well with him; the mercy of God is illustriously displayed, but the authority of the sovereign Ruler is prostrate in the dust. No more shall the heavenly choirs sing together, "Justice and Judgment are the habitation of thy throne. Just and true are thy ways, thou King of saints. Who shall not fear thee, O Lord, and glorify thy name?" Under such an administration rebellion shall not stop with earth. If there be some unheard-of sacrifice by which God's just hatred of sin and his determination not to suffer it to offend with impunity can be expressed, by which thus the guilt of the transgressor, being atoned for, may be pardoned, what force beyond all this shall undertake the renovation of human character, its resurrection from spiritual death into newness of life? "Oh, the depth of the riches both of the wisdom and knowledge of God!" God, in the person of the Son, took to himself a sacrificial humanity, lending it by such alliance an infinite worth, entering thus into a condition under the law, rendering there a perfect obedience, not obligatory on him who was above the law, shedding there the blood of expiation demanded by inexorable justice, thus lifting again the trampled prerogatives of the crown, and then plying the heart of the rescued sinner by the melting power of that cross, the might of that dying love, and moving upon it with the life-inspiring energy of the new creating spirit. This great transaction solves the problem. God can offer reconciliation in the fulness of his mercy, for his crown is protected, his government upheld. The sinner can come into a cordial acceptance of this offer, and be at peace with this offended majesty, being delivered by the righteousness of Christ from the pain and pressure of an evil conscience, won by the cross of Christ to penitence, gratitude, and love, his will subdued and his nature sanctified by the operations of the Spirit of grace. And so in brief this wonderful Scripture hath its fulfilment, — that God is in Christ reconciling the world unto himself. Indignant justice is pacified; obdurate rebellion is conquered; the penal sanction of law is sustained; the sentence is removed from the penitent criminal; with unfettered love God invites; with assured confidence the weeping sinner draws nigh. Over the bridgeless gulf the Mediator has laid his own body, and upon it a just God comes with life and peace to meet the now hopeful offender, forsaking all for that embrace of love. That which was symbolized in the person of Christ is thus actualized. A new, divine life, flowing free in this unobstructed channel, enters the dead heart of the race, and quickens it to live again. God accepts a suffering Christ as the condemned criminal's substitute. The sinner receives in his welcoming and believing soul that atoning Christ as his surety with God, bringing to him not only the seal of pardon, but a new force of willing, loving, and obeying. And so the song of joy breaks from his lips. Out of the miry depths his feet are raised to stand on the Rock of ages. What wonder that he sings of the Lamb that was slain! What marvel that we hear him after death chanting on the celestial hills, "Worthy the Lamb!"

My friends, the gospel which our churches hold and our ministry preaches is sometimes thought to be and represented to be a stern and harsh system, dealing sharply with human errors, covering with forbidding gloom the face of the Almighty Father, and pressing its unlovely austerities upon shrinking and sensitive spirits. How unjust and mistaken a thought! We preach God in Christ, "reconciling the world unto himself, not imputing their trespasses unto them." If we speak of the great divisive abyss the fall has sunk between man and his God, it is to unfold the necessity and the glory of that redemptive system, that mediatorial work, that throws its indestructible arch across. If we speak of a justice that demands for every sin the blood of expiation, it is to point to the Lamb of God that taketh away the sin of the world. If we speak of the carnal heart as enmity with God, it is to tell how Jesus died for you while you were yet enemies, to reconcile you to the Father. Our gospel is a gospel of reconciliation. Our ministry is a ministry of reconciliation. The glad evangel put into our mouths is this, "Be ye reconciled to God." There is no other portrait of the divine character so ravishing as this, no overture of God to man so tender, no voice from heaven the burdened conscience so leaps to hear, nothing that so lights the dying eye and comforts the departing spirit. No other system of theology can so demonstrate to earth and heaven that mighty Scripture "God is Love." "Herein is Love," not in the golden sun or soft dews or airs of spring or fruits or harvests or vineyards or all of autumn's generous bounty, — "herein," not in health and friends and social joys and daily good, — "herein is Love! not that we loved God, but that he loved us, and sent his Son to be the propitiation for our sins."

God is not your enemy. He would be your friend. You are afraid of him, but he will deliver you from all your fears; your sins cry against you, but he will blot them out with atoning blood and remember them no more forever; you dread the process of making peace with him. Did the father of the returning prodigal afflict him with hard conditions? But God is so great, so serenely holy, so girt with majesty and kingliness! Yes, but he knows what you are, and welcomes you to a perfect reconciliation. Would you approach, fix your thought on the Mediator. There he stands in human form, — no aspect of inapproachable splendor and power, — holding the Father's right hand in one of his, stretching the other to you, a bond between God and you, occupying and filling the whole distance; human on your side, divine on the other; shading off humanity into Deity from you through himself to God; shading off Deity into humanity, again, through himself from God to you; attaching you, by this mysterious, interlinked vinculum to his Father and your Father, and transmitting divine life and joy from the Father to your spirit. Still that outstretched hand, with the print of the nail in it, solicits your acceptance. When you clasp it, Jesus is yours and God is yours and heaven is yours. Holding there, Justice cannot strike you; you belong to the humanity of Jesus, and Justice has smitten there once, and is satisfied. Held by that hand, you are one with the Father and the Son. Those strange words of Jesus in prayer for his disciples on the sorrowful night of the betrayal are fulfilled, — "I in them and thou in me, that they may be made perfect in one." Come! Are you not ready? You are unworthy, you are weak, you are timid, you are conscience-stricken, you are shackled by evil passions and habits. Yes, all that is understood; but just such as you are God in Christ calls you, waits for you, by us beseeches you to be reconciled to him. Going hence to some secret place of prayer, will you not give your hand with your penitent heart to Christ, that henceforth, in life and death, in earth's travail and heaven's glory, you may, by that living link, be forever joined to God?

VII.

WEARING CHRIST'S GARMENTS.

AND THEY CRUCIFIED HIM, AND PARTED HIS GARMENTS, CASTING LOTS; THAT IT MIGHT BE FULFILLED WHICH WAS SPOKEN BY THE PROPHET, THEY PARTED MY GARMENTS AMONG THEM, AND UPON MY VESTURE DID THEY CAST LOTS. — Matt. xxvii. 35.

IT is a revolting scene of greedy cupidity which is here witnessed at the very foot of the cross. The Saviour, stripped of his garments, has been nailed to the wood, and the cross lifted and secured in its place. The mortal anguish has begun. On the right hand and the left of the chief sufferer hang the malefactors. The daughters of Jerusalem are weeping around. One would think that in the presence of such tragedies even the executioners would be sober and decent. They are inflicting punishment upon public convicts, it is true, but those convicts are human, and their dying groans, if unworthy of pity, might well touch a chord in the common nature that should hold observers at least gravely silent. But those whose bloody work has thus far progressed are not looking at the face of Jesus. They are looking for his garments. Those are their inheritance. It is a part of the usual price of the job. They are yet warm from his person; but the eager heirs cannot wait. While his sad eyes gaze down upon them, they make partition of the plunder. There are four of them, and they continue to make four parcels of what they have to divide. The division is equalized perhaps by severing the outer garment into its parts, fabric, fringes, and borders, so that each shall have his share. But when they come to the inner coat or tunic, it is perceived that it is not made in the common style, of two parts joined together, but is woven whole. To tear it into fragments would make it useless to anybody; so they cast lots for this, and one of them appropriates it as his prize. Look at them in their new garments. Will they know themselves? Will their friends know them? Have they not come to resemble Him whose well-known costume they have put on? Especially the man with the seamless coat, may he not be mistaken tomorrow for the Saviour himself, and startle somebody with the reappearance of the crucified Nazarene?

The resemblance goes no deeper than the garments. They are wearing what the Saviour wore, but they are like him in nothing else. They have his external appearance, but within they are unchanged, and carry still the hearts of thieves and murderers. They are his crucifiers; though they are clothed as he was while he walked among the living.

Is there anything significant in this incident? Is it not by itself a very meaning parable? Does it not hint to us that there may be many who put on the garments of Christ, but at heart they are no friends of his? May there not be many reasons why men should willingly and eagerly clothe themselves in the outward mantle of Christ's likeness, and yet rank all the while among those who put him to grief and shame?

Let us suggest briefly some of these reasons, and name some of those whom they are allowed to govern.

Few men who have a bad heart are bold enough to wear openly the costume that really belongs to them. If they were to expose all their vile thoughts and wicked purposes to the public gaze, they would be shunned as men shun pitch, slime, the plague, and other things that work defilement and mischief. They must put on some decent outside covering. They must cover up the corrupt desires of their heart. What can they wear so cleanly and unsuspicious as some garment from the vestry of Christianity? These are wolves in sheep's clothing. They learned this art from their "father." For Satan himself is transformed often into an angel of light.

It is respectable now to put on Christian raiment. The cross decorates imperial robes, and gleams in golden lustre on proud temple towers. The religion of Jesus has wrought too long and well in the earth to be despised. The man who has embraced its truths, and is guided by its principles, commands the confidence of his fellow-men. Wherever one can introduce himself thus habited, the garb carries with it a high and worthy indorsement.

There are some men whose idea of Christianity is that it can be put on as one puts on a garment. With them it is not, in its nature, an inward radical change, but an outward fairness, pureness, and saintliness. It consists in a decorous observance of the Sabbath and its institutions of worship, in a formal daily reading before the household of God's word, and a still more formal address to his presence, or in putting on certain ordinances supposed to carry with them gracious forces for the character and life. There is a desire to be Christian for the sake of standing well with God and our own esteem, and these light fabrics are easily fitted to us and are no burden. Conscience is pacified, hope is warranted, the heart at rest, and meanwhile there is no quarrel with the desire and the relish for natural good.

There are reasons enough in our day for being not only willing, but anxious, to appear invested with the badges of a faith against which none but the worst men openly contend, and the confession of which carries with it so much that conciliates universal regard. And if now we come to classes, and ask who they are who clothe themselves in this Christian costume, we may remark, —

1. There are some who make humanity their whole religion. They leave others to talk about the love of Christ. They love their fellow-men. They plead the rights of man. They argue the worth of man. They cultivate the habit of expressing sympathy for human sufferings, and extending charity to human want. They devise institutions to shelter the houseless and friendless; they spread tables for the famishing; they make garments for the naked; they carry about subscription books for all manner of humane enterprises. Their charity is chiefly a charity for the present life, a charity for the body; it does not busy itself much with missions, or gospel societies, but it throws its arms around the fainting flesh, and seeks

to better all the outward condition. Now this exact style of humanity is, as far as it goes, Christian. It comes of the gospel. It was born out of the teachings and life of Christ. We have learned to see the value of man, to pity the need of man, to comfort the sorrows of man, to understand the dignity of man, to feel the brotherhood of the race, since Christ came into the flesh and wrought for man all his works of love, and died for man on Calvary. And the very peculiarity of this charity, in looking after the earthly condition of men, makes it a closer copy of his kindness, all whose miracles of healing were to lift and straighten and nourish the poor human body. Here, then, is one of Christ's garments, clearly recognizable in fashion, texture, and hue as his, worn in the midst of human fellowships. Are the wearers therefore Christian? Outwardly and in doing they are. Are they inwardly? What if they join themselves to those who stoned him because he said, "I and my Father are one," and approve and pronounce again the same ancient reason, "For a good work we stone thee not," — they are advocates of good works, — "but for blasphemy, and because that thou being a man makest thyself God"? With Christ's garment on, and yet rejecting his doctrines, denying his divinity, refusing him as an atoning Saviour and expiatory sacrifice, are they not of those who crucify him and then part his raiment among themselves? From his cross he beholds them consenting unto his death, and putting on his robes for their daily wearing.

2. Again there are many who accept his doctrines, who call him, "Lord!" "Lord!" but who never receive him

into their hearts. They have been educated in the orthodox faith; they hold the orthodox creed; they attend upon orthodox preaching. Examine them at what length you will, and you will find them clear and strong in the truth that is distinctively evangelical. Let a stranger ask them at large, "What think ye of Christ?" and no confessor of Jesus could give, so far as the head goes, a fuller and more satisfactory reply. "The truth as it is in Jesus," they have put on entire. His seamless coat, unrent, clothes them. They walk abroad bearing his likeness to all who look upon their costume. Do they therefore love him? Have they joined their souls to him? Is he their life and joy? He is, in their creed, is he in their heart, their Lord and their God? In spirit are they transformed into his likeness? Oh, how many there are in all our congregations who have the doctrines of Christ, but who hold the truth in practical unrighteousness; who accept all that we teach concerning him, giving their assent to the whole system of his redemptive work, but never giving their hearts to his spirit, their lives to his service. You, too, my friends, wear his garments, but you are not like him; you are not his; he is not yours. What you yet need is to put on himself.

2. There are again some who have joined themselves to his visible people, and who wear openly the garment of a Christian profession, who yet seem to lack the inward life and power of godliness. Wherever they go, that garment of profession announces a Christian; they wear it into prayer-meetings; they wear it into the Sabbath assembly; they wear it to the sacramental table, while

the inward witness to what they thus declare is wanting. Their costume and their spirit are at variance. Their profession and their practice disagree. What they are contradicts what they wear.

One maintains externally the appearance of great sanctity. He is grave of countenance and careful of speech. He is punctilious in all formal religious observances. The household knows the length and comprehensiveness of his daily prayers. He is hard upon the errors of other men, and fastidious even about trifles which a more generous catholicity endures without disturbance. He is hard even upon himself. He keeps himself up by constant straining to this rigid standard. But there is nothing of the freeness and warmth of love about him. There is no fountain of tenderness in his soul. You would as soon put your infant to nurse with one of the Egyptian Colossi as to put a babe in Christ who wanted cherishing care into these granite arms. He is not a renewed man. Unawares he is a Pharisee, save that he is not a conscious hypocrite. He has great purpose and stern consistency; there is formed within him a conviction that this rigid dutifulness is piety, but Christ is not formed within him. Still another species of this outward sanctity does cover up conscious inward corruption. The long face is a mask. The man has found out that he is not what he thought he was, — a changed man. There is a tide of inward uncleanness surging to and fro in his soul, against which the floodgates are never shut. He cannot put off his sanctimonious habits; it is agreeable to be thought quite correct and eminently holy. It keeps curious eyes from peering into his bosom; the honest acknowledgment of what he is would be too deep a shame for his soul to bear. So he keeps on the garment, and harbors inwardly the carrion birds of impure passions.

There is another in the Church who has the costume of self-denial conspicuous on his person. That is a portion of the robe of Christ. "If any man will come after me, let him deny himself, take up his cross and follow me." And this man denies himself all the round of what are called the pleasures of life. These gay and costly festivities, that include rich tables, lighted saloons, music, and flowers, draw not one farthing of revenue from him. Is he not practising delf-denial? The personal and domestic luxuries of expensive furniture, elegant wardrobe, dashing equipage, a decorated and brilliant establishment, he lightly foregoes, though perhaps strongly importuned in one direction and another by those beneath his roof. Surely, a self-denying man.

His neighbors expend freely upon transitions with the seasons, — in winter into the comfortable city mansion, in summer out to a country retreat, or from place to place on travelling excursions, breathing the air of the mountains, sipping salubrious waters, taking the roll of the surf, pacing amid rural fields and beneath rural shades in inland rural towns. He calls all this "fashion," sets his face against it, and practises again his self-denial. And all the while that he seems to be dealing so abstemiously and rigorously with what others find to be their natural or acquired tastes, there is sitting within on the perch of his heart, a ravening cormorant, that devours everything its filthy beak can gobble. This man might love worldly pleasures perhaps, but he loves something else better. He might be fond of luxuries and festivities and seaside and mountain air and curative springs, but there is another thing dearer yet. He loves money. The cormorant is covetousness. The Christian virtue of self-denial was only a garment, the gilded outside of the cage where he keeps his cormorant. When he says no to a pleasure or a lust, it is not Christian self-denial that speaks, it is a croak of the cormorant. When he says no to the wife and daughters that plead for the beach in sultry August, it is not that he may have wherewith to endow God's poor, it is because his cormorant wants it all. Strange that Christ's robe should cover such a greedy spirit, the plumage of the holy dove this bird of prey!

Again there is often a very demonstrative religious zeal which really seems to consume the whole man, but which at some one critical point breaks down. It is very earnest for the souls of men; it will go all lengths for their rescue; it multiplies means and agencies and importunities to gather these aliens in; it can give time and strength and toil, will and money, too, to wield whatever hopeful instrumentalities for their salvation. The cause of Christ, the growth of the Church, the augmented fidelity and self-devotion of Christians, absorb it. Here is Christianity in full. The mantle reaches from the shoulders to the feet. There is no scantiness in it. Its ample folds wrap the whole person. Surely, here is a man with whom love is a universal principle. His soul is full of it. It must overflow upon every partner of the common humanity with whom he comes in contact. It will bathe and lave every hand he touches.

Let us accompany this friend as he goes out to make some trifling purchase. He is himself in trade perhaps, and understands that a man who lives by trade must have a fair profit. He sells on that principle. How does he buy? He calls for the article he wishes and examines it, as though disapprovingly. He asks the price. "What, so much for this?" His tone is offensive to a sensitive mind. Perhaps he remarks that he does not wonder that the sellers of this sort of ware get rich. He examines the article again, with increasing disapprobation. But there is no abatement of the price. He depreciates the quality of the material, the quality of the work, the style and taste of the goods, while all the time it is the thing he wants. He says plainly and bluntly, "You must take less." "You ask too much." "I can't give it." He is told finally that he is at liberty to leave it if he does not care to take. But that does not suit him. He wants it, and he wants to beat the seller down. He wants to get it at a cheaper price. He wants to feel that he has made a good bargain. He seems to forget that there are two of them that have the natural desire to secure a fair trade. He lingers yet and picks flaws, and half turns away and turns back and urges fresh subtractions from the value of the goods, and pushes hard for a reduction of price. It is not a very pleasant scene. I am sorry to detain you in it. At last the man is gone, paying down his reluctant money. The seller has a little heightened color on his face. He turns to us and remarks, "That customer is said to be a member so and so of such a church. I wonder what sort of religion they hold there. I desire never to see the man in my store again."

Well, we might call on domestics in families to testify to the impression which religious masters and mistresses make on them. We might call on a wife to give in evidence, if she only would, as to the sort of heart in a Christian husband that beats against her own. We might call on clerks and employees to stand up as witnesses and say how an intense Christianity develops in their direction.

But these points have been pushed far enough. Oh, it is so sorrowful that when we see Christ's vesture we cannot be sure that his lineaments are there too! It is so sad that those whose names are fairly written out on the roll of the church do under the Christian cloak what brings indelible reproach upon the Christian religion! It is a matter of such deep, deep searching of ourselves that, having on the garments of Christ, and having, as we humbly believe, something of the spirit of Christ, there may yet be so many things in us, such inconsiderate moments and actions, that a keen-eyed world protests, "We see the garments of Jesus, but we don't see anything else that is like him."

Oh, I beseech you, let the Church be searched to-day. If we keep underneath and mean to keep the qualities and practices of a worldly, greedy, and selfish spirit, let us strip off to the last fibre the vesture of the Master, that the reproach come upon humanity, and not upon the doctrine of Jesus. And if we wish a blessing upon us here in our Christian work, let us do more than run to and fro with swift-footed zeal, let us rectify our lives, put away every evil thing, find the dead flies in the ointment and extract them, for Christ wants clean hands as well as a fervent spirit to minister in the holy things of his altars.

VIII.

CHRIST'S CUP.

BUT JESUS ANSWERED AND SAID, YE KNOW NOT WHAT YE ASK. ARE YE ABLE TO DRINK OF THE CUP THAT I SHALL DRINK OF, AND TO BE BAPTIZED WITH THE BAPTISM THAT I AM BAPTIZED WITH? THEY SAY UNTO HIM, WE ARE ABLE. — Matt. xx. 22.

SUCH is human nature, even in discipleship, that it was certain that sooner or later the hearts of the chosen twelve would feel the temptation to human ambition. True, in the world's eyes, the Leader, whose person and fortunes they followed, was an obscure provincial, a man of no name or mark or rank, from a lowly family, a despised Galilean, concerning whose claims to honor and respectability it was enough to ask the contemptuous question, "Can any good thing come out of Nazareth?" To acknowledge him was to lose caste in Jewish society; to follow him, so far from quickening any ambitious aspirations, seemed rather the final crucifixion of pride. But the disciples knew more and better concerning the dignity of "the Nazarene." In their eyes he was an uncrowned king. The day of his coronation was not distant. The throne of his father David was his. He should sit and reign in a state more magnificent than

Solomon's. Where and what this kingdom was to be were questions upon which they had vague notions. Sometimes to their eyes its wide borders swept around the hills of Canaan, defied and repelled the assaults of Roman power, and their own Jerusalem was its royal capital. Sometimes it took on a more celestial beauty and grandeur, and was a kingdom not of this world; but Jesus was its Prince; that lowly head should wear this peerless diadem. And what should they be, — they who walked with this heir of royalty every day, who shared all his privacy, who companioned him under reproach and ignominy, whom he called his friends, whom he had himself elected to be with him and to compose his retinue, who were the only hearts on earth that showed him kindness and believed in his future? Would he not have royal gifts for them? As he rose into these high places of empire, should they not rise with him? Should they not be nearest his person, most illustrious in distinction of all who should then do him homage, be his councillors and senate, and share his kingliness as they had shared his lowliness? And which of them should be first and foremost in this coming elevation? Probably these questions found secret audience in each heart of this little band, and these visions of greatness floated before every eye. If there was an exception, it may have been the heart of him surnamed "Iscariot!" One strong, overmastering passion excludes, or at least subordinates, every other. There are not two monarchs of the heart. Avarice ruled in the breast of Judas! Fill his bag for him, and others might come between him and either side of Jesus. He was too covetous to be ambitious in that direction.

James and John were among the earliest called of all the disciples and on the same day with the calling of Simon Peter, and Andrew, his brother. They had already been distinguished by their Master, when he surnamed them "Sons of thunder." Perhaps, too, they were admitted all along to special intimacies with Jesus, as Peter and these two seem to have been selected to be with Christ whenever he reduced the number of his followers. It may have been John's place to have reclined next his Lord at every meal. In the distribution of the honors of his kingdom, will he not give them pre-eminence? The time has come for them to make the request. They are on their way up to Jerusalem, and Jesus has spoken plainly of the sufferings and death he shall accomplish. The two aspirants for chief places need an intercessor, and their mother willingly undertakes the office. She leads them near to him, and the three offer him their worship; and then the matron signifies that she has something to ask. "What wilt thou?" is the gracious encouragement, — gracious and encouraging, and yet it gives her time to pause, if she will, and inquire of her own heart what it is she craves. But her petition finds instant utterance, — "Grant that these my two sons may sit, the one on thy right hand, and the other on thy left, in thy kingdom." With a tender and pitiful look, we may suppose, and a gentle voice, — for so the words seem to read, — Jesus makes reply, "Ye know not what ye ask. Are ye able to drink of the cup that I shall drink of, and be baptized with the baptism that I am baptized with?"

And in this question appears the truth which it will be profitable for us, I hope, to revolve for a little. We understand the nature of that kingdom of which Christ is the head better than did the early disciples. We are not likely to make it a personal prize to sit on a throne with our Lord, either at his right hand or at his left; but it is a desire with many a Christian heart to come nearer unto the presence of Christ, to share a closer friendship with him, to know a more intimate communion, to drink in more of his spirit, to become more vitally and indissolubly joined to him, and to sit ever like Mary of Bethany at his feet, and learn of him. And we may. No voice rebukes this sort of ambition! There is a way in which this longing of the heart may be gratified and satisfied. And this is the doctrine of our Scripture. The price of personal and pre-eminent nearness to Christ is to drink of his cup and to be baptized with his baptism. The cup of Christ and his baptism refer to all his sorrowful and suffering experience in the work of human redemption. This twofold imagery divides that experience, perhaps, into two parts. Baptism is an outward rite, and touches us only externally. As a symbol it refers to that which comes upon us from without, that which the hand of another administers, or which some agency outside of ourselves brings in. But that which we drink we taste inwardly. Our own hand lifts it to our lips. Its flavor is inwardly appreciated; its bitterness lingers in our mouth; its fire burns in every vein, and its anguish courses through our whole system. So in the sufferings of Christ there was an outward and an inward smart.

Poverty and weariness and hunger and homelessness and buffeting and scourging and thorns and nails were his baptism.

The elements of his cup were mingled of the trials of his spirit. They were all the burdens he took upon his soul for man and among men; all his care, all his compassion, all his travail of patience and of grief, his experience of contradiction, ingratitude, misappreciation, rejection, and reviling. It was a full cup wrung out to him. There were strange ingredients in it, such as no other lips ever tasted, the dreaded bitterness of which wrung from him the strong plea, "Father, if it be possible, let this cup pass from me; nevertheless, not as I will, but as thou wilt." But in speaking now of our fellowship in the experience of Christ, we need not be careful to separate the symbols he employed. We may call that fellowship a tasting of his cup, or a participation in his baptism, as our thought shall most naturally take the one mould or the other. If we are to be near Christ, the first cup we are to drink with him is the cup of Consecration. One of his most distinguishing names is, by interpretation, "The Anointed One." As with holy oil he was separated and set apart for his work. We may conceive, for so the Scripture seems to intimate, that there were glories and functions and administrations belonging to him as the eternal Son of the Father which he laid aside, that he might be singly devoted to this work. There were certainly prerogatives and honors and sovereignties which he waived, that it might appear unto principalities and powers in heavenly places that he was engaged in this one thing, and had accepted all its conditions and limitations. When he comes into the field of human view, this entireness of consecration asserts itself with most abounding testimony. There was never for any scheme or object of any creature such a diligence as his. Temptation sought to make him swerve for its splendid bribes,— "all the kingdoms of the world and the glory of them," but he was steadfast there. Ease and place and fame paid court to him, but he would not turn aside. Weary nature and fainting manhood offered their plea, but plead in vain. His friends and followers interceded with him to persuade him off from pain and suffering, but he so rebuked this officiousness that the offence was never repeated. Whatever voice called him to any side issues, his reply was unchanging, "Wist ye not that I must be about my Father's business?" Every journey undertaken was for this sole end. Each morning renewed his tasks of teaching and healing, his labors of love, his pilgrimages of mercy. Far on into the night he bore still upon his heart the burdens of the day, and when he sends away his disciples on the sea-shore, and after the sun has gone down, it is not that he may rest, with no human contact to quicken or weary any nerve of body or soul, but that he may enter the shadow of some more straining and mysterious wrestling. True, the methods of his work were various. But it was one work. Its details were not such perhaps as we should have marked out for him. They sometimes stumbled his disciples. They raised a doubt in the bold breast of John of the wilderness, Herod's prisoner. Nothing seemed further from his thought than the assumption of any royal state. He was a travelling physician. He was looking after men's bodily maladies. He delivered wonderful moral discourses in parables. He roamed through Galilee and Judea, pronouncing these beautiful lessons for daily life, and opening the doctrines of his coming kingdom wherever he could find an audience. He was present at social festivals, dined with wealthy Pharisees, and mingled with marriage guests, but all and everywhere with one intent. Single-eyed, single-hearted, and in each variety of demonstration forwarding his great mission. He drank deep of this cup of consecration, and offers it now to our lips, as a bond and seal of union with himself. We are not to be tithed. All idea of self-ownership and proprietary rights we are to give up. We are to take the entire inventory of our personal forces and effects and lay at his feet. We may not check off and separate and divide,—this for Christ, this our own. We are not practically to arrange that one day in seven shall be set apart for God's service; that the evening and the morning of secular days shall be his; that the amount pledged on subscription books is sacredly to be reserved, and the balance is our own personal revenue from our toil, to be expended as we please, and plead, if special calls are made upon us for service and for charity, "I have not time; I cannot spare the means." In the modelling and mapping out of some professedly Christian lives, the claims of Christ cover but a small part of the whole. A little Sunday domain, rounded off at the corners, is staked out for him; his claim notches into the day's beginning; it touches hazily the border line of closing day obscured by mists from dreamland. There is a small mortgage in his favor upon the homestead, the interest of which only is paid, and all the rest of the estate is clear for the titled earthly master. Whenever he can steer clear of these definite and limited claims, the whole broad range is free to him, and every fruit that grows there is to sweeten his own palate and grace his own board. Does this man taste of the cup of Christ? Perhaps he does. He may just moisten his lips, but a deep draught he does not take. Oh, he must reserve nothing. He must write upon houses and lands, upon body and soul, upon heart and life, upon all his pleasant things, "Sacred to Jesus." He must lie down and rise up a consecrated man, a vassal set apart to the use of his Lord. He must go to shop and field and office and study and wareroom and drawing-room a consecrated man. Is it hard to make over all, to have nothing left, to be only a steward of time and money and personal presence and personal power? It is a great relief from care, for then neither gains nor losses are ours, and we may lay aside all solicitudes about harvest seasons, and spring and autumn trade, and the risks of the sea. Is it a stripping off of earthly authority and dignity, an abdication of the throne? Well, this is the cup. We can drink or we can refrain. But this is the price of nearness to Christ here and hereafter.

Again it is written of Christ that he pleased not himself. A brief and simple phrase, but let one attempt to appropriate and realize it as descriptive of his own style of living, what a breadth of sweep, what a world of significance, he will find in it! A young lady who had just joined herself to the fellowship of Christian people, and whose natural tastes and previous culture lay in the direction of social gayeties and musical entertainments, particularly of the dramatic order, was in conference with her pastor as to the restraints to be placed upon these tastes in future. "You have no one now to please but Christ," he said to her. "But am I never more, then, to gratify my love of music and of society?" she asked. "Never more in ways that would displease him, however exquisite the gratification might be to you," was the reply. "Am I to have, then, no pleasures in life such as others of my age enjoy? Is that which has been the light of life to me to become darkness?" "Can you not find your pleasure, then, in fulfilling the pleasure of Christ? Would you grieve him to gratify yourself? Would you not rather miss from henceforth the taste of every earthly joy to please him instead?" "But this makes life so dull and sombre," came, after a little, her sad and troubled answer. And then, after another little pause, her frank and ingenuous testimony lighting up her face with a look of joy such as mirth never wore, "But I would rather please him." Ah, my child, whoever you are, ready, like our first mother, to shed "a few natural tears" upon leaving your earthly paradise, take the cup; the first taste seems bitter, but a strange sweetness lingers on the palate. More grateful every day becomes the draught. The thought, "Christ's lips were on the brim before it came to mine," stirs into it an elixir of life no clusters of the vine ever yielded. His eyes have looked into it before yours. His face was just now imaged there. Drink next to him, and so come near to him, and be one with him.

And what a sentence is that written of him again, "He carried our sorrows"! His own hand offers us again the same cup, saying, "Bear ye one another's burdens, and so fulfil the law of Christ." We walk in the midst of earthly wretchedness and distress. We are not to go through briskly and carelessly, gathering our skirts unto ourselves, lest they should sweep within the grasp of some forlorn one and detain us. Here is one in affliction. You cannot restore his loss, but you can stop and weep with him. Here is one in want. Have you nothing to divide with him? I do not speak of your last crust. It is that which is usually handed out. Can you not share a fresh loaf? Here is one struggling beneath a weight of care, a pale watcher, who has not breathed a breath of pure, fresh air for many a day, a toiling widow with fatherless children, a deserted wife, or one worse than deserted, allied to brutality and shame. Stop and stoop and step under these burdens for a little, if you may, and let the released one take a run into freedom and open day, doubly cheered by the sunshine in the sky and on your kind face. Here is another struggling with temptation. Ah, the deep waters are about him; the waves will go over his head. Drop all, plunge in, drag him to the solid shore. All this will keep your hands full, — yes, and your heart full, and make your quiet home and your pillow so grateful. But you will never suffer from *ennui*. Time will never hang heavy on your hands. You will be furnished with abundant occupation. The last thought of the day coming to your soul, like the blessed balm of sleep to your eyelids, will be this, "I have wrought all day for others, dear Master; I have tried like thee not to seek my own." There's an opiate in that cup for weary nerves; you will sleep well.

Again, the cup of Christ includes misappreciation and ingratitude, as the return for good done and favors bestowed. Do you like that? We must not count largely upon human thankfulness when we put ourselves greatly out for another's advantage. There are not many that love the yoke of obligation. We keep our friendships best with those who owe us nothing. A quarrel is a cheap way to cancel all claims. We must be prepared to have our motives suspected, our acts misconstrued, our good evil spoken of, to receive a wreath of thorns for coronation, to be counted meddlesome, impertinent, obtrusive, and fanatical. The very faithfulness that springs from deepest love of the heart shall be reckoned uncharitableness, and the hand we freight deepest with bounty shall be the first to smite. Not a pleasant cup this; the mixture is acrid and stinging as the waters that lie above the "cities of the Plain." But Jesus drank this cup. Around him one day a hundred threatening hands were armed with missives of death. "Many good works," said he, with touching point, "have I showed you from my Father; for which of these works do ye stone me?" Would you stand with him there? Consent, then, not in a spirit of romance, not with a morbid, diseased fretfulness and suspiciousness, but with cheerful patience, that those whom you chiefly strive to bless shall wound you deepest. Christ gave uncalculating love. He bought every soul that denies him. The young man who went sorrowful and disobedient from his presence he loved, and left it on record that he loved him. He called the traitor Judas "friend," and the kiss of betrayal met a loving lip. He loved past all the wounding which secret or open hostility could inflict. It was a patient love. Those disciples were such dull scholars they needed "line upon line." "Line upon line" they had; but every lesson left them questioning among themselves, and brought out from them the stupidest comments. "Beware of the leaven of the Pharisees," he cautions them. "Ah," they say to one another, "the leaven of the Pharisees; it is because we have forgotten to take bread." But he led them on and up to his meaning with such unwearied patience, he took them apart and dissected for them his own words and reduced his wisdom to such simple elements, that these grown-up babes in spiritual knowledge at length could say, "Lo, now thou speakest plainly, and speakest no proverb." My brother, my sister, is your loving patience stoutly taxed? Take the strain with silent, placid lips. What a hubbub of childish mirthfulness or childish petulance there is sometimes in the home! How many distracting questions and instant and urgent calls are crowded into that chorus! It all pours in, perhaps, upon one sustaining heart that needs to be strong. One has a complaint to lodge, one has a hunger to be appeased, one has a thirst to be quenched, one has a hurt to heal, one has a pain to soothe, one has a perplexity to solve, one has lost something which must be hunted up, one has parted something which must be bound together, and one, the most importunate of all, does not know what he wants. All want a portion, occupation, something to interest, something to absorb. Yesterday's device is stale for to-day. The first suggestion is a failure, the second carries only a minority, the third leaves still a minority. The east wind is sharp without, or the rain is falling, and the sky is lowering. And this task, varied beyond all possible fertility of supposition, was the task of yesterday as well, and must be taken up again to-morrow. Oh, parent, guardian, teacher, are you able to drink this cup? Sometimes the weary nerves and aching head and heart will plead, "Let this cup pass from me!" Do you end your prayer there? There was a "nevertheless" in the form you are following. Try again. Remember it is the cup of Jesus. It will seat you at his right hand; it will make you one with him. He drank of it, and commends it to you. He does not taste cordials, and bid you season your drink with ashes. His cup, his own, he passes on. Raise it to your white, shrinking lips; take up that "nevertheless,"—"Nevertheless, not as I will, but as thou wilt." You look upon breaking fortunes, you look upon alienated friendships, you look upon withering hopes, you look upon failing strength, upon the dark shadow of adversity. Are you able to raise the cup perpetually "nevertheless, not as I will, but as thou wilt"? A beloved one droops; languidly the gentle eyes seek yours; whiter grows the thin cheek; a babe moans in your arms, and then is still. A stalwart boy goes up into his chamber and lies down, and comes not forth again. The desolation of widowhood darkens toward your door. Would you sit with Christ in his kingdom? Will you have, then, this baptism? Go down with him into swift-flowing Jordan, the chill of Hermon's snows in its waters yet. Take his cup, say your grace over it, "Nevertheless, not as I will, but as thou wilt," and drain it off, and you will find your Master at your side. His kingdom has come unto you. He is on your right hand and on your left; you will never more be alone. That last baptism of his was under the cold flood of death. There is something written above the Sufferer's crowned head on the cross beside that which is written in Greek and Latin and Hebrew. Its letters gleam down the ages, and one can read them here and now, — "Self-sacrifice, the law of Christ" — "the law of Christian living." The thorns are sharp, the nails rend cruelly, flesh pleads off, self-protection protests; but the hand of Jesus beckons. The last taste with Christ is of the vinegar mixed with gall. Oh, are we able? Have we been crucified with him unto this vain world? Do we know always what we ask in our prayers? Is it sanctification? Is it likeness to Christ? Is it unworldliness? Is it poverty of spirit? Oh, but if God answer any of these requests, it will be by a baptism as of fire; it will be by a medicined cup with gall in it. Do we still pray it? Yes, let us venture, for he can sustain while he disciplines. Behold the law of Christian advancement! the way of Christian honor the path to crowns and thrones. It is a way descending into the valley of humiliation. It stoops to service. Our Saviour announced it plainly, "Ye know that the princes of the

Gentiles exercise dominion over them, and they that are great exercise authority upon them; but it shall not be so among you, but whosoever will be great among you let him be your minister. And whosoever will be chief among you let him be your servant. Even as the Son of man came not to be ministered unto, but to minister, and to give his life a ransom for many." If the path climb, it climbs as the path of Jesus did on the day of crucifixion up the slope of Calvary. Let it be our constant prayer, "Master, take us into thy fellowship and strengthen our weakness for thy sorrowful but blessed baptism."

IX.

WAITING.

IT IS GOOD THAT A MAN BOTH HOPE AND QUIETLY WAIT FOR THE SALVATION OF THE LORD. — Sam. iii. 26.

THERE are countries where the climate of the year is divided into "the rainy season" and "the dry." But the former is not one uninterrupted period of "falling weather." Here and there, during its continuance, there are sweet, bright, calm days, with not a cloud on all the face of the heaven. The voice which I have taken this morning out of the old prophetic utterances I found in the midst of the Lamentations of the weeping prophet. But it is a cheerful voice. There is no sob of weeping in it. It was a bright hour amid that rain of tears when this word was written. And the sunshine lingers in it yet. We hear in it an echo of that earlier note struck by the harp of David. "Wait on the Lord, be of good courage, and he shall strengthen thine heart. Wait, I say, on the Lord."

But this word "wait" is a cold word for most human hearing. Even Faith often finds it hard to receive it, and passionate earthly desire meets it as the challenge of an enemy. It is a good word for all times and all hearts.

It is especially good for us here and now. As a people we do not find it easy to wait. A chronic fever of impatience is in our land, the universal epidemic. It comes partly of our stimulating climate, partly of our circumstances as pioneers of civilization on a new continent, partly of the rapidity with which we have seen great fortunes built up and golden dreams realized, partly of the straining competition on every racecourse for every goal, and partly of the natural ardor of the soul eager to touch its prize, and enjoy its good without delay. Speak to us any other word than this. Bid us "run," and we gird up our loins at once. Bid us "act," and the day shall not be long enough for our diligence, the season too short for our harvest. Bid us "dare," and no terror shall make us blench. But "wait,"—that denies all our longings, postpones our hopes, removes the feast to which our hunger hastened, dries up the spring to which our thirst was stooping. The salient, the energetic qualities of character are easily cultivated; the retiring, the passive come hard. Even with those who believe in God, his government, his promises, his faithfulness, his fatherliness, the virtue of patient waiting is of difficult acquirement. God is sovereign, wise, good, and true. He will perform where he has promised; but he is slow, and we chafe against the deliberate process of his providence. This fever of impatience burns in all the hearts of our American youth. They fret at all apprenticeship, whether to letters, mechanic art, or trade. They are in haste to graduate from all the preparatory stages, and to be launched at once upon the real, earnest life. They hurry through the ante-chamber to take their place within, with the jostling crowd struggling for the upper seats. When fully embarked on the voyage, they are impatient to see across the breadth of waters the harbor entrance. Blow, breezes, blow, and waft them over the ocean ridges to the destined port! How slow the log runs out! Give them a gale rather than a calm. Drive the steam hard, quicken the paddle-strokes to one continuous rush and roar; their eager feet would leap down upon the shores of their promised land. Our fathers were content to go slow, to gain by small and sure increments, to "retire" when age had silvered their heads, and their natural force was abated, glad and content to touch when almost at life's far boundary a competency. Not so with their children. We want to make one leap from the bottom to the top, forgetting that these large, adventurous leaps may also as easily reverse the process and carry a man from the top to the bottom. We want to be rich in a season, to ripen and reap our golden harvest, as Nature does hers, in a single summer. We want something left of our youth, and all our manhood at least, for enjoyment. We want to lay hold of our purses, not with the trembling hand of age, but with the firm grasp of a strength not yet on the evening side of noon. Give us the morning for toil, if it must be so, but give us a long, bright afternoon, with no unfinished task. Let us earn with sharp diligence and large profits while the hours are fresh and dewy, climbing with braced limbs while the sun climbs. Then from the splendid meridian, in a chariot like his own, gliding easily down the long cloudless decline toward the pensive shadow of the distant twilight. And this is not merely the fever of youth, the ardor of young men, the impetuosity of business adventure. It is found in every walk of life. It is the restless haven of every heart's desire. It waits upon every human scheme. It is in the strife of opinions, in the clashing systems of moral reform, in the growth of spiritual character and religious institutions. The progress of mechanical improvements seems to have infected every enterprise and hope of the heart of man. We travel in a day as far as our fathers did in a fortnight. It seems but fair, then, that there should be the same ratio in making our fortunes and winning our purposes. What took fourteen years then should take but one now. Nay, this is rather too deliberate. If there were any way of travelling by telegraph, we should most of us take the "lightning train." It chafes us that thought and spirit can fly so swiftly, and our gross bodies must lag so far behind. We shall never be satisfied till we harness electricity to our travelling-car, and take the risk of breathing on the trip. These advances of practical science in locomotion, the transmission of intelligence, and in almost every department of human progress, have made all old methods of living seem intolerably slow. Our veins are inoculated with mercury. Our whole system of life and labor is impregnated with a restlessness that can never fold its arms and be still. Of course it would be an utterly vain, as an unwise and uncalled-for, attempt to seek to arrest this ever accelerated tide of human progress. But the spirit which it engenders in the human heart, and its relations to morals and character, present matters of gravest consideration. This impatience betrays many a soul into crime. It is greedy of its ends. It seeks to reach them by swift, sudden courses. It would take the shortest cuts. Those which seem the shortest are often crossed by certain opposing barriers. There are laws of honor and rectitude, there are laws of the land, there are laws of God, that lift themselves against the impetuous desire. There is a terrible temptation to find a way over instead of taking the longer and slower way round.

Surmount these hindrances, and the goal is so near. Turn out for them, and the circuit is so weary and slow. Here is a premium upon transgression. A formidable rival may be removed or circumvented by a scheme that involves the sacrifice of magnanimity, the dishonor of some mean and dirty intrigue. Oh, would he were out of the way! How clear the track would be! Take care. If you consent, there goes the best of your nobility and your manhood. You will have come out ahead of your rival and — your honor. A false oath, — not so bad as that, — a piece of misrepresentation, a little stretching of what some men find to be the elasticity of the truth, and a grand success is possible. A triumph with stained hands, soiled garments, and the prostrate form of truth trodden under feet. Avaricious impatience does not mind the stains. They can be gilded over, covered up by and by with gold leaf. A little trenching on the Sabbath will round up a fruitful trip. An ungenerous advantage taken of superior intelligence and superior opportunity over a weaker brother, a forgetfulness in trade of the law we respect in moral codes, — loving our neighbor as ourselves, — will materially swell the aggregates of our profits, give us perhaps for a season or for years the control of the market. How can we postpone such an advance for our scruple's sake? Labor itself is a burden; the rewards of honest industry are often small; these steady, trifling gains will take years to foot up anything respectable, that will allow us to lay down our tasks and indulge our tastes. There is money enough with rich houses, in well-filled purses, in the vaults of banks. Another's name well simulated; a demand, with face and voice disguised, upon a belated traveller; a midnight operation upon the silver closet of a millionnaire, or the interior securities of, or the trustful day defenders of, the bank; or a midday operation, striking fraudulent contracts, or giving fictitious value to valueless stocks, and sudden riches and gratifications would reward this single, bold stroke. It is because desire cannot wait, because appetite is clamorous for instant indulgence, because the eager hands would clutch at once the coveted good, that crime, stepping in with its confident but delusive promise, flings its fetters over the soul. Again, this impatience of our hearts impugns the faithfulness of the divine Promiser. In respect to all earthly good, the sacred pledge of God is written in the ancient covenant, in the world's renewal of its youth, that "seed-time and harvest, cold and heat, summer and winter . . . shall not cease." The spirit of this promise repeats itself in many a gracious assurance concerning the great Father's care for the comforts and needs of the body, and our portion of natural good. But in some season of special trial the early and the latter rain fail us, the heavens are brass overhead, the earth powder beneath, the green blade pales to a sickly yellow. How shall we be fed? How will the garners of autumn be filled? The very necessaries of life seem to recede beyond our reach; prices mount on an ascending scale, speedily distancing slow climbing labor and its rewards. The implements with which we wrought are taken from us, and our hands left empty. The field of toil, for which alone we have training and skill, is thronged to repletion, and we are left out. It is deserted of all men, and we are left in it idle and alone, no man hiring us. Each turn we make reduces our strength and disappoints our hope. Inevitable want corners us, and no door of deliverance opens. For us all the divine promises seem repealed and forgotten. Is it not time for some daring, desperate, expedient? It is very well to hope if a man can see any light ahead, and "quietly wait" for salvation, if there is any coming. It may be written ever so fairly, "Trust in the Lord and do good; so shalt thou dwell in the land, and verily thou shalt be fed." But a promise wont spread a table, or light a fire, or weave a piece of cotton, or make up a garment, or pay a note, or satisfy the grocer on the corner. We must look out for ourselves lawfully or lawlessly. Necessity knows no law. Then is God forgetful or faithless? Nay. All the while he is working unseen and silently. Behind the curtain his hand is busy. From afar converging lines are bringing up relief. Separate forces will unite at the point intended. That point will be perhaps man's utmost extremity. But at that point hopeless destitution and the divine fulness will meet.

You remember how, in last autumn's campaign, upon Alltoóna's thinly-defended works, in Sherman's line of communication, moved a whole division of the rebel host. One of Sherman's resolute leaders, by hard marching, flung himself behind those works. The greatly outnumbering assailants demanded a surrender to spare the effusion of blood. The Union commander was willing to meet the effusion of blood, and the storm broke upon him with devouring fury. Seven hours it raged and seven times his own numbers pushed the fierce assault. Single-handed he fought it out. Where were the tens of thousands of his comrades? Was he left to his fate? So it seemed. Why, then, maintain against such odds the unequal strife? Why not yield while there was anything left to save? Ah, he was there to fulfil a sacred trust. And nobly did he discharge it, till unexpected victory came at last, and the baffled enemy retired. Was he left to his fate? Sherman's eye, from the top of Look-out Mountain, was on every white puff that surged up from those well-served batteries. The strong columns of the army, under laurelled generals, were moving on through all those hours and closing in, and well-nigh encompassing the rebel bands. The whole loyal host was engaged in bringing succor to that brave company in the beleaguered town, though they knew it not. So watches and works the all-beholding, faithful God, preparing the fulfilment of his pledges when our hearts are ready to faint. Let us be rebuked. Wait, in whatever extremity, and we shall see that "God is not slack concerning his promises as some men count slackness." Again our impatience outruns the divine Providence. God covenants with believing Abraham that in his seed shall all the nations of the earth be blessed. But Abraham is an hundred years old, Sarah is ninety, the promised heir is not, and Eliezer of Damascus stands gaping and ready for the inheritance. It is vain waiting longer; Abraham must help Providence. So he allied himself with the Egyptian bondwoman, bringing sore trouble and sharp discord into his house, and embittering his age with domestic feuds. And at last how simple and easy to almighty power the redemption of his pledge! how all-sufficient the sovereign providence! It was revealed to Rebecca, even before she looked upon the faces of her twin boys, that the elder should serve the younger. But dim-eyed, gray-haired Isaac is on his death-bed, and still Esau holds the birthright. Wait, oh, impatient mother, God's word will not fail. But she cannot wait. She must help God by a lie and a crime, and so she puts up Jacob to that act of cruel deception, that almost broke that aged heart, exiled Jacob for many long years from his home, sowed bitter hatred between the brothers, and brought upon the younger a keen reprisal when his own head was bowed with the snows of life's winter. This is the great temptation with an impatient spirit to outrun Providence, to set up its own devices in the place of Providence, and so defeat the nearest methods of God's chosen plans.

Again this spirit of impatience misses in its haste the higher good. Samuel, the prophet, anointed Saul king over Israel, and sent him before him to Gilgal, bidding him wait seven days till he himself should come and offer up the sacrifices. Seven days Saul waited, but the Philistines were mustering strong at Micmash, the men of Israel were falling away from the king, battle was imminent, and the sacrifice yet postponed. The seventh day is nearly spent; the host of the uncircumcised approaches. Samuel will not come, and the rash, impatient king himself offers the sacrifice. He has gained this preparation for the battle, and stayed perhaps the desertion of his people. But what has he lost? Scarce has he ended the rites before the prophet comes, and announces that, for that act of public disobedience, God had rejected Saul from the kingdom. Obedience is better than all which disobedient haste can hope to secure. Strength of character is better, patience is better, calm submission is better, heroic endeavor is better, the steadfast passive virtues, born of trial and made tough and abiding under the strain of some wearing delay. How often in trouble we are blind to this truth! Oh, give us relief! Take off the burden! Relax the tension upon nerve and spirit! Give us an antidote for the pain! Come, Lord, ere our brother die! Ah, sisters of Lazarus, let the Saviour linger. Two days he abode still in the same place where he was. It seemed indifference, cruelty, anything but love. But the marvellous experience of the next four days, those precious, precious tears of Jesus, the grand and gracious miracle that stirred all Jerusalem from centre to circumference, were well worth waiting for. Bear his absence a little longer. Oh, tired and troubled spirit, the larger shall be your deliverance, the sweeter your joy.

Over the delays of our personal sanctification we are sometimes weary of waiting, impatient of our slow progress. It seems to us fitting that we should be. So many weak sides, so many vulnerable points, so many redoubtable and unhumbled foes, such frequent falls, such shameful defeats. Oh, shall we ever grow strong and have the mastery of our spiritual enemies? Yes, by successive conflicts; wait till the appointed hour brings them on; by oft-repeated trials they will rise upon us one after another, by God's wise methods and seasons of spiritual nurture. Let him introduce them, each in his time, and we shall wear at last the victor's crown, and sing his song.

We are impatient often in our own sphere of Christian labor, that the gospel seems so powerless. There are so many yet resisting souls that we long to see brought in as the trophies of its conquering efficacy. Look how they stand up in the midst of us, — men, more than we count, on whom the truth has broken many a lance without ever piercing their shield. Oh, for more frequent appeals for a sharper weaponry out of the sacred arsenal, for more puissant hands to wield it, for new modes of attack and new secrets of overcoming. "Wait," said Jesus, to the assembled disciples, ready to storm Jerusalem and sweep over India, "tarry in the city, wait for the promise of the Father which . . . ye have heard of me." And they waited, and with a sound "as of a rushing mighty wind," though all the air was still, and no leaf stirred on Olivet, came the descending spirit, and then each flame-crowned apostle went forth clothed with might and with salvation.

Let us wait as they waited, — wait in faith, wait in prayer, wait in submission, wait in confident expectation, hopefully, quietly, with zeal and labor like Paul's, with courage like Daniel, and we shall see in every field of hoping and of toiling the salvation of the Lord.

Difficult but precious lesson, — the lesson of patient waiting, of cheerful content under divine delays, of joyful assurance, though the desire of our heart and the God of our promises do linger long.

X.

INCOMPLETENESS OF LIFE.

AND THE LORD SAID UNTO HIM, THIS IS THE LAND WHICH I SWEAR UNTO ABRAHAM, UNTO ISAAC, AND UNTO JACOB, SAYING I WILL GIVE IT UNTO THY SEED: I HAVE CAUSED THEE TO SEE IT WITH THINE EYES, BUT THOU SHALT NOT GO OVER THITHER. — Deut. xxxiv. 4.

AS we move onward in the journey of human life, there are many reminders by the way of the coming end. The sickness that lays us up for a while in the midst of our vigorous days, the decline of each setting sun, the death of summer verdure and the autumnal fall of the leaves, the lapse of the year, the passing of each of our life's four seasons, the dropping from our side of the companions of our way, — each of these is intended, and usually serves, to turn our thoughts forward to the final arrest of our steps, the mortal sickness one day to seize us, the going down of our last earthly sun, the winter of our year. There is nothing unkind in sending us such reminders. We need them. And they are given in faithfulness and mercy.

And one of the impressions most vividly produced upon us at such seasons is of the disappointing incompleteness of our life on earth. The fever comes in the midst of our plans and toils, the closing day reproaches us for many a brave purpose of the morning unfulfilled, and the waning year cuts short the schemes which we had hoped to see rounded with full success. This impression is probably present on every heart as we stand here together on this shore of the last Sabbath of the year and see its months, like waves broken and spent, all behind us. How much that we meant to have effected before we were called to stand by the pillow of the dying year is still unachieved! What good that we hoped to have attained to is yet in the future! What dear desire eagerly followed is yet unpossessed! And as it is to-day, so it will be at the last. Each human life, longer or shorter, wherever it pauses, and however it be protracted, will be visited at its close with the sense of disappointment and incompleteness. If Moses had been told, when he led out the tribes from Egypt, that he should never lead them into the promised land; that he should march at their head forty years in the wilderness, but should never cross the Jordan with them; that he should come in sight of their goodly inheritance, but should never set foot in it, never taste of the milk and honey, never sit under the shadow of its fruitful vines, it would have been so sad and depressing a sentence that faith and resignation could hardly have struggled against it. There was always before his eye and his hope the vision of that great triumph when he should stand at the head of a redeemed nation on those sacred hills of promise, and be permitted to lift up with his own hand the banner of the holy people higher than all the ensigns of earthly royalty. But it was never to be. He was to come near it, but short of it. It was to be almost within grasp, but not touched. One only narrow stream of all that had separated him from this prize still flowed between; across it and far beyond he could see with his eyes, but he was never to go over with his feet. There he stood on the very border, the gate ready to open, the goal before him, when God said to him tenderly, but firmly, "Come up into this mountain and die!" It was a trying word to Moses, and for one moment he plead against it. "O Lord God, thou hast begun to show thy servant thy greatness and thy mighty hand. I pray thee, let me go over, and see the good land that is beyond Jordan, that goodly mountain and Lebanon!" And then came the final word, fatherly but sovereign also, "Let it suffice thee; speak no more unto me of this matter." There followed indeed the glorious compensative vision from that salient summit of the Moab range, but the work and the hope of a life seemed to miss of their crown. Touching illustration of that incompleteness attending every human career in this world, upon which we may briefly meditate as we are held awhile in the grasp of this old year so near its end.

There is more than one sense, to be sure, in which the briefest and most fragmentary life may be considered filled out to utmost completeness. As to God's providential purpose in it, it is as long and as productive as it was meant to be. Just as it is, it fits accurately into the ever-developing divine plan; no more and no less was expected from it. It is complete as a link between the generations of men and the stages of human progress. It takes the living torch from the hand of its predecessor and passes it over to the hand of its successor. Then its function is ended, and it may cease to be.

It is often complete in the balance of its own proportioned seasons. It sports in the sunny hours of childhood. It drinks in the fervid inspiration of youth. It shares the consciousness of manhood's strength. It wears the white and honorable crown of age. It is a full life year. It has had a spring, a summer, an autumn, a winter, treading the full round of all the circling months. There is sometimes, too, whatever the heart has longed for, not yet attained, — there is sometimes, let us thank God, a full-orbed sense of satisfaction with our work and the length of our working day. A dying patriot and statesman could say as he faltered in the midst of the toil which, gray-haired and bowed with years, he still maintained, "This is the last of earth; I am content." And another gray-haired laborer on whom the hand of power was laid with despotic violence could write it as his peaceful testimony, "I am now ready to be offered, and the time of my departure is at hand. I have fought a good fight, I have finished my course, I have kept the faith."

Still how much that this same heroic veteran had hoped to secure of the victories of the truth must have rested upon his mind as visions, upon whose fulfilment he might look down from another world, but was never to see in this!

This incompleteness will come into clearer recognition if we consider how little a human life accomplishes in comparison with the plans of God. Those divine plans are large. They reach from age to age, from generation to generation, "from everlasting to everlasting." They cover the beginning, the progress, the final periods of all human history. They take up, employ, and dismiss successive workers, while yet some miner detail only is wrought out, and the vast integral scheme is scarcely at all set forward. A single task may fill and weary the hands of one laborer and another and another before it is concluded, and in its completion seem only a trivial contribution to the general progress. Measured by the colossal, slow-moving system of God's providence, the turning of this vast wheel that rolls on the designs of the all-wise Mind, — a wheel so high, so broad, that, though always moving, its motion, like the growth of the seasons or the procession of the constellations, is imperceptible to our eye, — how brief, how fragmentary, how evanescent is the little life and work of man! God will call him out of the families of earth a peculiar people. Who shall have the founding and building of this elect nation? How much shall any one chosen instrument accomplish in the piling of this slow-rising architecture? Abraham hears the voice of God on the plain of Mamre, and moves out to begin the work. He dies, and Isaac's hand catches the slackened thread of progress. Jacob goes over Jordan with his staff only, and comes back a double band. Joseph disappears beneath the dark portal of an Egyptian prison, and reappears in the second chariot of royalty. The babe of the Nile turns his back on the court, choosing rather to suffer affliction with the people of God. Joshua inherits the captaincy of the tribes after him. Warriors, judges, and kings in long succession follow on. Jerusalem itself sinks under sorrowful judgments; the abomination of desolation stands in the holy place, and from the loins of David's line comes forth a later and a mightier Leader to conduct the lingering but sure march of the Church unto that triumphal hour, when "the kingdom and dominion, and the greatness of the kingdom under the whole heaven, shall be given to the people of the saints of the Most High." But what hero of the leadership, whose truncheon so many hands have borne for a while, can say concerning this imperial conquest, "Behold what I have wrought"? How small a space in such vast reaches of progress does the span of a single life cover! How broken and fragmentary, compared with this sublime whole, must that life appear to itself and the great Supreme One! We rise up and deliver a stroke or two, and then sink faint and overborne almost at the point where our toil commenced. It is to compare great things with small, as though all the tillers of earth had it in charge to makes its rough places smooth, and to convert its deserts into gardens of bloom and fruit. But the most that each can do is to bring a single field into culture, and, having sown his first harvest, which another shall reap, the night cometh and his work is ended. How insignificant the plat which has compassed his utmost of diligence, as compared with the broad continents and the boundless Saharas yet to be subdued! How incomplete the earthly life as judged by the all-comprehending plans of God! We had thought, in our day, to help forward the kingdom of truth, to supplant wickedness on the earth with righteousness, to carry the light of salvation out over the dark seas and unto the dark isles, and to help Jesus to his throne, and see him begin to reign ere our eyelids should droop in the final sleep; but the evening twilight has descended, and our lips can do little more than repeat the old challenge of our enemies, "Where is the promise of his coming? For since the fathers fell asleep all things continue as they were." What incompleteness in such living! What a fragment is such a being! What an humbling consciousness must possess it at last of the unattained, now forever beyond it!

So it will be also, not merely in reference to God's plans, but in reference to our own private schemes, of working, whether for earthly fruits or spiritual. You shall hear some aged patriarch say, as he walks feebly forth into the sun from his cottage-door, and gazes upon the acres over which his hand has guided the plough for half a century, "I always meant to have blasted out that ledge of rock, to have levelled that ridge, to have drained that swamp. It has been my purpose for years to have cleared that boggy and stony pasture field for tillage and meadow. I have often thought of opening a vista through that forest growth; of sinking that steep ascent in my carriage-path, by a cut to the heart of that knoll, into an easier grade; of digging a well in that upland range for my herds; of breaking that abrupt slope on one side of my lawn into terraces; of detaching my barn from my house, and adding to the mansion a wing for more capacious domestic accommodation; but I have never seen just the time when I could enter upon these improvements, and I am too old now. My sons after me may perhaps effect some of them; but I shall never undertake them." And he turns back to his easy-chair with a sigh over his interrupted work. Age and infirmity caught him before his dreams were realized. The end is near, and what remains undone must, so far as he is concerned, remain undone forever. He has seen it with his eyes, but he has reached a bound over which he may not go to possess it. And where these hopes and plans have reference to spiritual interests, the experience is the same. We had hoped to have seen some one puissant enemy of the truth subdued, and to have had a hand in the triumph; to have secured the evangelization of certain spiritual wastes always appealing specially to our heart; to have witnessed the growth and establishment of some Christian enterprise, whose foundations we had hoped to lay; to have rejoiced over the conversion of some dear friend and neighbor; to have had a jubilee in the home over some lost one found, some wanderer returned to his father's house and his father's God. But we have gone as far in our instrumentality for these precious ends as we are permitted to go. The end is near. Our words are feeble. A few more prayers, and we must lay our burdens down and rest, where nothing shall disturb or gladden us any more. These unfinished holy endeavors, we behold their consummation in vision, but we are not to touch them with living hands. So also there is personal good, long-coveted privileges, we hoped to have enjoyed, but the taste of which is never to sweeten our mouths, that valley stream of Jordan meeting our feet sooner than we had thought. What the failure will be none of us now can say; but we may be sure our life will be incomplete in respect to some of these crowning expectations. Hope always outstrips pursuit, and "Hope springs eternal in the human breast." Some hope will reach across the river, and the swift current will forbid our crossing over. We had hoped to have carried our children through their process of education, or to have seen them settled in their calling and winning good successes, or to have sat beneath the new-sprung roof of their home life, to have taken their children into our arms and read the future of our lineage in their young eyes. We had hoped to have cleared off certain incumbrances from our earthly estate, and to have accumulated a certain definite sum as our competence for age and an inheritance for our sons and daughters. We had hoped to have seen certain great aggressive movements in the redemption of man from the bondage of prejudice, appetite, and vicious habit prevalent, before our eyes should close; the true meaning of Christ's gospel settled and accepted by all professed believers; the salvation of benighted parts of our land coming forth out of Zion; the final overcoming of our own spiritual enemies; the full conquest of evil passions in our heart; the peaceful settlement of some long perplexing, practical question of our personal religious life; our full conformity to the image and will of Jesus. But when we stand there on the bank of the river, we shall assuredly see some of these hopes beyond us. Pursuit will stop at the water's edge. Possession will mock us from the farther shore. There will be some good our hearts have intensely craved, our hands wrought for diligently, our feet hastened after far and wearily, which we shall see only with our eyes, and, seeing thus, know that it is not to crown our earthly lot, and confess in this baffled search, this postponed desire, the incompleteness of this mortal life.

And if we ask now for the lessons and the uses of this sense of incompleteness, how obvious it is that it is meant to impress us with the conviction of God's all-sufficiency. He does not lean so heavily upon his human helpers that, when they fail him, his work pauses and his plans are arrested. He does not build so confidently on these frail pillars that, when they crumble beneath the load, the fabric of his great scheme of Providence totters. His stoutest champions, his foremost agents, the leaders of movements that carry in them most of the conditions of human progress, and the richest promise of human welfare, may vacate their trust and lie down in silence and darkness, but the divine counsels and the divine resources suffer no bereavement. Men ask, How can such great losses be made up, and who is worthy to succeed to such honors laid down? But God is not disturbed. His plans are not hindered. He can call whom he will to the vacant posts. He has his successors already in view, in training, and under appointment. His own all-sufficiency impresses itself upon us through this, his independence of short-lived, frail, and fainting human workers.

In the same view his sovereignty appears more august and kingly. It is his hand that fixes the limits of this fragmentary human life. He has appointed to each man his bounds, which he cannot pass. He breaks in upon our plans, our vitality, our strength, and decrees the arrest of all our hopes and labors. He does it in ways so varied, so unexpected, so startling, so discriminating, as to leave the impression on men's hearts that there is a supreme Disposer on the throne, who takes counsel of himself in such arbitration, and acts his wise and sovereign pleasure.

Another use of this dispensation is to quicken our diligence. Oh, all the voices of the frailty and brevity of life bid men be up and doing. The morning and the evening, the evening and the morning, in their quick succession, the rapid flight of the seasons, the swift tread of the years, the lapse of fleetness and vigor in the human frame, the changing shadows as our sun crosses the meridian, — all unite in this salutation with every dawn, repeating it with each stroke of the hours, "Work while the day lasts, for the night cometh in which no man can work!" Some tasks are sure to be crowded out of life, some labors commenced to be left unfinished. Then "what thou doest, do quickly!"

And again the lesson is that, while redoubling our diligence, we moderate our expectations. We are sowing for magnificent harvests. We are toiling for splendid successes. We are investing for richest returns. We are climbing toward loftiest and most radiant summits. For all our present hardship and rigor, there shall be a golden future, and in the light of it, as it rises above the far horizon and advances to meet us, our eyes glisten and our step is more buoyant. Ah, how many have gone forward, their feet sandalled with such hopes, and stepping as though they trod on air, who found that the river intercepted their path before they reached the goal; that their confident expectation was only a view from Pisgah's top; that fruition lay beyond the stream, and their feet touched those cold waters while yet their hands were empty. Be moderate in desire and expectation. Tone down this brilliance and eagerness of life's hopes, so shall life's disappointing incompleteness be less bitter to our spirit when the cup is raised to our lips. There is a peculiar chastening for age in this arrangement of Providence. Age is the harvest time for which we have sowed, and in which we expect to rest with our sheaves thick around us. But how often does age stand by its empty granaries with no field on all its estate yet to reap. The land of promise toward which it travelled so long is beyond it still. Instead of sitting beneath its vines and tasting the grapes of Eshcol, it is sitting on the bank of the river somewhat desolate and alone, waiting rather than enjoying. We wonder often why good men, whose years have been given to works of beneficence and piety, should have such sharp discipline in age, — the loss of health, the loss of property, the loss of those on whom they expected to lean, the grief that comes from looking upon the sorrow or the shame of some whom they love and being powerless to help them. Ah, they were not quite weaned from earth, not fully ripe for heaven! These last touches of a gracious discipline are for their final perfecting, — the mellowing of the fruit before angel hands gather it. And under this earthly completeness our eyes look forward and upward for what is denied us here. We shall not indeed go over this Jordan of disappointment and inherit on the other side; but there is another Jordan which we shall cross. We shall not have our home in the earthly Canaan, nor tread its vine-clad hills; but we shall enter that celestial land of promise, and sit on those serene heights where angels cluster, and on which shines the light of God. We may not inherit fully here; we may advance only into the cold shadows of poverty and neglect, as we go forward leaning on our staff; but there, as heirs of God and joint heirs with Christ, a full and satisfying inheritance will crown and gladden every desire, and all earthly disappointment be swallowed up in eternal satisfaction. This lifts the people of God out of all the sadness that settles on life's shattered hopes. On this mount of faith their feet can stand as on Pisgah's top, and all the glory of the goodly land appear before them, and loftier and whiter than the snowy crown of Lebanon the dazzling mount of the throne of God, and no voice of stern interdict pronounces the decree, "Thou shalt not go over thither," but a welcome of soft music calls to them, "Come, ye blessed of my Father, inherit the kingdom prepared for you from the foundation of the world."

XI.

JOHN'S FAILURE.

AND HE SENT AND BEHEADED JOHN IN THE PRISON. — Matt. xiv. 10.

WHEN the angel Gabriel announced to the aged Zacharias that his old age should be no longer childless, the announcement carried with it this assurance concerning the unborn babe, "Thou shalt have joy and gladness, and many shall rejoice at his birth, for he shall be great in the sight of the Lord." And when that more illustrious prophet heralded by the son of Zacharias had commenced his public work, he bore his witness to the dignity of his messenger and forerunner, — "Verily, I say unto you, Among them that are born of women, there hath not arisen a greater than John the Baptist." But how brief was the earthly career of that greatness! How suddenly it paused! In what obscurity it went down and went out! It seemed to end, too, in failure, — a failure all the more disastrous and reproachful (perhaps in our eyes) because it would appear to have been met off the track of the preacher's legitimate calling, and might so easily, with a little care and prudence, have been avoided. "See what comes," we say, "of his interference with the morals of sovereignty and power. He was not court chaplain. He was not the keeper of the conscience of Herod. He was not sent to regulate the domestic relations of the Tetrarch. He had one message to deliver, one cry to lift up. He was a herald running before the coming of Zion's King to proclaim, "Repent, for the kingdom of heaven is at hand," "prepare ye the way of the Lord." If he had confined himself to that, kept within his sphere, preached that doctrine of repentance and wrath to come, and the near advent of one mightier than he, he might have escaped the prison and the axe. "Possibly." And what effect had his rash and obtrusive protest upon those implicated in the evil? It kindled a revengeful and remorseless hate in a woman's heart. It drew into sympathy and fellowship with her in a new crime the heart of her daughter. It led the guilty Herod, not to repentance and reformation, but to a deeper and more tragic guilt. It must have held up the name of the chief magistrate to obloquy and odium, and brought a scandal upon the ruler of the people. It set the example of disrespect to dignities, and tended to insubordination in the subject. It ended in the silencing of a voice to whose stirring words thousands had listened, and the sacrifice of a life that might yet have gathered unnumbered trophies of its earnestness and fidelity. "Yes, all that." He had a field of labor. It was broad and unoccupied. No man disputed his precedence in it. His sway there was without a rival. There was no narrowness in its limits to make him feel shut in and straitened. Up and down the Jordan valley, across the length and the breadth of the Judean wilderness, he could range at his pleasure. He was bishop there of all the desert, and he was fitted for his place. He was at home in the desert life. His lungs played freely in its congenial air. He had taken upon him, in body and soul, the rude, stern, grand type of its nurture. He coveted no purple robe. The locust of grassy valleys was to him instead of fowl and fatling, and the wild honey was sweet to his taste. He could dispense with the home, the city, and social life. Night in the wild was his pavilion, and the stars above the river his companions. Brave, bold, rugged, strong, and young, he was the man for this missionary work. He had gained a hearing too. He spoke not to the echoes of the Moab mountains. Jerusalem and all the region round about had heard of him and gone out to him. He had touched the popular heart. He struck, and every chord vibrated. And it was not mere curiosity or sentimental interest that he excited. He roused the conscience. He alarmed the fears. He won his hearers. They forsook their sins. They came to his feet broken-hearted penitents, and were baptized of him in Jordan unto a new life. There was no flagging of this power over them. He was in the full-tide of this popular movement on the crest of the wave. And if this field had suddenly become barren, and yielded no longer any harvest, he might still have pushed forward in the van of that conquering kingdom, uttering to new people and tribes the word, "It is at hand," and pointing over his shoulder to the shadow of one whose shoes' latchet he was not worthy to unloose.

All this opening for a life of usefulness, this splendid

harvest which he had begun to reap, he staked and lost on one adventurous throw. He must needs intermeddle with matters of state. He must go up from the Jordan to Jerusalem to rebuke wickedness in high places. He must beard the lion in his den, adulterous Herod in the very insolence of secure crime and unlorded power. In this he failed, by this one step he lost all. Was it a mistake and an error? Did he lose all? Was the life of John in this turn of it and sacrifice of it a failure? That is my question. We cannot so conclude because he died early and by a death of violence. Then are the death of youthful patriots who fall in victorious battle a mistake and a failure. Then were the death of martyrs at the stake and in the amphitheatre a waste of generous blood. Then were the sacrifice of Christ himself what it seemed to his murderers, the defeat of his work and the final triumph of his enemies. No. Death itself is often the noblest victory. We may give much for a good cause, and keep back life. We may give toil and prayer and gold, and testify thus our sense of the soundness of its claims. But when we throw in this final contribution, when it is seen that we count life itself cheap before the preciousness of some holier and worthier thing, that is a testimony that silences all gainsaying. It is not certain, then, that life given in sacrifice is thrown away, goes out in waste and failure. John was true to his convictions. At once we side with those convictions. We are sure that he was in the right. Our hearts front the tyrant who had inaugurated adultery as the morality of the court and echo the calm, steady utterance of those unfaltering lips, — "It is not lawful for thee to have her." It is a great and rare thing for a life to be true to its conscientious judgments, to swerve from them neither from fear nor favor, to refuse to be bribed or awed into dishonest silence, to act and speak as the free soul, the untrammelled thought impels, to keep that soul free, and that thought without a shackle, and carry the sustaining consciousness that the outward and the inward correspond. This noble assertion of moral liberty may bring the body into chains. Is it better, then, to wear the fetters within, to have no shackles on the limbs, to boast, "I am at large," while the spirit is imprisoned in its own cowardice, and thought and speech are in the ignominious chains of falsehood? Which is success, and which is failure, — to sit within dungeon walls a true man, or to stifle the moral sense in a deeper darkness and ride in a chariot? The man who abides by the right, who confesses it with heart and life and lip, who moulds to these inward facts of his moral convictions the outward shaping of his way, who keeps life true to this inward light, who will have it, and who makes it at any cost correspond with what God has given him to know and believe and feel, has gloriously succeeded, whether he be canonized living as a saint, or be broken on the wheel. By this test the life of John was no failure. He kept his truth. He brought his convictions into the incarnation of action. A fire burned within his bones, — a fire of indignant remonstrance against a public and notorious wrong. He would not smother that fire. He would not be untrue. No fear, no policy, should mark his face in flattering and smiling obsequiousness before the face of Supreme Power. He maintained his freedom, and the voices of the ages say above his headless trunk, "Here lies a true man." I cannot call that a failure; I call it immortal success.

Again, John was a witness to the disinterestedness of truth. If it had been seen in that trial of his constancy that truth could be bought and sold, that truth coveted preferment, that it ceased to be truth when danger and suffering threatened, that it was a bidder like avarice and ambition and every light and false thing for personal gain and popular favor, that it loved ease and comfort and emolument better than its own purity, that it was what it was only for the sake of what it could win by it, and when threatened with loss, changed sides like a politician, — if this had been the witness of John, it would have been more corrupting than the sin of Herod. But he stamped it on his life, he stamped it on this historic page, he wrote it on his prison walls, he preaches it still with the voice that pierced the heart of the desert, "Truth has no price." Again, the testimony published then and left to us is that Truth is no respecter of persons. If when publican and harlot appeared before him, when the humble and nameless crowd surrounded him, John had preached "Repent," ringing it rough and full, — "repent, flee from the wrath to come!" and when the sensual and cruel Herod was in presence, spoke not at all, or spoke softly, rounded off the angles of that sharp word Repent, and spoke of the desirableness of some improvement, of the probability that his excellency might some day reject the infelicities of his present position, and begged permission, in courtly phrase, to point out some of the consequences of what he hoped he should be pardoned for saying he could not regard but as a grave and serious error, that majesty of Truth would have been brought into contempt; he would have been a traitor to her queenly dignity. He would have interpreted her message in one dialect to an obscure offender, and in quite another to the man who gilded over his crimes with the gloss of wealth and station. That would have been a failure for the world's pity and scorn. The other was a success for the world's admiration, for God's encomium. And now who knows the whole effect at the time of that fearless and noble protest? It was needful in God's dealings with Herod that this rebuke should come in as a part of his history and experience. It brought a holy God near to him and before him. It held up right and lawfulness in outlines clearer and a demand more audible than princes are often permitted to see and hear. It was instead of a public sentiment, anticipating judgment upon the vileness of a crowned potentate, and dared to come near enough to make sure of being heard and understood. It was the hour of God's mercy to this ruler. It gave him one of those golden opportunities which come to us all to acknowledge and forsake guilt, to fall down and pray, "God be merciful to me a sinner." It may have arrested the evil influence of that vicious example in a station so commanding and influential, and have kept back multitudes from following in the path of so bold and shameless a demoralization. It set up, we cannot say before how many minds, a divine standard of what is lawful, and educated the conscience of thousands, perhaps, to reverence and obedience. "Thrown away and wasted!"—that earthly life may have been instead of the eternal ruin of thousands of its contemporaries,—may have held back a nation from lower deeps of debauchery, and have saved from relapse, and have confirmed in the faith and virtue of a new religion, the tens of thousands of converts whom John had baptized. We are not competent yet to pronounce that life a failure. We are too distant, too ignorant, so to pronounce. Again, it may be well enough to remark that the great work assigned in Providence to this life seems to have been achieved. His herald task was performed. He had seen the hour when he could say, "This is He of whom I said, After me cometh a man which is preferred before me." Publicly he had baptized to an infinitely more glorious and eventful mission than his own that greater and mightier Prophet. The way of the Lord had been prepared. The forerunner had turned the attention of the people to this illustrious advent. His final discourse had weightier tidings for the world's ear than any he had previously pronounced, "Behold the Lamb of God which taketh away the sin of the world." He could add nothing more to that. It was time to hear another voice speak. There came a revolution in the popular heart, and instead of the eagerness to rush forth into the wilderness to see that more than prophet, the new quest was, "Sirs, we would see Jesus." Already it had been told to John by some of his own half-zealous adherents and followers, "Rabbi, he that was with thee beyond Jordan, to whom thou bearest witness, behold the same baptizeth, and"—

oh, hard trial to the natural heart — "all men come unto him." Not thrice, nor twice, has there been in all the annals of humanity a nobler victory over self than the answer of John evinces, "A man can receive nothing except it be given him from heaven. Ye yourselves bear me witness that I said, I am not the Christ, but that I am sent before him. He that hath the bride is the bridegroom. But the friend of the bridegroom which standeth and heareth him rejoiceth greatly because of the bridegroom's voice. This, my joy, therefore, is fulfilled," and he adds, without one rebellious thought, his self-triumph moving us almost as deeply as that of Abraham before the altar of Mount Moriah, words that poor human nature finds it hard to speak calmly, but with the same great joy on his face, "He must increase, but I must decrease." It was not an incomplete life pausing where it did. As truly as Paul the aged after him, could this youthful hero sing, "I have fought the good fight, I have finished my course, I have kept the faith." His work was done and well done. His crown was won. Herod's hand placed it on his head. His doctrines remain. His utterance sounds down to us. What it is to prepare the way of the Lord, what preaching it is that rouses and changes men, he has taught us. A finished, consummated life, nothing fragmentary, no failure here. We are wrong to measure success by outward and visible results. The true measure of success is in one word, FIDELITY. When laurels are distributed by God's hand to the victors of earthly warfare and struggle, the eulogy of the divine lips does not recount the trophies of that valor, more or less in

number, — "Thou hast been faithful in few things, I will make thee ruler over many. Enter into the joy." It is not, "Thou hast been successful, thou hast been popular, thou hast drawn crowds of followers and disciples after thee," but simply, "Thou hast been faithful." · The world says, perhaps, of some obscure laborer, if indeed she speak of him at all, "This man has toiled in vain." The Church may ask, if she will, "Whom has he converted?" The year books shall bear record that others have made and baptized more disciples than he. Against ill-success, against discouragement and false judgment, he may have wrought all his life, and seemingly at last succumbed to the difficulties and impracticabilities of his position, and the first cheering word he has ever heard may come to him when God beckons him across the river and greets him with, "Well done, good and faithful servant." But we should omit perhaps the grandest refutation of the idea that the life of John was a failure, if we should neglect to notice the power of it for evermore as a kindling and inspiring example. Ah, there stood a hero. There was no blanching in him. So should truth front wrong, his example declares. It should dare first to speak, then to seal its testimony with blood. For us he was constant, faithful and fearless. It did not conquer Herod, but it has waked and kept on fire the martyr spirit in other lives all down the lapsing ages. It has rallied steadiness and endurance; it has animated Christian boldness and courage since, in hearts no man can number. When the pinch comes, the sight of one resolute face, one form that quails not, puts manhood into a thousand breasts. Men have looked back to John in many a crisis of hard-fought fields and dubious days. There he stands, between the prison and the headman's axe on the one side, and incestuous Herod on the other. He seems to see neither prison nor axe. God above and duty before him are all he sees, and he wavers not for one uncertain moment. We catch his spirit. We copy his deed. We see him in the same line with later and earlier conquerors. This side of him, Peter dauntlessly saying, "Whether it be right in the sight of God to hearken unto you, more than unto God, judge ye." Beyond, far up the ages, is Daniel, with one window of his chamber looking out toward Jerusalem, the other toward the den of lions, and the voice of prayer rising from his kneeling form. Had Peter died then and there as he stood, had the lions had the mastery of the young Jewish prince, doubtless illustrious and kindling would their example have been. It were not well to have earthly deliverers attend always upon Christian heroism. That would mix an earthly element with the triumph of faith. Let some of these conquerors pay the penalty of their faithfulness, refusing deliverance. So shall their championship of truth and right be a purer and more unquestionable witness to an inward power sustaining them against nature's weakness.

Sometimes we have in current earthly histories examples on the field of strife of so-called failures, worth more as quickeners to valor and helps to a soldier's virtue than most brilliant successes. Such was the scene in the late Crimean War when, on a dull October morning, thirty thousand Russians appeared over the hills of Balaklava, in the rear of the allied armies of France and England, and swept the feebly-defended Turkish redoubts crowning the heights. Retiring then a little to choose their ground, plant their batteries, and reform their army, they seemed to be making preparations to bear off the captured cannon of the allies. A somewhat confused order was given from the English commander-in-chief, confusedly transmitted and confusedly interpreted, for the cavalry to advance and frustrate the enemy's design. The effect of the order thus understood was the world famous charge of the Light Brigade, that hurled a little band of gallant gentlemen against an army of horse, foot, and artillery in the chosen position. Surprised at the order, misgiving alone, unsupported, but lending their hearts to the work, they rode through grape and shell, trampling under feet a cloud of skirmishers, right over the fatal battery, cutting through a mass of five thousand Russian cavalry, and turning on their course, each man matched against a host, pierced by lance-thrusts, hacked by sword-cuts, and riddled by bullets, regained the camp by twos and threes, riding out six hundred and seventy strong, returning with scarce two hundred saddles filled. A waste of heroic life and gallant blood we say. And yet it struck a chill through Russian hearts, and bannered every English warrior in every succeeding fight. It taught lessons of the soldier's obedience, the soldier's loyalty, and the soldier's truth which the wars of centuries and a hundred gazetted triumphs could not teach so well. It stirs the warm blood in a soldier's bosom, more than the general's word or the bugle's note. The memory of it will be the pride of the English soldier, and fire and sustain his noblest daring, so long as men shall learn the art of war. There is to-day no aristocracy so peerless, no order of nobility so illustrious, among all England's titled ranks, as that little surviving company, concerning which men say as they point out a solitary passer-by, "There goes one of the 'Light Brigade.'" There is no victory on all the plains which English blood has moistened the island bards shall love so well to sing, the plumed cohorts shall boast with so generous an emulation, as this wasteful, useless, unequalled charge.

> "When can their glory fade?
> Oh, the wild charge they made!
> All the world wondered.
> Honor the charge they made,
> Honor the Light Brigade,
> Noble six hundred."

No, my friends.

Nothing that is true to honor and courage and fidelity, nothing heroic and self-devoted, is ever in vain. The hearts of Christ's warriors on earth shall ever feel the thrill of brave blood at the name of John; the bards of Heaven shall celebrate his failure as one of the grandest victories of God's human champions. Young men, brethren, fellow-workers, go and do ye likewise. If you stand for a truth, a principle, a sample of conscience, a price of morality too high and pure for your associates to appreciate; if in any of these issues you stand alone; if for your persistent virtue the narrowing circle of neglect and want shut in about you like prison walls; if well-meaning friends chide your too fastidious conscientiousness; if you fail to carry your principle by the acclamation of majorities, and find that you must suffer for it instead in a minority of one; if you are moved to give your young life to the country that calls now for all her valiant sons, and the thought of finishing your career so soon, on some fatal field day, instead of living on in serene tranquillity and amid household ties to a late old age, wrestles with your spirit, look back again to that lonely prisoner, that heroic youthful preacher and confessor, done to death for his faithfulness, and accept your lot, listening the while to this watchword from overhead, "Be thou faithful unto death, and I will give thee a crown of life."

XII.

FRIENDSHIP.

. . . . THERE IS A FRIEND THAT STICKETH CLOSER THAN A BROTHER.—
Prov. xviii. 24.

WE speak a very tender and sacred word when we call one our "brother." But a brother may not be a friend. All the household ties may be complete upon a heart that yet feels that it has not one friend. The intimacies of the home may be coupled together, leaving this heart unmated. And where love is not denied, the love that is rendered us in the natural ties scarce seems to us the tribute of the free heart. It is mixed with instinct. It comes not so much as a matter of choice, because the eye has seen and the heart has felt a charm that cannot be resisted, but as a matter of natural instinctive prompting, quickened by common blood, strengthened by common interest.

It may not be a personal homage when those who are cradled together are found content with one another's society. Nature has joined them rather than elective affection. The fellowship is close often rather by force of habit than by clinging tenderness and mutual sympathy.

The heart wants more than this. It wants one upon

whom it can bestow its love and esteem, to whom it can impart all its confidence, and from whom it can receive the same, as a voluntary offering, the expression of a good will which it has won not by blood, but by its own qualities, not the dictate of nature, but the full, free choice of the heart.

Sometimes this want is supplied within the circle of the home, not as the fruit of nature, but above nature. More frequently, perhaps, I had almost said more naturally, this intimate friendship is with one outside the home, the soul exercising its liberty, finding its happiness in giving without the constraint of nature, and craving in return that which is spontaneous and unconstrained. It would love and trust, not of debt, but of free will.

Give me a friend. I am not myself till I have a friend. My nature is locked up; my friend has the key. Till he open, how can I know, how can another know, what my heart is capable of? I am restricted, stifled, suppressed. I do not grow up and out to the light and the air. I do not think my own thoughts, nor speak my own language, nor warm into true, loving, and genuine confidence till my friend come. If I have no friend, I shall be likely to remain unexpressed, and so to be less and less what I might be. My friend carries my development beyond all my old consciousness of capacity. What does a stranger or a mere acquaintance do for my truer self? He takes a careless greeting, a light courtesy, a civil word, a touch of my listless hand. Is this all I have to give? Is this all I am?

What a transformation one hour of intercourse with a friend effects; how my heart opens; how I venture down for its deepest mysteries, and lead them up to day; how I dismiss the shyness that kept the sanctuaries of my soul veiled; how the soul itself walks forth like Adam in the garden, unrobed but not afraid, meeting in the paradise of friendship no eye that brings a blush; how I speak what my lips never uttered before; how I feel what my heart never felt before; how the hidden fountains at this breath of spring — the rigid frost all dissolved — well up and pour forth their fresh, unchecked streams; how my nature revels in this genial clime, whose brightness is the face of my friend! Is this myself? I knew it not. I should never have known it but for this touch of friendship's magic wand. It is not my old solitary self.

It is my occult, my begotten, my possible self, and I come into actual and demonstrative being in this natal hour. I was never fully born until now, and knew no complete maternity till I knew the cherishing nurture of friendship.

How much, then, do I need that friendship itself should do for me? If I can put into speech all that my soul, in its deepest asking, wants of a true friend, what shall I plead for?

I want a friend that shall meet the craving of my heart for a perfect loveliness and beauty. I cannot be satisfied with loving fair and beautiful things that are inanimate. The rose is perfectly beautiful in its way. My heart springs toward the faultless arch and brilliant coloring of the rainbow; the wooded lake, far away from the haunts of men, and unvexed by the intrusion of human life, is quietly and exquisitely lovely. I admire these charms of nature; I stand fascinated with gazing upon them; I pronounce their loveliness without a blemish, but I am alone while with them. There is no tenderness in my love, no warmth of sympathy in it; there is no exchange of soul. My taste is educated and refined, but I have seen no face that answers back to mine.

I want an incarnate beauty, a loveliness living and vocal, moving in the plane of intelligence, capable of appreciating and reciprocating what I feel, so that I can love and be loved after my kind. I want a being, a character, a person, a soul, to whom I can say, "Thou," and who will understand my offering when I lay down there all that I have. And I want the fairness to be exceedingly fair, the loveliness exceedingly lovely. I want to gaze and gaze and see no blemish. We all have within us an ideal of a grace and beauty that are faultless. Matching this ideal and kindled by it, we have all of us an aspiration to find and obtain this perfection, making the prize ours forever. We are looking for it on every hand all our life long, — a nature all truth and purity and gentleness and tenderness and benevolence and strength, with no false thing, no harshness, no prejudice, no fickleness, no weakness in it. Shall this ideal mock and elude us always? We question each bright face of earthly kindreds to see if it be there. We hold a moment each hand that touches ours. Is this the ideal friend, constant, loving, sympathetic, above all meanness, selfishness, deceitfulness, and mutability? We listen to each tone that falls upon our ear, if haply that one true heart still searched for spoke there. Where we give our love and confidence, it is as much our ideal we love and trust as anything real which our eyes have discerned, often more. We think we are looking upon the real when we have only projected out our ideal and flung its charm over the object of our gaze. And the disappointments of life come often from the growing perception that the real fails to coincide with what we thought we saw and were about to possess. Indeed, we have learned, most of us by experience, even the most favored of us, that in the real we must subtract more or less largely from the ideal, consent to imperfection, find our best friends and truest not all that we thought them, at least, not all that we could conceive, come upon qualities or limitations of qualities that demand our forbearance, even as we must ask, for ourselves, from them, large forbearance in return.

This consciousness and discernment of mutual faults makes our human friendships very tender and touching, secures many sentiments in loving hearts, the exercise of which would otherwise have found no place, — sentiments of generosity, carefulness, forgiveness, and charity, — but it denies to us forever our ideal. That perfect image unmated anywhere, finding amid all varieties of human life no mirror for its fairness and symmetry, comes back to our hearts, like Noah's weary dove to the ark, and hides within the chamber of our soul. We gaze upon it still, but it is only an image. We refresh ourselves by the contemplation of its surpassing attractions, but it is a picture, and no more. Is there no original for this picture? Shall we never behold this image realized and vitalized? Shall this hunger for a perfect loveliness nowhere and never be satisfied? Is it merely an internal aspiration, a standard which our own soul has set up, and is it to help us only as an educating ideal, but never to gladden and enrich us as something with which we can make a close and satisfying alliance?

Let us rest this question here, unanswered, for the moment, and pass on.

We want again, as a natural and inalienable demand of the heart, a friendship that shall draw out our whole capacity of loving. The heart delights to give love, to go on giving so long as there is no check, to feel that it can give without restraint or limitation. But suppose it presently find that where it has begun to bestow love, it cannot love there any more ardently; that it has exhausted or outrun the attractive power; that it is like a forest tree growing in a box in a greenhouse, its roots hemmed in and confined by that narrow crib, and its boughs met soon by the low roof and clipped to that dwarfish standard, — roots that would pierce the earth for many a rod, seeking deep springs of remote watercourses, — boughs that would rise into the mid-air and toss with a giant's strength in dalliance with the full gales of heaven. Suppose the heart awake to this consciousness that it has given to its friendships all that those friendships can command, and has yet an indefinite capacity for loving unemployed; that it could give more love and yet more, but cannot give more to these objects, outreaching and overgrowing them as a luxuriant vine outtops and overruns a low and scanty trellis; what, then, shall comfort and portion it? What shall it do with this superfluous capacity of loving? Is it superfluous? What was it given for in such excess? Shall this fountained fulness find no outlet, and for want of channels set back and stagnate and breed the malaria of ceaseless discontent, a perpetually chafing restraint. When the heart questions, as it must if it make no positive discoveries, if it were willing to love on blindly; when it questions, as at times it cannot avoid doing, the wisdom of bestowing such vast affection upon the frail, perishable, and imperfect objects of earth, and the still outreaching vine seek something loftier and larger to climb and spread upon, that it may show what a vigor of life and productiveness is in it, shall it forever droop unsupported to the ground, and plead with all its vacant tendrils in vain?

We want, again, a friendship that can enrich us indefinitely. This is not a selfish desire so much as a noble aspiration. Being incomplete in ourselves, we seek to draw completeness from our friend. He must have what we have not. He must not fall below what we have. If he be poorer and weaker in everything than we are, he will not help us up, but will drag us down. If we choose as our friend one whom we can contain and measure on every side, we shall either some day despise him or shall sink content to his level, wronging our own more vigorous soul. He that chooses wisely chooses where he will have gain of something that he lacks. A true friendship should be mutually improving. We also may give, though we acquire. We may have something to impart where we have much to receive in this interchange of bounty. We want a friend, therefore, whom we cannot exhaust in a day or a season, one in whom we can make new discoveries of wisdom and of worth every day, one who has something beyond still in every disclosure he makes to us of his thought and of his heart, one whom we can never fully read as we peruse a printed volume, coming at last to the end and saying, "I have finished," as we close it and lay it down. We want to feel that he gives us richly of his abundance, and that, had our want been greater, he could have given more, or that he gives all, and yet could give again, as a cloud empties itself, and passes, and returning on a changed current, pours a fresh deluge down.

But while we desire thus a superior for our friend, we want one who cannot despise us, one whose wisdom, where he is wise and we are ignorant, will bear with our ignorance; whose strength, where he is strong and we are weak, will bear with our weakness; whose address, where we are untutored, will guide and teach without humiliating us. We want to feel it safe — safe for our self-respect — to show him our deficiencies, that he may supplement them, and yet not look down upon us. We have even a longing to show not only our weakness, but our corruption, to confess that we have moral diseases at heart, to beseech that we be not better thought of than we deserve. We may indeed exercise modesty and humility in our earthly friendships, but we cannot show there the evil imaginations that haunt us, lest we sully our friend's purity too. Were there one to whom even this infirmity might be disclosed and our soul have help, and yet our place be secure in his esteem and affection, oh, what a friend were that!

We want in a friend quick perception and intelligent sympathy. He must not stride in with rude and blundering steps among our delicate sensibilities. His offers of help must not be in a voice that jars upon our hearing when we are sensitive. He must understand us, not after long and reiterated and wearisome explanation of our feelings, — he must understand us instinctively, read our mood at a glance, penetrate to our trouble or our joy with one diving look, adapt himself to the changes of temperature beneath the sky of our soul without too keenly feeling himself the variations of climate, — know how, in one word, to rejoice with us when we rejoice, and to weep with us when we weep.

We want one, and here is where our quest among our human kindred utterly fails, who can come in upon that region of interior loneliness, where we are so often weak and desolate with none to help.

We have sorrows that we can never tell to any mortal ear. Oh that there were one who could sit down and hear the long sad tale and pity us and comfort us!

We have burdens to bear to whose lifting we can call in no human hand. Oh that there were one who could come to us when we are bowed and our strength is spent, and with friendly hand lift at those burdens or sustain us as we falter beneath the load.

We have temptations pushing us hard in unseen conflicts, to whose withdrawn battle-fields we cannot invite any with whom we associate to repair, lest they also receive some wound that will be henceforth reproachful to us. Ah, if we knew a friend who could be our champion then, himself invulnerable, and his friendship unchanging, not to be forfeited by such a fellowship in our struggle with evil, what a note of triumph we could sing!

When friends have counselled us and entreated us, and shown us the way of safety and the path of honor, we have still a remaining weakness in which they cannot come to our aid,—a weakness of will, an infirmity of purpose, a wavering heart, a halting choice, which is often fatal to our peace and welfare. Ah, if there were one who could show us duty and counsel us to walk in it, helping us to will and to do the unerring right, what a friend were he in the crises of our life!

When my frame is prostrate in sickness, when I cannot lift my fainting head, nor scarce stretch out the right hand of my strength, when it is too great a task to speak aloud, or to frame question and answer for any who come to my bedside, give me then a friend whom physician and nurse can safely admit to my presence, who can salute me without disquieting me, sit with me without imposing the burden of his presence, whose presence itself is a benediction of rest and peace, who can interpret my feebly-murmuring lips without making me repeat my whispers, who is calmly wakeful when other eyelids droop, who watches as vigilantly and tenderly the pulses of my soul as the physician those of my body, and gives me the sweet and reposeful sense of being always cared for, the comforting assurance that neglect is impossible, and I can bless the painful captivity that shuts me up with such a friend.

There will come some day a sickness that cannot be healed, a hurt that is mortal. The final hour draws on. My friends are about me. I see their love and sorrow. I am setting out on a strange journey. Will any of that weeping circle go with me? No, they are there to see me off while they stay. They take my hand not to join me as I depart, but only to say "Farewell." They bend over me, not to whisper the sustaining pledge, "I will never leave thee, nor forsake thee," but to breathe a last "adieu."

As I enter the shadow of the dark portal, I see them clustering together behind me, leaving me to go forward alone. "Oh, my friends, desert me not now, walk a little way with me on this fearful unknown road." But however anguished my appeal, not one of them passes to my side to bear me company. They weep, but their feet remain rooted to the ground. To my outstretched hand they extend theirs, but it is only to wave the parting signal.

Must I tread that shadowy valley with no companionship? Is there no rod, no staff, that can comfort me? Not one of all that have loved me to whom I can then say, "Thou art with me, I am not afraid"? And when I have gone down thus to the dark river, and have crossed over, what do I know of the farther shore? Must I land a lonely stranger on that shore of eternity, that dim vast shore, with no guide, no welcome, no kindred, no tie from the past, that holds firm and strong, no familiar friendly voice that shall make me feel at home?

These are some of the thoughts and questionings of my

heart when I muse upon the friendship I need, and as I muse and question, I perceive more and more the difficulty of securing such a friend. Oh, rare and precious treasure that should fill this great want of my soul and my life! Where shall I find him? Who is he? What is his name, and where his home?

And I turn to read my Scripture again. "There is a friend that sticketh closer than a brother." Does not Solomon mean more here than the failure of natural affection, and the exalting of real and abiding affection above natural ties? Is he not writing more grandly than he knows? Does he not hold a prophet's pen? Is he not sketching a likeness, the original of which should come afterward? Is he not publishing an unconscious testimony which one who was to arise in the fulness of time should take to himself? How is it that all hearts agree that this ancient utterance fits now but one name of all that have been spoken among men? Jesus of Nazareth, the Son of Mary, the Son of the Highest, the Friend of man, is this "Friend that sticketh closer than a brother."

He is "fairer than the sons of men." I can find no spot or blemish in him. In him is no excess and no deficiency. All that I have ever conceived of innocence and purity and goodness, of patience and gentleness and sincerity, are realized in him who did no sin, neither was guile found in his mouth. My ideal is met at last.

There I can love without qualification and restriction, with no guilty sense of idolatrous extravagance. I can expend my whole power of loving. My heart cannot enlarge itself beyond the attractiveness of this beloved object. Love as I may, growing in loving capacity and fulness through all immortality, I can never feel that I have loved him enough. I only feel how mean, how poor the offering of affection which I bring when compared with his inexhaustible worth, and sing at last when my one heart is emptied at his feet, —

> "Had I a thousand hearts to give,
> Lord, they should all be thine."

And as I cannot overtop this attractive power by any luxuriance of my heart's love, so neither can I exhaust the fruitfulness of that friendship for me. Successive harvests may reduce the fertility of the soil; the drought may drink up river and lake; but however much I draw from the bounty of Jesus, from his love, his light, his power, his faithfulness, I feel that there is an infinite fulness left. These resources, and the kindness that makes them mine, I cannot drain.

And pensioning my wants on this enriching friendship, I never feel my relations to it degrading. I am never despised, never reproached, never treated as a mere hanger-on, a wearisome dependent. The more I ask of this friendship, the more it gives, and the better it is pleased, and there I may show all the indwelling corruption of my soul, and hear no word and catch no look that puts me to shame. I may show it as freely as one with a hidden cancer betrays the secret to a trusted physician, receiving in return only an access of healing care.

Here I am understood. What I cannot express is known. The sympathy of Jesus makes no mistakes.

Deeper than my consciousness is his insight into my trouble, and his manner as gentle as his intelligence is wise, — soft words tenderly spoken, rest for weariness, strength for weakness, comfort for sadness.

In the solitudes of my soul, where no human footstep can tread, he is at home. I can find no chamber so interior and secluded where a grief may hide from him, or a wounded spirit lie tossing without his knowledge and presence. The balm which no human hand could reach me for my secret hurts his wounded hand brings in; the temptation, whose severity I could not make known to any intimate of my earthly fellowships, he foils with his ever-ready skill and power, for I am willing that he should know, and he is more than willing to defend. The weak and wavering will he steadies and rallies and girds with conquering energy.

He makes all my bed for me in my sickness; comes in with a step that never jars; exacts nothing of effort and action, but only asks peaceful trust; excites no sensitive nerves, but only calms both body and soul; keeps unwearying vigils while he "giveth his beloved sleep;" makes every wakeful hour bright with his dear, comforting presence, so that the silent, dark night is a chamber of radiant communion with him, and when my eyes question him of the issue, lays his finger on his lip and smiles till I am satisfied.

And on that lone, last journey, when friend and lover and brother retire from me, he gathers my arm in his, he leads me on through the darkness. I feel no weight of the sable gloom. I feel no fright at unseen awful terrors.

I am with him, and a dawning light paves soon my advancing path, and I see a pearly gate, and I enter a golden street, and my Guide and Friend presents me faultless before the presence of the excellent glory.

Is not this the friendship we want? Can we live without it? Can we die without it? If it were offered, could any heart that was not mad reject it?

They gave him his name of old, — scornful lips, but they spoke the truth, "Friend of publicans and sinners." He stands near us now and makes his gentle overture, "Ye are my friends if ye do whatsoever I command you."

Will you have his friendship? Will you sacrifice everything else to make him your friend?

Take this hymn of trust and make it yours : —

"O holy Saviour, Friend unseen,
Since on thine arm thou bidst me lean,
Help me, throughout life's changing scene,
 By faith to cling to thee!

Blest with this fellowship divine,
Take what thou wilt; I'll not repine;
For as the branches to the vine
 My soul would cling to thee.

Though far from home, fatigued, oppressed,
Here have I found a place of rest,
An exile still, yet not unblest,
 Because I cling to thee.

What though the world deceitful prove,
And earthly friends and hopes remove;
With patient, uncomplaining love
 Still would I cling to thee.

Though oft I seem to tread alone
Life's weary waste, with thorns o'ergrown,
Thy voice of love, in gentlest tone,
    Still whispers, "Cling to me!"

Though faith and hope are often tried,
I ask not, need not aught beside;
So safe, so calm, so satisfied,
    The soul that clings to thee!"

XIII.

FAITH'S VENTURES.

BY FAITH ABRAHAM, WHEN HE WAS CALLED TO GO OUT INTO A PLACE WHICH HE SHOULD AFTER RECEIVE FOR AN INHERITANCE, OBEYED; AND HE WENT OUT, NOT KNOWING WHITHER HE WENT. — Heb. xi. 8.

IT was a sublime venture in the strength of which Abraham went forth from Ur of the Chaldees in search of a strange land to be shown him of God. No geography of that unknown country lay before his eye. All the map he had of it was this misty sketch, without features or outlines, in the divine promise, "A land that I will shew thee." His home was in the rich, alluvial pastures of the lower Euphrates. That was his country, the place of his nativity, the place of his kindred and of his father's house. All the pleasantest and all the strongest ties of his life held him fast to that spot. Ancestral associations made the place sacred to his heart. There he himself had lived till he was now seventy-five years old. He was not a young man, standing alone, just beginning the world, and free to strike out whither he would in search of good successes; he was a man of family, with wife and aged father and youthful orphan nephew and a considerable household attached to his movements and sharing his fortunes. The Canaan toward which the heavenly call bade him journey was at least four hundred miles away. All between was a pathless wilderness; there was no public road along which he might take his domestic tribe, following securely in the track of travellers who had gone before him. Swift streams unbridged, mountain chains with passes unexplored, secluded valleys, the hiding-place of robber bands, and the horrors of desert-life were certain perils to be encountered. And what precisely should be the reward? Something large, but vague.

But Abraham's faith was equal to the test. Ah, he had the strong, sweet comfort of a sure call from God. He knew what voice had spoken to him. There was no doubt about the word of command. That was audibly divine. And he so believed the Promiser that it was easy for him against all dissuasives to obey, or, if not easy, that great faith won the victory.

I think it was well for Abraham that that call was to an unknown future. It would have been a tougher strain upon his faith if he had seen what was to be written of him in the years to come. Doubtless he would still have triumphed, but it would have been after a sharper conflict. The promise that leads him out is this: "I will make of thee a great nation." When he arrives in Canaan, a stranger amid its powerful and populous tribes, the covenanted blessing in its repetition seems to recede. "Unto thy seed will I give this land." He flits about from mountain to mountain and vale to vale, building an altar here and another there, but not settling or pausing by any of them, moving southward, a pilgrim from day to day without a home, and presently driven quite out of the country by a grievous famine. Is this the goodly country, the land flowing with milk and honey? From the pursuing jaws of the famine he hastens down into Egypt, and is soon in trouble with the court and the king, and in peril of his life. Then back again into the south of Palestine, in trouble on account of Lot, from the invasion of hostile kings, in trouble in his own family, in trouble for the doomed cities of the plain, in further and stranger trials of faith, and dying at last with nothing of all that splendid inheritance his own but a tomb, which he had bought with his own money, in which lay his dead wife, Sarah, and in which he himself, but for that one field still a landless exile, was buried at her side. Truly he went out not knowing whither he went, and not imagining. Among all the pictures which, under the inspiration of his faith, he drew of the future, probably not one of those hard realities was sketched.

And this has been, ever since the peculiarity of our earthly trial, the one record of every man's story. He is called of God at each stage of his way to go forth, he knoweth not whither. The call he hears, but what it leads to he cannot foretell. The consummation he may feel sure of; but the method, the process, the path that lies between, even the nature of the prize he is to touch, described in material terms and as though close at hand, but changing for possession perhaps to some remote spiritual interpretation, — all this is hidden from him, an enigma which only the future itself can solve. Each morning of our life, each fresh enterprise for a day or for an hour upon which we embark, is a call to us to enter into the unknown, by simple faith in God.

I wish to dwell upon the influence of this peculiar feature in our earthly trial, this venturing of faith upon the unknown that lies outward from the present.

It is, in the first place, no dissuasive from going forward. Every man has it to say as the light of morning flashes under his opening eyelids, "I know not what the day will bring forth. It may have some great disaster in store for me. As I go out into the street I may encounter some shock of violence that shall shake the very citadel of my life, — my wareroom and all that it contains may be shattered into wreck; the day's business, despite my best sagacity, may prove the most unfortunate stroke of industry my hands ever delivered. It is all uncertain. My whole labor may be vain and worse than vain." This is not the mere musing of a hypochondriac. It is all the soberest truth. Shall this man, therefore, add, "I cannot take a step amid such hazards. I cannot go forward till the mist clears up. This walking I know not whither is too rash. I will not rise. I will keep my pillow. I will adventure nothing because I cannot see the end!" Would you commend him for his wisdom and prudence in such a decision? Would you not bid him shake off both his fears and his sloth and, taking an inspiring draught of faith, gird himself for his day's journey and his day's work! Shall the husbandman, because he knows not what floods or drought or blight may come upon his fields with the season's progress, refuse in the young summer to plough and sow, lest there should be, after all, no harvest for him. Shall there be no enterprise of pith and moment undertaken because the issue lies hidden under a cloud? Shall our ignorance of the future paralyze all our diligence, and will none but the headlong and desperate venture to plunge forward into the dark? Faith never gives such counsel, nor worldly wisdom, borrowing her lamp for the darkness of the way. Faith says, "Go forward!" She tells us, "God knows what is coming," and he bids us be up and doing. His eyes survey all that is hid from us, and ours can look into his. It is enough that he is not blind, and cannot be taken by surprise. From shore to shore the wide, dim sea lies level to his gaze, and he calls to us to sail on. There are storms ahead, and sunken rocks, and fugitive icebergs, and ships steering to meet us in our own track, and red-handed pirates, and hungry swarms from foundering vessels, and ten thousand other nameless perils of the deep. Yes, all these possibly. But there is God overhead, observing all, controlling all, guiding all. That is enough for faith. And as to the matter of prudence, why, our dangers do not come exclusively from motion. Sitting still may keep us in the very focus of harm. The flames may wrap the house from which we refuse to go out, the bed from which we refuse to rise. There is no work of life on which we do not proceed without knowing whither; but the believing heart simply says, "God knows," and moves cheerfully and trustfully forward.

Again. The unknown of faith's heritage saves our

weakness from being crushed. We can bear our griefs and disappointments, by God's help as they come upon us, one by one. "Sufficient unto the day is the evil thereof," — sufficient for our strength, sufficient for our knowledge. And only one day's evil can in the present divine arrangement come upon us between the rising and the setting sun. But God has not made us strong enough to take upon our hearts in one burden all the evil of life. That vision would quite break us down. Suppose in entering upon the family relation we saw at one straight glance forward all the trials that are to wear our strength and make our hearts bleed, the pain and grief of little children, their wrestling with strong diseases, anxious days and sleepless nights on their behalf, the dimming eye and whitening face of one and another, and the dreary hush as they fall asleep, the heavy solicitude that comes later when the problems of their character and destiny are waiting solution, the sharp anguish of praying for them in their times of temptation what seem to us unanswered prayers. All the changes of that coming and unwritten family story, its migration from scene to scene and home to home, its struggles in dark days when want is doorkeeper of the house, the infirmities of human temper that sometimes darken its interior lights, the perplexing questions it is to stagger under for burdened months before responsibility sees an open path of duty, we could not go to the bridal hour with so bright a face and light a heart as now. We should turn pale with dread and misgiving, and ask ourselves doubtfully whether we should be found sufficient for such a future. And yet who of us in looking back over such a record would wish he had otherwise chosen? Gathering in one all our sicknesses, all our labors, all our sorrows, all our defeats, wringing all life's bitterness into a single cup, and offering that cup to our lips to be taken at one draught, who could lift his hand to that cup and welcome that draught to his palate? That would make a Gethsemane darker than nature's midnight. Whatever the alternative were, we should be tempted to plead, "Let this cup pass from me!" It is better that we go forth not knowing what lies before us.

Again. The unknown to which faith leads us out stimulates hope and aspiration. If we were not quickened by the view of grand possibilities, there is little we should attempt. Cold, absolute, certain knowledge would be the blight of hope, the death of aspiration. We do not know the future, but we can paint it. Give us our colors and our brush, and stretch the canvas for us, and move our easel near. Our way is to be onward along sunny vales, by pleasant river banks, through gardens of delights, with richest fruitage hanging low to desire, and all hearts that beat in contact with our own ·catching strength and joy from ours. You need not tell us that this is a fancy sketch. For once it may come true. Say not that scenes as fair have been painted before, but have been uniformly overlaid by more sombre hues of reality; we are going to the unknown, and the unknown may be even more radiant than our vision. Other men's lives in the past have failed of their ideal, but ours may come nearer. We see where they mistook; we shall avoid their errors, and achieve the success they missed. The flight of other men's hope has been amid cold clouds, pelted by storms, beaten down by the great rain and hail, and has come fluttering and out-wearied to the ground, but our eagle will spread a more soaring pinion, and ride the tempest with a stronger stroke, and hold his steep way straight on for the sun. There are better prizes than human hands have gathered; we may reach them, — loftier heights than human feet have trodden; we may stand upon them. Many a gallant ship has struck in the voyage; ours shall come into the harbor. It may be the divine will that the successes denied to those who have gone before us shall crown our endeavors. Our friendships shall prove more constant and prosperous than those of which we have read. From our bridal altar a pleasant highway shall lie onward amid bloom and verdure unfading. Ah, what may not God purpose for us of triumph and enjoyment? Faith takes hold of his whole power and goodness. The unknown is what is possible to him. Believingly, hopingly, faith-inspired, we go forward, not knowing whither or to what, but dreaming of the brightest.

And then again, going thus in faith to meet the unknown, we are saved from the bitterness of disappointment. The particular hopes we have cherished may miss of their fulfilment. But, then, we did not stand upon hope, but upon faith, and that rock is steadfast still; that never moves. Our bright dreams fade out one by one, but God does not change. Our ignorance, in which we drew pictures, has not affected his wisdom. The real ground of comfort and of confidence has not yielded by one particle. He has brought to pass what he would. It is not what we expected, but it is what he saw to be best, and therefore it is best. It is better than the gay, flimsy pattern our pencil sketched. It has undiscovered connections with a richer and greater good than we have seen. These trying events, so different from what we had hoped for, are not final ends of God's dealing. They reach forward into a future still unrevealed and worthy of our most ardent aspiring. They are parts, humble parts or costly parts, of a whole, which no eye but God's has yet seen, and whose majesty and grandeur will fill the soul when we apprehend them with infinite content. You cannot convince us that failures are what they seem. They are simply such uses as the great Designer chose to make of us and our working for a scheme that cannot fail. Faith's unknown is capacious enough to hold within its globed sphere such issues of the divine beneficence, such rewards for hoping, believing, and toiling, as shall make all our anguish in journeying toward them a forgotten travail in the joy of their new birth. In this view disappointment has no deep sting to wound and rankle in our souls. It is only in faith's rendering a correction of our misconception as to the methods by which God will reach through us his full, transcendent ends.

The effect of this arrangement upon character is one of its most peculiar and most precious influences. If at the outset of our way, at the threshold of every new enterprise, we could climb some height from which all the coming road were visible, the long reaches to be traversed, the hills to be climbed, the streams to be forded, the sharp angles to be turned, the dark ravines to be threaded, from which also the distant end lay full in view, it would be natural for us to keep our eye upon that revelation. At every forward step we should recall that map of the road, and measure our progress and graduate our expectation by what we could retain of that vision of the whole journey. We should be looking steadily and sharply for the features and way-marks of the road which had impressed themselves most deeply upon our minds. We should thus walk by sight, and make our eyes our guide. But now, as we turn our eyes forward, there hangs before us the thick, impervious veil that separates us from the unknown. We can look back and gather the record of the past, and listen to the voices of experience. But as to coming events, we can only look up. There is but one Being who sees the end from the beginning. For our comfort and guidance, he offers us, in our weakness and ignorance, the alliance of his perfect knowledge, his infinite wisdom, his overcoming strength. We are taught thus to walk by faith. We cannot see, but we can trust him. We know not the road, but we can follow him. We cannot tell what is coming, but we can look to him to prepare us for all. The road forks, and we are utterly at a loss which hand to take; we peer into either opening, but the unrevealing mist lies thick on both; we can only watch our Father's face, and lift our hand to touch his, and wait the intimation of his choice. These necessities keep us near him, awake our concern at anything that divides us from his presence, and hold us in suppliant and dependent intimacy with him.

If a promised blessing, some expected reward, seem to recede as we advance, we study the promise more deeply, we find new capacities of meaning in its terms, we get glimpses of some better thing than that which we thought so near at hand, and look forward to a grander consummation than our life histories had ever dared to hope for. If that which we dimly saw, and supposed just before us, is yet afar off in some untravelled remoteness, like a mountain peak, which at dawn of day we thought we should reach ere noon, but find even as the day wanes that it seems as far away as ever, what a majestic pile must it be, to keep itself so along above the horizon, and send forward its kingly salutation to such distant travellers!

We have a Canaan in pledge and in prospect. We travel on toward its border. Our feet are on its soil. The land we touch is called Canaan, but it does not seem our land of promise. It has sweet vales and goodly hills, its vines are fruitful, and butter and honey flow down its rocky shelves, but we are not put in possession. We are a hungered and unportioned still, and must journey on. Why, then, our Canaan is still beyond and before us, and its vales must be fairer than these, and its hills greener, and some goodlier Lebanon lift its white crown above it, and clusters richer than those of Eshcol be ripening for our coming. We are looking for a home and a rest, for the soul is sure "a rest remaineth;" that cannot fail us. And we have come, we think, upon our sweet possession. Now, soul, be comforted, and, heart, be at peace. Now let the dear, strong ties of kindred, manifold bands of love and sympathy, gather upon us, fasten their clasping coils around body and soul, intertwine their thousand-fingered tendrils with the chords of our very life. Here we are at home. Our pilgrimage pauses here. Our tent life is at an end. We shall have no more any feast of tabernacles. Let us build of stable and durable material, and bid our household gods accept their permanent shrines. God is good and has kept his promises well. We will take the harp and sing — But what is that he says? "Arise ye and depart, for this is not your rest; it may by and by be your tomb, but never your restful home." Why, then, we must strike our tents again and take our staff and journey once more. But a rest remaineth, and it is across the river, and its name is Canaan! Yes, it remaineth, but we are learning to think, we are beginning to know, that it is that other and darker river which we are to cross before we find it; that we are to tread the celestial heights, that we are to enter the promised rest, the sure inheritance, only as we enter the city of God.

Truly each pilgrim of faith goeth forth not knowing whither. He pitcheth at close of day as though at his journey's end, and is not aware that he must move again with the morning. God keeps his hope still just before him, — just before him, but never grasped, — so that he may run still with outstretched hand and eager desire; and then the hope is lifted higher, and God's lips smile the assurance, "Here it is at last," and we see that we have been running for nothing less than an immortal crown, — for no transient home, but for an eternal heaven. This is faith's large and full inheritance, her magnificent unknown. The earthly disappointments are only stepping-stones each toward these serene final summits; the restlessness of earth, only the traveller's enforced diligence in pursuing his road quite to its goal. Our ignorance, that stumbles and halts so often, and catches up such inferior good as though it could be content with it as a portion, and grieves so to lay it down, covers this heritage of everlasting joy and peace. All the busy, earnest years that lie between the starting-point and the goal, all the rich investments of our heart's deep love, — the fond, warm covenants in which we pledge a union not to be sundered, — all personal and domestic ties, all social bonds growing out of our life with the full vitality of nature and of grace in them, are but the training and discipline for our nurture unto his great and blessed purposes ready to be revealed in us at the last.

If we saw now and beforehand as clearly as we shall see the meaning of each particular part of the grand scheme, we should miss the full power of its ministry upon the growth of our souls toward the stature of their immortal manhood. Let us give faith's rendering to the poet's rhymes.

> " When another life is added
>   To the heaving, turbid mass;
> When another breath of being
>   Stains creation's tarnished glass;
> When the faint cry, weak and piteous,
>   Heralds long-enduring pain,
> And a soul from non-existence
>   Springs that ne'er shall sleep again;
> When the mother's passionate welcome,
>   Sorrow-like, bursts forth in tears,

And the sire's self-gratulation
  Prophesies of future years, —
    It is well we cannot see
    What the end shall be!

" When across the infant features
  Trembles the faint dawn of mind,
And the soul looks from the windows
  Of the eyes that were so blind;
When the incoherent murmurs
  Syllable each swaddled thought
To the fond ear of affection
  With a boundless promise fraught,
Kindling great hopes of the morrow,
  From that dull, uncertain ray,
As by glimmering of the twilight
  Is foreshown the perfect day, —
    It is well we cannot see
    What the end shall be!

" When the boy, upon the threshold
  Of his all comprising home,
Puts aside the arms maternal
  That enlock him ere he roam;
When the canvas of his vessel
  Flutters in the favoring gale,
Years of solitary exile
  Hid behind its snowy sail;
When his pulses beat with ardor,
  And his sinews stretch for toil,
And a thousand bold emprises
  Lure him to that eastern soil, —
    It is well we cannot see
    What the end shall be!

. . . . .

" Whatsoever is beginning
  That is wrought by human skill, —
Every daring emanation
  Of the mind's ambitious will, —

Every first impulse of passion,
  Gush of love or twinge of hate, —
Every launch upon the waters,
  Wide horizoned by our fate, —
Every venture in the chances
  Of life's sad, oft desperate game,
Whatsoever be our object,
  Whatsoever be our aim.
      It is well we cannot see
      What the end shall be!"

"It is well we cannot see
What the end shall be;"

but best of all that, not seeing, we can both hope and trust.

XIV.

PLEA FOR THE MONTHLY CONCERT.

AND WHEN THEY WERE COME, AND HAD GATHERED THE CHURCH TOGETHER, THEY REHEARSED ALL THAT THE LORD HAD DONE WITH THEM, AND HOW HE HAD OPENED THE DOOR OF FAITH UNTO THE GENTILES. — Acts. xiv. 27.

FOR graphic and even romantic interest, there is no other book of the Bible that surpasses this book of the Acts of the Apostles. As its name indicates, it is a book of action. You are led by it along a story of marvellous adventures. There is not one dull chapter. Every page is stirring and eventful. Neither history nor fiction ever traced a chronicle more crowded with strange and thrilling scenes. And the line of adventure is not, either in its inspiration or its consequences, frivolous and transient. The scheme that marshalled the journeyings and the sufferings of these heroic actors was nothing less than to "open the door of faith" to nations ignorant of Christ and his salvation. What a lyric and picturesque touch of the pen of Luke in this expression, — "opening the door of faith"! A door of light upon deep darkness, — a door of deliverance for the bondmen of superstition and idolatry, — a door beneath whose grand arch, and through whose stately portals, the long, bright procession of the Christian virtues should enter in and possess the realms of barbarism, degradation, and cruelty! Perhaps it will be popularly, though it cannot be to Christian hearts, a less taking version if we say it is a record of missionary labors, missionary trials, and missionary successes. It is the first volume of the long work of the Church in obedience to that command, at once so full of the love and the authority of Jesus, "Go ye into all the world, and preach the gospel to every creature."

In the scene outlined in our text, we are introduced into a missionary meeting, whose special purpose is the communication of missionary intelligence. To the disciples at Antioch belongs the honor of the first mission ever sent forth by a Christian Church. Moved by the Holy Ghost, with fasting and prayer, and the laying on of hands, they had set apart Barnabas and Saul to the missionary work. (You read concerning this inauguration service at the beginning of the present chapter.) From such "Farewell" these two intrepid brethren had gone forth from city to city, with various fortune, through perils and sufferings, with ever increasing boldness, preaching the death and resurrection of Jesus, and salvation through him. At length, after persecutions and stonings, rejected of the Jews, but with great and good success among the Gentiles, they had completed their tour, and now stood again among their brethren at Antioch. The whole Church came together to hear these returned missionaries. There was no need of urging an attendance upon that meeting. None said, "It is only a missionary meeting; it will be dull and tame." There were no attractions within all the city that could divert a disciple from the scene where these missionary laborers were to tell their simple story. Their hearts were bound up in hearing how it had fared with those whom they had sent out to preach the new gospel, and how that gospel was winning its way in the earth. No strains of music, whether sacred or profane; no lips of eloquent orators, charming never so wisely; no scenes bright and pleasant with social festivities, could compete with the interest of that rehearsal which was to tell how a Christian mission had prospered. They had not prayed and fasted and commissioned their brethren to this work, to be indifferent to its record, and turn carelessly away from the story of its progress, its difficulties, and its triumphs.

In nearly all the elements of interest attached to this occasion of long ago, and in some additional elements of a grander scope and deeper power, we have this scene repeated in our own times every month, in that "CONCERT OF PRAYER" now so widely observed by the modern Christian Church. Eighty years ago last June, the observance of this Concert began with an association of Baptist ministers of Nottingham, England. Forty years earlier an attempt had been made, by a number of Scotch ministers, to secure more united and concerted prayer for a general effusion of the Holy Spirit "on all the churches of the Redeemer and on the whole habitable earth." The Saturday afternoon and Sabbath morning of each week, and more solemnly the first Tuesday of each quarter of the year, were specially commended to Christians for such seasons of agreeing intercession. Many pious hearts in Great Britain, and some on this side the ocean, caught the flame of this quickening influence, and "praying societies" were gathered and maintained in various places in both countries. The sacred fire touched the heart of our own Jonathan Edwards, who was moved to write an elaborate essay, entitled "An humble attempt to promote explicit agreement and visible union of God's people in extraordinary prayer for the revival of religion and the advancement of Christ's kingdom on earth." These efforts and influences culminated at length in the adoption of a resolution by the Nottingham Association, in 1784, "recommending the setting apart of the first Monday evening in every month for prayer for the extension of the gospel." The circle of churches acting upon this suggestion widened, though somewhat slowly, every year. A few American churches, it is believed, kept alive the old Quarterly Concert from its institution, before the middle of the last century. A few more began the observance of the Monthly Concert at about the time of the sailing of the first missionaries of the "American Board." But the observance of this Concert did not gain very general prevalence until the year 1815, when it was urged and enforced by the Panoplist, and almost immediately welcomed by large and increasing numbers of local churches. After some twenty years, it was found that not a few pastors and churches, from the difficulty of gathering a full attendance upon Monday evening, had transferred the Concert to the first Sabbath evening of the month. Several missionary and ecclesiastical bodies favored this change; the subject was discussed at the meeting of the American Board in 1838, and though no action was taken, it would appear that this change had been widely though not universally approved.

With such a past, this sacred season has come down to us. Its observance, maintenance, and transmission are now in our hands. It is no longer a novelty; neither is the Sabbath, nor Christianity itself; but none the less for that ought our interest in it to be fresh, lively, and tender. Our fathers and mothers loved it and honored it. They would as soon have turned their backs on the Lord's day and the sacramental supper as on this hour of prayer for the conversion of the world. The first Sabbath of each month was with many of them the communion Sabbath. Most appropriately they came from the table of their Lord to pray that the memorials of his love and death might be set before all the perishing. In their sacramental hymn these two verses came always together:—

> " 'Twas the same love that spread the feast
> That gently drew us in;
> Else we had still refused to taste,
> And perished in our sin.
>
> " Pity the nations, O our God!
> Constrain the earth to come;
> Send thy victorious word abroad,
> And bring the strangers home."

There is some reason to fear that, with the present new generation of Christian believers, this Concert has less interest and sacredness than with the generation retiring. They felt that it was as divine as the very institution of missions; that the Church at home could not otherwise obey the command to go forth preaching the word to the ends of the earth; and that it was treachery to the Lord, and to those whom they had sent forth in their name to disciple all nations, to lay upon them such a commission, and send forth with them no volume of united, agreeing prayer. They had too faithful a spirit, too tender a conscience, toward this observance, to allow in them the omission of any possible respect to its most honored keeping. We wear the bands of fealty to this venerable ordinance more loosely and lightly. With us it is only one of a great many ways of spending the evening of the Sabbath, between which one and any of all the rest we are free to choose, as convenience, ease, and personal inclination may dictate. The Sabbath evening has come to have a thronging pressure upon it, such as our fathers never dreamed of. It is our evening for sacred operas, — I mean concerts, — for oratorios, for paid declamation, for every department of humane and moral enterprise, for the recitation of perilous adventures in our modern land of bondage, for inaugurating new police regulations in the metropolis, for well-nigh every cause that can find an advocate, hire a hall, and that wishes for an audience. These manifold channels, with others less questionable than some of these, sluice off the attendance upon the venerable Concert of Prayer, and leave it sometimes stranded dry and high, like an abandoned hulk on the shore.

Such a depletion and desertion of this meeting is a great loss to the cause of missions, a great subtraction from the power and faithfulness of the Church in this main artery of Christian life and labor, a blast and a blight upon the intelligent and principled piety of the youth of our communions, and a sad omen for the type of piety that shall hold the ascendency with us in coming days.

Let me now take some one of you by the hand, whom I see here this morning, but never see on the Concert evening, and set before you the persuasive claims of this Monthly Concert of Prayer.

Consider, first, its contribution to your intellectual culture, and to the amount of your positive knowledge. Missionary explorations have now been pushed out over the four quarters of the globe. They have traversed the length and breadth of the continents. They have searched the sea for hidden islands. They have made the acquaintance of every barbarous people. They have occupied the seats of ancient civilization. Toward the poles, they have gone as far into arctic and antarctic winters as the most dauntless navigators. Under the equator, they have braved the heat of tropic suns. The men who have conducted these Christian marches have been men of good ability, of studious habits, and of disciplined mind. Most of them have been graduates of our colleges, and not a few of them men of the highest promise in scientific tastes, literary accomplishments, and intellectual force. These men have gone out into these varied regions of the earth, with their eyes open and their minds alert, to observe and record all that came within their field of vision. They have told us of the novel aspects of these strange shores. They have opened to us the interior of these mighty continents. They have mapped out these island groups. They take us up picturesque valleys, and over rocky ridges, and across nameless rivers, and pause with us on the margins of inland lakes, veiled hitherto from all but native sight, and climb with us the dome of volcanic mountains, until we see with them all that their eyes have gazed upon. They tell us the growths of the field and the forest, — what the hand of nature rears, and what the hand of tillage. They paint the portraits of the races dwelling in these far-off scenes, introduce us to their houses, their social life, their temples of worship, their religious rites, their traits of character, their governments, their manners and customs. They are not flying tourists, skimming over the soil as by express, and sketching only what they see by daylight from the windows of a lightning train. They go into these new climes to dwell there. They make themselves at home among the people. They observe deliberately, and by many a verification, all concerning which they testify. They have the deepest practical interest in studying the hearts and lives of these strange races, and they are men whose testimony can be taken as the witness of truth and honesty. The rehearsal of these testimonies, from beneath the face of the whole heaven, must needs bring together a vast amount of the most wonderful and the most reliable contributions to human knowledge which our enlightened age can boast. It is knowledge not merely of the dead past, but of the living present. On parallel lines with our life at home, all these distant nations and tribes are moving forward in their own current, daily histories. And every month, at least, we may look over, eastward and westward, into these contrasted courses of human progress, and keep a calendar of the whole drift of the race. There is no periodical that comes upon the table of the *savant* that contains within the same space a juster, wider, more varied view of man as a mortal and an immortal being — his condition, his dwelling-place, his graduated interrelations on the full scale of humanity — than the monthly "Missionary Herald" of the American Board. Scholars quote it, ambassadors pay tribute to its writers, science, geography, history, study and appropriate it. These are the pages, such are the facts, that come month by month before the minds of those who attend these missionary meetings. To some extent these facts would be accessible without such attendance, in the printed periodical; but, practically, they would not be gathered. If read, they would not be made so impressive and memorable. A young man who should resolve, for his intellectual enriching alone, never to fail of attendance upon this monthly *résumé* of the world's getting on, might, to his advantage, accept it as a substitute for libraries and lyceums and lectures, and would, when in years, find himself possessed of a sum total of mental acquisitions which no pecuniary value could measure. No young man who desires any breadth of intelligence concerning the day in which he lives, and his contemporaries of the great common family, can afford to neglect this one source of intellectual training and furnishing.

But it is more vital to the idea of Christian culture to say that nowhere else can you obtain such vivid conception of the depth of man's moral and spiritual ruin. Human nature is the same with all the races, and in every land and clime. But we see it at home under the ameliorating power and the decent restraints of the Christian faith. Take away these restraints, go before this renovating power, where the dawn of this travelling day of light and order has not yet risen. Oh, how deep and total the darkness! What forms are moving about in it! What scenes are veiled in it! What degradation is there! Follow the missionary's torch as he lights up dimly the revolting reality. What faces are there! Are they human? Is that the mouth made to smile with sweet and gentle affections? Is that the brow piled as the throne of thought? Are those the eyes filled with the light of intelligence? Look upon the retreat where that life kennels, translate its speech, trace out the rudimental family relation, speak to them such words as virtue, goodness, purity, benevolence, truth. Verily you are talking in an unknown tongue. Are these our fellow-men, children of our own ancestors? Alas, what has sin wrought! This is the world that has departed from God. This is what God saw and loved. This is what Jesus saw, and died. Can any of us see it and think sin a little thing? Can any of us see it and doubt the doctrine of man's depravity? Can any of us look upon it habitually, and not appreciate the world's need of the gospel? If there be in our modern Christian development a less burdensome sense of man's utterly lost and ruined condition than our fathers had, if we have come to speak pleasantly, tolerantly, and hopefully of human nature as only needing a little smoothing and polishing to be acceptable to a holy God, may not this defection be traceable to a neglect of these dark exhibitions of human guilt and shame?

Here, too, perhaps, as nowhere else, we learn to appreciate the power of the gospel as a restoric system. Can it clothe these naked savages? Can it lift these dull and sensual eyes heavenward? Can it transform these brutal instincts to holy aspirations? Can it change these ferocious tempers to meekness and love? Can it lead out before these gross and debased minds God and good angels and all the purities and sanctities of Christian living? Can it displace the kennel with a Christian home, and establish within the decent order and propriety of a Christian household? Can it change the wild, vile speech of those untamed lips to words of prayer and songs of rhythmic tenderness and worship? Can it harness tyrannic and domineering idleness and improvidence to diligence and thrift, and turn the wilderness into a garden, the desert into a fruitful field? Can it lift up the swarming tribes of such human outcasts, and build them into the fair proportions of a Christian nation, and set it as a gem of light and beauty on the bosom of the deep, the loveliest thing God's eye looks upon on the broad Pacific Sea? How such a view exalts the gospel before us! How it rises and towers up — God's great work — with new sublimities of power, more kindling, inspiring, and quickening to our homage than we have ever elsewhere seen it! If we would know how much God has invested of his wisdom and greatness in this redemption scheme, these are the scenes in which to acquire that knowledge. No month shall pass without bringing some of these amazing triumphs of the love and grace of Jesus before us, to move our wonder and excite our adoring praise.

What other scene helps us to come into such full and tender sympathy with Christ as this? How does he feel toward our lost race? How does he look upon these "dark places of the earth, full of the habitations of cruelty"? What are his thoughts of this vast, sunken, heathen world? Is it for us only that he died? Does he long for us, and none beside? Are not his compassions waiting, waiting, waiting, till some voice speak his name in the ears of these far-off ransomed ones, and some hand lead them to him for pardon and crowns of life? What is his dearest wish, what is his grandest purpose, on the earth? Is it not to be known as the earth's Saviour and Lord? Can a Christian heart be in sympathy with Jesus and indifferent to missions? Can that heart enter into the feelings of that divine bosom, and prefer, on the Concert eve, to spend the hour somewhere else? Find me a place upon which the regard of the Saviour is more intensely fixed upon the first Sabbath evening of the month than that scene where the Church assembles to pray, "Thy kingdom come," and to watch and listen unto the answers to that prayer. Whither will you guide me? Shall it be where light hearts gather to be exhilarated by artistic singing? Is Jesus present there with warmer sympathies than where those prayers ascend, and the ends of the earth send in responses? Shall it be where some question of municipal polity is discussed?

Shall it be where trained elocution is reciting the sentences of famed orators for our literary entertainment? Shall it be where an indolent household circle takes *négligé* posture in easy-chairs and on soft lounges? What other purely religious gathering even, however solemn and spiritual, can have an object so grand, so comprehensive, so near the deep core of the heart of Christ, as this that has met to take up his great commission, and to bring him his chief and long-delayed joy and reward? If our personal predilections, our itching ears, our roving propensities, our thirst for outside spiritual stimulus, our desire for self-gratification, control our movements, why, we may go hither and thither, as far as our vagrant feet and our more vagrant fancies shall carry us. But if sympathy with Christ marshal our steps on this one Sabbath evening, if we mean to be where he lingers with tenderest interest, and to come under the most welcoming glance of his eye and his warmest smile, can we doubt that this scene of conference and prayer concerning the evangelizing of the nations is the scene whither we should be led?

It will be acknowledged, of course, that the Church owes a duty to Christian missions, and that each individual member of the Church shares in that debt. What is it that is owed? A little treasure, an annual gift, an occasional utterance of the Lord's Prayer, without any special emphasis on the missionary petition therein, more than we put on that for our daily bread, a glancing of the eye over the missionary column of the family religious newspaper, if such a column can be found? This cannot be all. And yet it is likely to be about the whole, if one neglect the Monthly Concert. It is, with multitudes of professing Christians living in such neglect, practically the whole. Nay, we are to meet and hear freshly, again, that great missionary command, with all the stress of Jesus' heart in it. We are to meet and send out our cheer to the faithful brethren who have gone in our place to the distant idolatrous tribes, and who look back with straining eyes to see whether they are remembered still, and how many of us come together to hear their salutations, and to waft them, in prayers, our united benedictions. We are to meet to kindle in our souls afresh the missionary ardor, to draw in a deep inspiration of the spirit of self-sacrifice, and of the rescuing pity and yearning love of our Lord. The missionary life, which is, more than any other form of expression, that which embodies and conveys most of the heart of Jesus, — most nearly identical with that spirit of Christ without which no man is his, — cannot be vital and earnest with one who chooses to live in habitual non-attendance upon this scene of sacred missionary interest.

If there is any one scene that secures the full and symmetrical development of the Christian character, crowns and wreathes it with all its graces in full bloom and fragrance, it is still this scene of the Missionary Concert. Here is height, for we go up to the throned heart of Jesus. Here is depth, for we gauge the abyss of man's ruin. Here are length and breadth, for our thoughts and sympathies and prayers run swiftly from pole to pole of the habitable earth, and wrap the globe around, like the tidal wave of its oceans. Here Christian pity is taught to weep her softest tears. Here Christian endurance faces its sharpest conflicts, its heaviest strain, and Christian heroism wins its greenest laurels. Here our faith wrestles with hardest problems, and again looks upon its brightest rewards. Here we come to feel that we are nothing, and less than nothing, before the mountain barriers that bar the gospel's way, and again that our faith, instrumentally, is mighty through God to the pulling down of the strongholds of error and sin. Here the love of souls becomes a consuming passion, and the longing insupportable that our crucified Lord should see the fruit of his anguished travail and be satisfied. Here our search grows eager for the ancient promises, and we sift the word of God to trace out that covenant of the Father that pledges to the Son the heathen world as his inheritance. Humility, patience, perseverance, self-denial, ceaseless gratitude for the things wherein we are made to differ from our benighted kindred, the spirit of importunate prayer, a discernment of, and a consecration unto, the true and noble end of Christian living, — all these receive here, every month, a fresh baptism, wherein they are sprinkled from the dust of earthliness, and show a divine purity and beauty. The hold of our ambition, our greed, our craving for luxuries, our all-encroaching worldliness, are relaxed; and here, if anywhere, here almost assuredly, we write upon body, soul, and estate, "All for Christ." This makes a broad, vigorous, healthful Christian development. Nothing narrow, sickly, and dwarfing in this experience. Here the disciple grows to his full stature. He lives not in the confining cell of his own prejudices and his selfish enjoyments. He lives in the wide world over which the cross-bannered host of God's elect is marching, beneath the open sky, where the shadowing wings of the missionary angel bear on that glad heraldry, calling down, through the airy spaces, "Peace on earth, good will to men," and within the full circumference of that large love that bought the world with a sacrificial death.

My dear people, I do not think any of us can afford to dispense with this school of Christian nurture. I think many of us need a higher appreciation of its priceless worth. I believe there is nothing that we can do for our Christian growth, no influence under which we can sit for our personal quickening and enlarging, no service which we can render to the Master and the great scheme which he carries on his heart, in any one hour of all the month, at once so profitable to us, so fruitful for human good, so grateful to Christ, as this attendance upon the meeting for missionary intercession. Will any of you say that these meetings are not interesting? That is your mistake. They are. You cannot tell in any tone, by any utterance, from any lips, the story of the struggling and triumphing gospel, the story of man's degradation and sinfulness and woe, the story of our Christian comrades pioneering the paths of saving truth in the far-off lands of superstition and darkness, without interesting any heart in sympathy with Christ. Will you stay away because the meetings are thinly attended? Is that a remedy for that evil? The single element of a thronged house, without one other feature changed, would fill the meetings with life and power. The presence of numbers, the warmth of so many hearts beating together, the ascending clouds of intercession from so many souls in unison, the interacting inspirations from so many sympathies, all drawn out in one direction, and coursing together through the changes of the meeting, would make the place as solemn and privileged as the council-chamber of the Deity.

It is one evening of a month. Give it to this service. Set it apart and consecrate it, and make it sacred to this observance. Write a vow before God, in your closet, to keep this Concert. Let nothing but his peremptory hand upon you keep you away. I would have no regular engagement, of whatever sort, that should bereave me and Christ of this attendance. Come, young and old; come in fair weather and foul; come fresh or weary; come though angelic choirs give concerts in pavilions of gold, though silver-tongued orators promise strains of eloquence sweeter than song. Come, to please Jesus, to take upon your willing hearts the tender pressure of his last command, and your souls shall reap a full reward; the welcomes of your waiting Lord shall greet you and rest upon you, and the world's redemption shall be hastened on.

XV.

HUMAN LONELINESS.

IF THOU BE WISE, THOU SHALT BE WISE FOR THYSELF; BUT IF THOU SCORN-
EST, THOU ALONE SHALT BEAR IT. — Prov. ix. 12.

DRIVE at midnight through the mazy streets of some great centre of human life. Here and there a lamp is faintly burning. The crowds have melted away. Silence has settled down between the dark ranges of mansions and warehouses. The eye glances up and runs along the surface of the tall, dim walls. What is hidden there within? What secrets do those shuttered homes enclose? If one could look into all that seclusion, what strange elements of society, what varied and perhaps startling experiences, personal and social, would meet his view! High up, half shaded, but struggling feebly out, a light burns obscurely. What is there, — sickness, wakefulness, plotting crime, or only deep slumber watched over by that friendly ray? Imagination revels at will. But night, silence, and the dark masonry, with its curtains and blinds, keep their secrets. We cannot explore or know. And if all those windows were to flame out with a sudden illumination, if we could take the wings of the bird of night and fly over the thronged city, and every roof were transparent, we should know not much more than we now know while pacing slowly and wonderingly along the dark street. The interior scenes of those guarded shelters would be visible, — passages, stairways, and the furnishing of occupied apartments. We should look upon faces and forms, hear the heavy respiration of sleepers, or perhaps human voices interchanging murmuring confidences. But the real mystery of life is more darkly shrouded. Wake all the unconscious thousands there, and let them offer their opened eyes and their ordinary daily face to our gaze, we should be but little nearer the solution. There are more impenetrable walls, there is a deeper night around that mystery, than the retiring day and the hand of man have made. Only God above and the heart within know the facts of experience and character.

Each human life is an isolated life. It may have its alliances and its contacts, but it never loses its identity and its individuality. The stars are by our science, for convenience' sake, set in systems, grouped in constellations, but each is, for all that, a separate sphere, with its own unexplored interior world. So the human soul is an orb by itself. Its peopled chambers compose a world apart from all other worlds. Amid crowds or amid solitudes the man sits ever by himself in the solitariness of his own uninvaded consciousness, with secrets which he could not, if he would, make clearly intelligible to any fellow-man, with questions and issues which he must meet alone.

I wish to lead in our thoughts out of the world of broad

and general sympathies, to disengage each of us from our associations and clanships, to separate us from the sweep of the tide, in which we seem blent with kindred drops, our career and our destiny merged with those of our classification and fellowship, and to bring us in face to face with our own single selves. That is the intent of our Scripture to single us out from a massed humanity, to isolate us within our own personal orbit, to discover to us the singularity of that orbit, to make us feel that undivided responsibleness that burdens ourselves, and to recall us to the conviction that we are to meet the real problem of life solitary and alone. The solitariness of human life is the point specially to be illustrated.

1. Each man is alone in the original, native singleness of his being. He was born alone into this world of his kind, a unit of life, a single fresh soul from the Creator's hand, with his own private and personal outfit of mental and material forces, his own adjustment and proportions of mind and body, their interchanges and relations of offices and effects special and peculiar to him. His cerebral development is his own. The intellectual and the animal divide him up and share him by appointments never exactly repeated. The physical serves well the rational, or disappoints and cripples it, or shades off toward the one extreme or the other. He is of a hardy or tender spiritual constitution; his sensibilities, frigid and stern, or warm and sympathetic. His temperament is his own. The whole balance, poise, and composition of his manhood are individual and unique. The elements of the common humanity are there, but differently mingled in

him from what they are in any other fellow specimen. God's creative versatility and variety never run low. In all the forest no two oaks in limb and trunk and shade stand alike. On the seashore each grain of sand is individual and distinct. The wintry air is full of falling snowflakes like blossoms shaken from the trees of paradise, but each is crystallized with a conformation of its own. In breadth and height and hue the grass-blades vary, and "one star differeth from another star in glory." The diversity of the human form is a symbol of the real diversity of the human life, and of itself helps by no mean contribution to constitute that diversity. Souls are as unlike as bodies. One may seem twin to another, as in the fleshly form, but in stature, color, texture, or whatever expresses the dimensions and qualities of spirits, each has its own specialty and vindicates its separate type.

The very object of creating men single and distinctive, that their function and work may fulfil the Creator's design, keeps them in their identity apart. They may touch at many points, they may compose little societies, they may join their voices in the same strain of music, they may lift together at the same burdens of human travail; but each voice has its own tone, each nerve its own force; this singleness of their own individual make always attaches to them. In that, each is forever himself, — himself alone, and not another, and those limits and boundaries, those descriptive lines that mark him off from the world at large, shut him in to a personal and perpetual solitude.

2. Again, each man is alone in the citadel of his own consciousness. He has an outward eye and an inward

eye. With the outward he looks, and this map of earth is unrolled before him. There rise the mountains, there spread the plains, there the valleys are scored, there wave the forests and murmur the brooks, and chase one another in the play of Titans the colossal waves of lights and shadows over the harvest fields of summer. There heaves the sea, now in stormy tumult, flinging its angry billows against all its bounds, and now sobbing itself to sleep like a child wearied out by its own passion, and again bright and sparkling in the gleam of sunny weather. Above bends the sky, sometimes gusty and howling with winter winds, or all still and black with a rayless gloom, or curtained with impenetrable and chilling mists, or weeping softly in summer rain; and then again, with a deep, pure, and unfathomable blue, across which the crescent moon cleaves her way, or the sun rides royally, or through which, as a transparency, the starry lights of celestial windows and avenues show far and clear. This is the outer world, with its sea and sky, its landscapes, seasons, and changes. And I have outlined its map, because it has its counterpart within. The inward eye looks over an inner world as broad, varied, and marvellous as the outer. There rise the ridges of its controlling thoughts, its grand and stable beliefs; there gush the fountains and murmur the streams of its sensibilities. There wind the channels of its habitual purposes and courses of soul; there is the expanse of knowledge over which the mind ranges; the long, branching vales of memory; the heights imagination scales; there come and go the April lights and shadows of its changeful moods; there surges up in tossing swells, or lies in calm repose, the great deep of its emotions; the forests are musical with birds, or silent and gloomy above the covert of the passions that have their lair there as beasts of prey. Above, to Hope and Faith, in the atmosphere of this soul, there are sometimes clouds and driving and bitter blasts; sometimes blessed revelations seen remote like stars, and sometimes the effulgence, the full splendors, of glorious sunlight. This can hardly be called a fancy sketch. The outer perpetually symbols the inner, — nay, it scarcely has any meaning or reality save as the soul finds correspondences for it and glasses all its features and vicissitudes in its own more conscious life. Upon this inner world of consciousness there rests only one human look. The soul walks therein alone. It never can admit society there. It is not in its power to open up these interior vistas to any other eye. We may notice an air of abstraction come upon one of our companions; he seems lost in revery; he has forgotten our presence. But that is all we see, — his face and form and vacant, assorbed manner, no more. But what does he see within the narrow chamber of his brain, whose walls and dome we can cover with our two hands? There is a world broader and statelier than earth itself. His thought glances across continents of wondrous being, ferries itself over oceans all quivering and throbbing with vitality, soars to a cope no eagle's flight ever touched. Who can follow him? Who can read the strange chronicle of his musings? Who can watch the processions that sweep along those covered highways, and say how they are draped, — whether in mourning sable or festive white? In the sphere of consciousness each man dwells alone.

3. Again. Each man is alone in the daily current of his existence. I mean he lives his own life. It is himself, and no other, that wakes where he lifts his eyelids to the light of morning. It is his own feet that begin again his journey, as he takes up his pilgrim staff, girds his loins, and sets forth. He thinks his own thoughts; he summons before him his own aims; he feels a craving that reports itself to him alone; his ideal good, his ideal life, flit before him, visible only to his own eye, and beckon him on. He has something to achieve every day which is his personal prize for the day. He walks with his own gait; the footmarks left are his; he lifts in his toil his own strokes, hurried or measured, strong or feeble; he has gained or lost as the day closes in a sense which touches him as no other life. He may have yoke-fellows in his toil, closest intimates in his schemes and dreams and affections, but still his stream of life flows by itself. If it join some companion stream, it shall be like the union of the Aar and the Rhone. They have united, they fill one channel, they flow on between the same banks, but far down below the point of confluence, they are seen to be as distinct as when the one slid from beneath its mighty glacier, and the other came roaring down the Grimsel pass. So for many a league they pour onward, side by side, the blue Rhone, the yellow Aar, — one, yet divided. Each man has his own moulds of action, in which he runs all his conduct. His method of viewing motives, of reasoning upon premises, of arriving at con-

clusions; the springs within him, whose play is the most constant, whose volume the largest, upon which whoso would move him must lay a finger; the force he expends hour by hour, and the direction in which he advances; the threads he weaves in and the threads he drops, and consequently the pattern that grows under his fingers, — all these constitute and proportion his life, but no other in all the compass of humanity. When he hears the record read out at last, when that one leaf is turned in the eternal book, and the original of that biographic story is summoned, there will be no need to call his name; he will know the portrait; he will step out of the throng to own that life as his; no other man will move; the identity will be so clear there can be no mistaking.

4. And each man, again, is alone in his sifting. There may pass over his head peaceful and happy years; fair behind him lengthens out the pathway of his life, but the night of his wrestling shall come. The one distant terror, unknown for half a lifetime, or known and forgotten, or remembered and yet postponed, in God's providence kept aloof, suddenly approaches, like Esau and his armed band sweeping down from Mount Seir upon Jacob and his company. It was years ago that the younger had so grievously injured the elder brother, and fled for his life. God has greatly blessed him since, and he has prospered exceedingly; but the crisis he has shunned so long at last darkens toward him. To-morrow that avenging presence will be upon him, that brother's dreaded right arm must be met. And the night leads him into that terrible and mysterious conflict. The struggle must

come for every man. There is that in his nature, there is that in his story, there is that in providence of testing and trial, which he must meet. The ghostly shadow will assume that one form which he feels he has chief cause to dread. He must grapple with it for his life; no eye shall look on; no crowds shall cheer; no champion shall come to his rescue. Alone, the night about him, singly contending against a strength whose resources he cannot measure, no release till a determinate issue be reached, — that issue, life or death, glorious victory or shameful defeat, — he must fight it out. There is a temptation before which each man is personally and peculiarly weak. Perhaps we have battled with it already, possibly that sorest conflict is yet before us; but whenever and wherever we meet it, we meet it alone. It will sift us; God will let us feel our weakness. Another man's trial we could lightly bear; that which vanquishes him we could easily put to rout. No wonder, perhaps, he was so soon overcome by such a foe. But there is some spiritual antagonist as formidable to us. Just when we are reproaching, perhaps, our fallen brother, our own Goliath of Gath enters the valley to meet us. Ah, if we could know the history of every tempted and sinning man, — the long, weary wrestling, the slow, sad night shutting in the strife, the manful resistance, the waning strength, the inward anguish, the self-loathing, the shame like that with which naked Adam fled and hid in the garden, — if we should consider that a stress may yet be laid upon us beneath which our best powers shall wither, no words so gentle, tender, and loving should ever pass our lips as those we should utter over the erring. Let us remember it. So far as human strength goes, each must wrestle alone with the most triumphing temptation that can assail him. Job's three friends sat by his side, but they left him still alone; the toils were his, and not theirs; and so with all the evils of his lot. So will it be with us, each of us sifted and tested by himself.

5. Each man is alone in dealing with God's truth and spirit. The gospel is preached by one utterance to a thousand souls; but to each man it is as if he sat there uncompanioned in the house of God. God has only spoken to him. The question raised is, What will he do with this divine message? Personally will he have Christ to reign over him? The sun shines for him and his neighbor; the air is their common inheritance; the same fragrance of flowers they may inhale together. But out of all that hear the offers of pardon and life only the soul that in the solitude of its own voluntariness yields to the moving spirit, steps forward for itself, and takes and kisses the hand of the Sovereign, will find itself included in the amnesty. Each must hear for himself, each must resolve for himself, each must act for himself. Alone with God, singled out from a world gone astray, God's eye upon it, God's love wooing it, the bleeding hand of Christ stretched out to it, the world, the flesh, and the devil pleading against it, the soul must conclude in that solitude this high debate, and choose for good or for evil, for the death that never dies or the life that is everlasting.

6. Alone the soul must encounter the struggle of dying. The hand may be held in some warm, loving clasp;

underneath the drooping head may glide a strong embracing arm; the white cheek may rise and fall to the breath of some cherishing bosom, and the friends dearest in life may stand around; but the soul enters upon that dread path alone. The fleshly hands meet, but no spirit of its fellows walks hand in hand with the departing traveller. What it sees, it only sees; what it suffers, it only suffers; the progress is all its own, — the opening marvels, the clearing shadows, the awful verities; the other attendants, though so near, are by the breadth of worlds behind. We may have stood many a time by the side of the dark river, and seen others go down into the chill waters, and the way may seem familiar; we may think we know it; but when we assay the current, when the cold waves rise higher and higher, and we gasp and falter and feel for firm footing, and look to see what welcome waits us on the further shore, what forms come to meet us and environ us around, that experience we must try alone and by ourselves. It is coming to us, that solemn hour; it will take us into its solitary custody; it will single us out from the crowd and whisper in our ear, unheard by any other, either this inspiring message, "The Master is come and calleth for thee," or this stern arrest, "Thou fool, this night thy soul shall be required of thee."

7. Alone, too, each shall rise in the great day; alone each shall be judged, each sentenced alone. Though that trumpet blast shall wake all that sleep, each shall open his eyes with sensations all his own upon the scenery of that day. Though all the generations of earth shall stand together before the judgment-seat, yet each man's story

shall be recited amid the hush of a listening universe, and the final word, "Come!" or "Depart!" shall fall on each heart as though none beside knew such joy or such grief.

So solitary, though amid dearest fellowships and closest intimacies, is human life in all its stages, from its dawn of being till its destiny is fixed forever. Come, then, my friend, and look your isolation full in the face. You stand a single individual soul in God's sight, responsible for yourself, living your own personal life, moving toward your own definite future. No crowd conceals you, no general movement sweeps you in, no vague fellowship provides for you apart from your personal, individual acting. Alone you have sinned, alone you must repent, believe, and obey. Oh, the vital question of salvation is one between you and God! It must be settled in the chamber of your own spirit. You yourself are to confront all the weighty issues of your being in time. Religion is your own personal matter, a life that is to be special to you, a new vitality to come into the privacy of your own heart.

The deep solitariness of your whole existence admits of one grand qualification. Into those lonely chambers one glorious Being may come. Over the fields of consciousness you may stray with one Friend by your side, who shall see and know and feel all that you feel and know and see. In the weighty conflict, this healing and victorious presence may succor your fainting strength and wounded form. Along the changeful highway, in the shade, in the shine, the meek Pilgrim from Nazareth may keep you company and share your experience. In all trouble and anguish one tender Heart shall pulse with yours, as truly at home at the core of your sorrow as you that suffer. You shall enter the shadowy vale singing, "Thou art with me." As all of earth recedes, you shall whisper again, "These have left me alone, yet am I not alone, for my Saviour is joined to me, and we twain are one spirit." And passing on and out, your watchword at heaven's gate shall be, "Forever with the Lord." Come, O lonely life, and be united to the Lord of life. O solitary spirit, be made one with the Father and the Son, your solitude opening thus upon infinite riches of sympathy, love, and communion.

XVI.

THE MINISTRIES OF TIME.

I THE LORD WILL HASTEN IT IN HIS TIME. — Isaiah lx. 22.

GOD is sovereign and omnipotent, but he waits the ministration of Time. He could force seasons and laws, but it is his way rather to work through them and by them. He has ordained them as servitors of his will. His purposes on the earth, in the conduct of human affairs, had, in respect to their accomplishment, a germination, a process, and a harvest-hour of consummation.

Time is the prime-minister of Providence, and brings to pass in due order, at their full periods, and at the appointed juncture, the patient counsels of the Most High. There is no hurrying and no sickness of deferred hope on that eternal and tranquil mind. "One day is with the Lord as a thousand years, and a thousand years as one day." It lends a new dignity and a sterner and loftier majesty to Time, when we consider it thus, not impersonally, as the passing away of our days, — the swift, mute lapse of the stream of life sliding down the vale, — but as a strong, executive angel, a sceptred and conscious force, that has it in charge to reveal and fulfil the hidden plan of God.

Man is strong, and works great changes upon the earth and his fellow-man. Art is strong, and produces its rapid marvels. The forces serving the human will are nimble and muscular. Heat and frost lift up monuments of their might and magic. The fires of earth's centre, the winds that sweep over the surface, the seas that thunder along her shores, — these have their power and their trophies. But Time is the great magician. All these latter forces are sinews of its own arm. The changes, the revolutions, the histories of this world, are only chronicles of the vice-regency of Time.

It is fitting, as the swift shuttle glances past again, drawing another thread into the woven fabric of God's scheme for earth and man, bringing out yet more clearly the parts in the pattern for the whole, that we pause to consider

This ministry of Time in accomplishing the divine pleasure.

If the whole scope of the supreme administration may not be known thus, we may gather at least some of the principles and particulars that unite at last to perfect that consummate whole. We shall see that Time is, among men, the revealer, the attester, the vindicator, the rectifier, the fulfiller.

Time tests the principles of human conduct. I speak here of avowed principles consciously, perhaps boldly, proceeded upon, set in contrast or antagonism with one another. There is a difference among men, both in theory and in practice, in respect to these principles. The diversity and the divergence illustrate themselves in innumerable ways. Look in upon two scenes of family training. In one of them the idea is, with the controlling head, that the true end of domestic nurture is social success. Special stress, then, will be laid upon the accomplishments whose chief grace is external. The manner is a matter of first concern. The gloss of an outward polish is of great price. The step must be put under tuition. Motion must be artistic, graduated to rule and canon. Exits and entrances must be fashioned after a model. The introduction into society is a grand and solemn crisis. Acquaintances must be made. The young lives must be launched upon the social world. What if they should be neglected, thrown out of the current, stranded high and dry upon the bank, the stream of their generation flowing merrily by, and leaving them, as it were, only to serve as landmarks for the progress of the gay, iris-tinted bubbles that float, with music and laughter, ever on amid greenness and bloom? This must not be. A social triumph must in some way be achieved. And all the care and painstaking converge to this issue. In the other the commanding object is the formation of a right character. The interior life of gentle manners must be gentle thoughts. The only external polish that will never grow coarse is the outshining of inward purity and kindness. The law of love is the sufficient code of politeness and etiquette. The best social furnishing is the wealth of the soul's virtuous intelligence, an appreciation of what is true and beautiful in nature, in mind and morals, the utterance of generous sensibilities and of a self-respect that prefers its own calm approval to admiration and flattery, and sets the price of its modesty too high to offer itself as a prize for social bidding. You shall hear now the first of these two systems remonstrating with the other, predicting social isolation, social failure, urging the demonstrative and forcing culture, adopting it for the sons and daughters under its guardianship, and resting cheerfully and complacently in its superior discernment and wisdom. This subject carries me back in thought to my own early rural home. I look in again upon the families that were so ambitious of social conquests. I see the youths and maidens there planning festive entertainments, and delighting in gay assemblies. The fashions and the gayeties were, to be sure, somewhat on a rural scale; but it was our world, and a miniature in all essential features of the most brilliant metropolitan life. And, to be sure, the sober, puritanical portion of the rising generation there were left quite outside this conventional society, — their faces were not seen, nor their hands sought in the ball-room. The winter evening ride, the rural party, and generally all scenes of youthful merry-making in which the set came together, were made up without their presence. Here there were smiles and laughs and romps and dances and cards and all the staple of vain and thoughtless fellowship and enjoyment, from which our graver style of young life was self-exiled. And so the issue was made, and the trial of the two systems entered upon. And in the one circle, quick friendships were formed, a score of acquaintances were added to one's list in a single evening. No danger of being lost sight of socially, dropped out of social recognition; here the doors

21*

stood wide open to social settlements and domestic alliances. And sometimes it was felt, I know, on the other side, that all such doors were shut against them. They seemed isolated from those of their own age; their seclusion was uninvaded; they could improve their minds, cultivate their taste, study the secrets of happy, dignified, and well-ordered homes, quite to themselves. Who would know ever whether they were prizes or blanks? The drawing would be all in the other circle, and the more worldly policy looked like a success. There all was bright and glittering. Here lay a shadow. There, there was mating and marrying and giving in marriage. Here all relations were undisturbed. Taking life as it is, this more select discipline promised to be barren of results. But principles are everlasting verities; they change not; they are of slow development often; their seed lies cold and motionless long; their harvest comes late, but it comes. Such issues are not to be settled in a day. Their trial takes in, in its progress, more elements than are at first seen to be included. The earlier appearances are not reliable exponents of the final consummation. Across the breadth of years I look and read the story truer. The paths of life from those two circles, the streams from those separate fountains, are visible before me. The gay, brilliant type quickly darkened and degenerated. That was its best. It never rose higher. There were early excesses, there were early and dishonored graves, there were floating wrecks of vice and dissipation, there were sad, sad tales of shame and anguish, there were miserable disappointments. Those that were specially decked and tutored for proudest triumphs, somehow, always missed their goal. What they won was trash, or worse, and for the most part they drew utter blanks. It all came to nought. The glittering bubble burst, and there was nothing in the hand but the stain of defiling moisture.

And on the other side, once more, there was always a wealth of personal resources; there was a growing but unconscious refinement; there was fostered a selecter and more discriminating taste; solid and abiding qualities grew with the passing youthful season, and when more difficult and fastidious minds came searching for fresh, unsoiled natures, and an outfit for wider and higher spheres, they found the golden fruit hidden beneath the over-shadowing leaves, and gathered it with pride and joy. I have lingered too long upon this, but it is a most instructive page. And the record is repeated at ten thousand social centres, only it cannot be written at once, or read at a glance. Like Chinese writings, the lines stretch down the lengthening scroll of Time. Time is the slow scribe, the sure expounder.

One man argues that, "Take the world as it goes, and you must practise upon it to gain your ends. You must manage a little; you must move subtly and dexterously toward your aims; you must not show your hand; you need not tell the whole story out; you must ask more than you expect to get; you must put the best face on a thing it can be made to wear; you may well enough leave sharp eyes and keen wits to explore and interpret your silence. The universal system is such that if we do not adopt this policy, we shall be left hopelessly behind." Another man plants his foot immovably upon the conviction that honesty is the best policy. He must be frank, transparent, true. More or less, his gains must bring within his doors no reproaches. Poverty is a pleasanter household companion than remorse; strict right with a crust, rather than wrong with princely dainties. And the two procedures start together on the track. The first success is almost always on the side of cunning. Slow-moving, downright honesty is speedily distanced. One holds a court, the other sits in solitude. The proverb hardly expresses a truth for "the life that now is." Ah! wait a little. Hear the witness of Time. Intrigue and practising cannot always escape the light, and the light they cannot bear. Men once bitten grow shy of traps. Nobody loves to be practised upon. Wily natures always come at last to be distrusted. These little business and social treacheries invariably, in the long run, lose the operators their richest capital, — confidence. And the tides ebb away; and now it is honesty's turn. It comes late, but it is final. There is nothing after it. Here is perfect trust, unsuspecting security. Here we find bottom, and stand firm. The proverb was altogether right. Principles have had their development, and each after its kind borne its fruit. Time has ripened and gathered it, — apples of Sodom for the one; apples of gold, — nay, golden-globed sweetness from the tree of life for the other.

This is the demonstration of principle that cannot be set aside, — the demonstration of Time.

Again, Time is the test of friendships. Where is the

love that never grows cold, that outlives youth and bloom, that was founded on deeper and more vital attractions than those that pass away with life's roseate morning? Where are the hands that used to clasp ours? Have they warm and welcoming palms for us still? Where are the lips that smiled upon us once? Do they keep smiles or sternness for us now? We used to listen to such earnest and tender expressions of interest in our fortunes, delight in our society, regard for our persons, and appreciation of our characteristics. Are all those utterances silent now? How much of youthful and ardent friendship has survived those summer days? How many of our later associations have kept their first gushing promises in truth and faithfulness?

And yet we must not judge harshly. If there is any lesson which Time letters most legibly on all the pages of our story, it is, that our hard, reproachful judgments, our morbid protests that all is false, deceitful, and hollow, that truth and honor have forsaken the earth, that none can be trusted, that no heart is sincere, that real kindness and genuine good-will are not to be found among men, are extravagances that would be ridiculous if they were not so false and injurious. We have been deceived and betrayed, but we must not generalize from that instance. We have broken through the ice here and there, but there may be yet broad fields of it as firm as a marble floor. The very hearts that we pronounce alienated and estranged may rather have become wearied than chilled. Dislocated from one side, the broken fibres of social affections must cling somewhere. Thrown upon other fellowships, the tendrils have caught and twined about fresh objects. Once they were all free to turn and choose as they listed, but they have been pressed long since into new alliances, and have responded to the new appeals as once they responded to ours. But in this very fact they show that their nature is unchanged. To human love, if not to our personal memory, they still are true; yes, and bring back the old relations, and we, it may be, should not find them wanting. This is what Time teaches.

And then, again, Time tries his tests upon character. Sorrowfully, often, we are made to watch this process. All seems fair outwardly. We have unbounded confidence. We surrender our gravest trusts. We rest upon this tried and approved integrity. It becomes a standard-bearer in the most salient advances of Christianity. It wins a good report. It stands a pillar, straight, strong, and upright. Lay your weight there, build thereon; and we build, and feel secure for solid years. And, one day, there is a crash. It was only the shell of a pillar; either within it was all rottenness and hollowness, or a sudden and violent wrench twisted it out of place, and down it came, fallen and broken. It is a mournful lesson Time has read us. Whom shall we trust? What shall we build with? Character that has stood seemingly all severer tests, passed unsullied amid youthful passions and summer temptations, met the hour and call of solemn duties, took on the sober livery of its autumn staidness and ripeness, cannot this be confided in? Are life-long victories over manifold forces of evil no security? Ah! one test remains. It is a silent, patient, long-waiting detective. At last it gives in its report, and we are stricken dumb with surprise and grief. Hastily, perhaps, we say, "All is over; this is the end; there is nothing left there; here shuts down the gate of life and hope." And Time may yet correct this too hasty conclusion, and read us an unpublished story that would draw deep upon our tenderest sympathies, and forbid us to pass capital sentence upon our brother on one indictment only, when we are impeachable in many points, and lead up out of the valley of humiliation a chastened penitent, a restored wanderer, whose lore in divine grace and infinite compassion shall surpass all that we have known, whose fitness for rare and special service shall be tempered in this fiery furnace, and whose evening of life shall yet show a serene and glowing west. Hast thou, O Time! and thou, O wondrous Grace of God! such revelations in store? We will pause, and hope and pray till the future draw back its veil.

Is there a ghost in every house, a phantom dogging every man's footsteps, a secret in every bosom? Here and there, there is a seemingly calm and self-possessed spirit, that faces tranquilly the light of day and the gaze of all-searching eyes, as though the waters flowed transparent with crystal clearness over a pebbly bed, in which the while there is yet beneath this surface-sparkling, a deep, dark pool, and at the bottom a grim, slimy monster that never comes to the light. There lurks that leviathan for unsuspected years. No ripple above, no commotion on the surface, gives signs of the horrid life in the dark depths. The man walks amid his fellow-men as though with a consciousness never disturbed. No infirmity of nerve ever sets him to trembling. No pause in his unsleeping vigilance betrays him into fatal admissions. In his utter solitude he sometimes faces this untold story. But no lips can ever tell it. It lies within the compass of no single knowledge. It is broken into fragments, like a shattered ring, or a fatal bond torn apart and distributed into remote and alien hands. Can those fragments ever be gathered, those parts ever be reunited? Alone and by itself, each means nothing, reveals nothing. What simultaneous impulse shall move these "disjecta membra" to come together? The thing can never be; and the keeper of the shameful secret passes on reassured. Then Time waves his wand. The hand that held one fragment moulders in dust, and the eyes of executors scan curiously the torn and yet ominous leaf. From opposite meridians, as though led on by fate, come up, at the only juncture that could serve the issue, the remaining witnesses. The mutilated memorial is again a whole, but it is written in cipher, and the dream of security lingers yet. And the magic wand is lifted once more, and the hidden key drops from its hiding-place, and all is legible and patent. Time has become the minister of justice. And the last words of every dying year wake in guilty breasts this dreary echo, "There is nothing covered that shall not be revealed, and hid that shall not be known."

And yet there are those to whom this word is not dreary, but animating; not a menace, but a long-sustaining promise. They have been under a cloud. Their character has been unrighteously aspersed. Men have believed evil of them. They have been the victims of mistakes or of circumstances or of malignant conspiracy. The baleful torches of calumny have flared upon them and blackened them all over. Their simple assertion of innocence has been taken as brazen-fronted hardihood. Many a hand has been withdrawn from them; many a face has turned away. Friends once trustful and beloved have passed by on the other side. So they have walked on in the cold shadows of the long night, waiting for the dawn; and the slow hours rolled away. They had no hope but in God, and God sent to them this championship of Time. And one day the solution of the mystery was suddenly uncovered, and men saw how they had been deluded, and how falsely they had believed. And this patient innocence shone forth like a rising sun, the brighter for its obscuration, all the more revered that it had suffered long in uncomplaining silence. And it is seen that character is not committed to human keeping. No enemy can take it from us. We need not fear, in our innocence, the face of mortal, the malice of infernal. We can calmly defy all machinations; and when girt about with hissing serpents, who boast that they have us in their own den and power, we can stand in the heroism of this single truth: "The Lord is on my side, I will not fear; what can man do unto me?"

Again, the real struggle of a man's life, the crisis of his moral history, Time often holds in reserve. It comes not in his sheltered boyhood, over which bend only bright and genial skies. His youth glides past him, a peaceful stream flowing on through gentle meadows. Manhood takes him by the hand, and there has been as yet no faltering in his step. He seems to have conquered in the fields of life, to have mastered his passions without a conflict. And, perhaps, gray mingles with the native hue of his hair, the seal of his confirmation in settled integrity. He knows not, and no man knows, the strength of his propensities. The hour of trial has never fairly fronted him. What a mutinous crew slumber under the hatches there he suspects not! What combustibles are gathered beneath the fair fabric of his unsullied name! What a train might be fired, what a fight he might be called to maintain, with upleaping and furious foes and flames, he never for a moment dreams! It may happen to him to know better by and by. The ripe hour hurries on. It is all the more perilous that he has never faced real and mortal danger. He has no lore of warning experience. The train is fired, and the tumult begins. Let him gird himself like a man. The combat rages. What a fearful strife! Forward and backward the tide ebbs and flows. No such strain as this has ever tested the might of his arm. He has called himself a soldier, but he has never had a field-day till now. What if it should go against him? He pants and bleeds and falters. Oh! woe the day, if he have not a divine Helper, or if he forget to look up for heavenly succor! Let no man speak harshly of the fallen; let no man plume himself upon his own immaculateness. Our day may come. Low behind the bending west the distant cloud may even now be rising. Be meek, charitable, watchful, and prayerful.

God even commits his own vindication to Time. He delays, both to visit for daring wrong and to reward patient faith. His threatenings and his promises seem laid aside, forgotten. The impious cry, derisively, "Where is the promise of his coming?" and the believer, "Lord, how long?" But there is no demonstration from the silent heavens. That sovereign hand begins its work afar off. It rolls up not a single event, but an ordered and massive system. The good die while yet the consummation hoped for lingers. The vile triumph, and their seed seems established in the earth. Then on the vast, dim dial, the index points to the appointed hour, and vengeance and deliverance do their work; and amid blasphemy confounded and righteousness exultant, sounds the blessed voice, "I the Lord will hasten it in his time."

In the individual life the grandest spiritual truths are learned late. Here, as in all learning, there is an alphabet first, and more wondrous revelations afterward. For these deeper and more radiant mysteries there must be often a peculiar preparation. The soul must have a past to look back to, to build upon. The path up the snowy Alps is at first along rugged and earthy ravines; by and by it emerges, and the dazzling peak shoots heavenward. The time of need, the hour of trial, the crisis of sharp experience, must bring the moment of revelation. We must suffer our converts to be babes; we must expect for ourselves more glowing and rapt discoveries of God's grace and loving-kindness than our poor attainments in the past have ever mastered.

But these ministries of Time touch heart-nerves in passing. They play sorely on tender chords. The music is solemn, wailing, and dirgelike. There are weeping kindreds here who dreamed not a year ago, in their glad security, what Time had in store for them; that he should lead their best beloved away from their circle; that he was weaving ever, while they smiled and slept, a winding-sheet for tender, fair, and manly forms; that, in the silence and in the darkness, he was digging a grave, and lettering some sweet household name in marble; that soon he should shroud their joyousness in the darkness of the tomb, their festive garments in the sable of mourning. But this he had in keeping for them. He has lent strength and grace to many a life; he has piled up bounties at every door; he has filled our garners with his loaded wains; but, alas! he has stolen from hearthstone and fireside what he can never replace.

And yet Time has a ministry of consolation too. He heals where he wounds. It is of God that his touch has such a balm in it. He wipes away tears; he unknits the furrowed brow; he brings back the smile to the quivering lips; he leads the captive forth into the sunshine; he gathers upon the bereaved the tender and soothing spell of memory; he plants flowers in the path where bleeding feet have walked, pierced by the thorns.

O Time! what dost thou yet keep back from us? What commissions hast thou to execute upon us in these fresh, opening days of the new-born year? Whither along this track that glides always into the shadow of to-morrow dost thou lead our feet? What of joy or of sorrow, of conflict or of suffering, art thou marshalling even now? Vain guess! No voice answers. Into the mist opens no vista of light. But this we know, Time is a creature of God. It waits upon that sovereign will. It comes to us a guide sent from heaven, to conduct us onward into the good pleasure of One whom in life and in death we can trust with our mortal and immortal hopes.

O Time! roll on the year, bring up the forces of the hidden future. With one hand clasping the divine hand, and a mutual good cheer, which we make a prayer to-day, we go forward in faith and hope.

XVII.

SORROWS OF JESUS.

. . . .'. A MAN OF SORROWS . . . .—Isa. liii. part 3.

WHEN mention is made of the sufferings of Christ, our thoughts turn naturally to the scene in the garden, where nature, overstrained, gave her witness in crimson drops, and to the slow agonies of the cross, killing, not by any single mortal stroke, but by the sharpness of conquering pain. This habit of thought fails to appreciate the deep significance of such an expression as that we are to dwell upon now.

It need not, necessarily, be a mournful and saddening subject for us to consider. There is nothing depressing in recalling the hardships and wounds of a soldier who has come home victorious and laurelled from the wars, nor in speaking of the storm and wreck and thirst, the great fight with the elements through which the much-enduring mariner has returned safely and prosperously to port, nor in listening to chronicles of the long, dreadful arctic night from one who sits at our warm fireside and tells of the conflict and the triumph. Our Saviour has endured the cross, passed beneath the shame, carried his sorrows and ours, and gone home to his glorious throne, made perfect by sufferings, filling out thus the whole spherical idea of substitution and personal sympathy, and announcing himself as "he that liveth and was dead, and is alive for evermore." To speak of his "sorrows" may fill our eyes with tears, but they will be tears of grateful tenderness, of glad thanksgiving, and will leave the eyes that weep clearer and brighter to discern his peerless exaltation who thus suffered and triumphed for us.

The expression we are contemplating of its own force indicates, not the crowning and closing specialty of suffering which Jesus endured, but the tenor of his life, the current of his daily experience, the habitual consciousness of his soul. It takes in, of course, as a part of its meaning, that consummation of extreme and dying anguish, but it covers the whole story beside. When we say of one "he is a man of few words" we mean not that he of whom we speak was particularly silent on a given occasion, but that he is of a reserved and unsocial habit at all times and everywhere. Our description has the same breadth of extent when we speak of another as a man of strong passions or prejudices, of another as a man of keen observation, of another as a visionary man; we refer to the general character and experience, and not to isolated instances.

The life of Christ was a sorrowful life. It moved from beginning to ending in that zone. Sorrow was his meat and drink. It bathed his spirit with daily immersion. In that shaded and thorny vale his feet walked always. He never rose quite clear from this valley mist, this atmosphere of sorrow that drooped about him and clung to him. Ah, it makes our hearts ache, not, indeed, with a sensation all of pain, but with a tender and burdened fulness, which has its witness in our eyes, to follow this Master thus, and remember it was all for us. The human in him was altogether sorrowful. The expression fastens our eye upon his humanity. He was a man of sorrows. Those experiences of life which in us are mingled of lights or shades, those avenues of entrance into the human soul which in us are avenues to many a joy as well as to here and there a grief, were in him experiences altogether on the shady side, — avenues along which trooped and pressed for admission a thronging procession of griefs. To share the bright lot of our human nature in its frequent providential story, to sit in our earthly sunshine, to taste the sweets of our earthly vines, to inhale the fragrance of our earthly flowers, to be ministered unto by seasons and climes, to hold delighted converse with congenial spirits, and see the smile of friendship and hear the words of love, — humanity with such an allotment, if this were all, were not so great a trial even to an exalted spiritual nature. But to take it with its capacities of joy and suffering only to have them filled with the latter; to take it with its deep sensibilities alive both to pleasure and pain only to find it all sensitively thrilling to pain, — this is another sort of transformation for a blessed and holy nature, and it was with such an experience of manhood that Jesus entered.

Let us glance down the catalogue of these sorrows and name such of them as meet our eye with most prominent lettering. We shall not have time to dwell, only to let the list linger a moment on our rapid hearing; and those unnamed will seem to some more worthy of commemoration, perhaps, than those to which we now lend speech.

We need not make much of his poverty perhaps. Other men have suffered and do suffer poverty. They are pinched and distressed. They see the sad eyes of unprovided ones looking up to them daily, and cannot look back with an eye that relights the lamp of hope. They are hungry and cold and have the faintness of want and the heartache of despair, and all without any consciousness of some high and infinitely blessed end to be thus served and compassed. We know not that Jesus' sufferings of destitution were more acute or in any wise a sorer tax upon patience and manhood than that of many over whom the heart of charity bleeds amid our own homes. And yet we do not know all the history of that poverty. Not much is said about it in the Gospel histories. There are glimpses here and there. We know what the circumstances of the family were when that infant form was cradled. We know that Jesus wrought with his own hands, probably through a long and toilsome youth, to add something to the comfort, or take something from the sharpness, of need in his own father's house. A single line tells us in plaintive confession, "The foxes have holes and the birds of the air have nests, but the Son of man hath not where to lay his head." But there are wide, blank intervals of his life, in respect to the comforts necessary to the body, where the narrative is altogether silent. The more refined and sensitive a nature is, the more delicate in its perceptions and tastes, the more the coarseness of poverty's rude shifts must chafe and press. As the humanity of Christ seems to have been left to feel to the full its earthly experience, there may have been under the shadow of this meaning silence such ever wearing trials, such single scenes of intense suffering as we cannot easily conceive. But we have said enough about this.

Look at that sorrow of loneliness. His own family understood him not, and his loved and loving disciples were perpetually puzzled about him. All whom he chose, and between whom and himself there were ties of kindred and friendship, were yet so far off from him, looked upon him with wondering and doubtful eyes. Even the mother who held him in her arms, held him as it were at arm's length, and wondered over her strange babe. John might lie in his bosom, Peter might touch his hand, the twelve might sit around him at table and feast, but within the humanity that came in contact with theirs, in his own thoughts and feelings and cares, there was another and inner sphere into which no man entered with him. There was no equal, congenial, and brotherly companion into whom his eyes could look, without speech, all the contents of his heart, and read in return a perfect intelligence and sympathy. He need not have gone away from his disciples to be alone. He was ever alone.

> "Cold mountains and the midnight air
> Witnessed the fervor of his prayer."

But his loneliness was a mere solitary mountain height, a deeper midnight for his uncompanied soul. It seems to have come over him now and then, and he speaks it with such a voice it would seem as though the thrilled and startled earth might give back a groan. "Alone," and yet I am not alone, for the Father is with me. Think of walking over this earth and through the midst of its circles and kindreds without one companion for a day or an hour of a lifetime!

We have spoken under our first head of his spirit as gentle and refined, and of its hard and harsh contact with the coarseness of want. But think now of its coming into contact with all earth's rude and coarse types of life, its nameless abominations, the things seen and heard and understood which we cannot write, — sharp speech, evil railing, mutual suspicions, wicked jealousies, taunts, revenges, ugly and tyrannical tempers, plottings and counterplottings, the looks which a human eye can give, the expressions which a human face can wear, the words which a human tongue can utter, sharper than daggers, more brutal than blows. Go on in your own imagination, of which however you need not much help. Only fling the coloring of facts upon the canvas, and then see what to such a spirit must be the sorrowful mingling with such a race.

Think, again, of the sorrow of his sympathy and compassion. If he could have gone through the world hard-hearted, he could have escaped this pain. But all grief was his grief; every woe came upon his inheritance; he bore our griefs, he carried our sorrows, he entered into the burden of every tried one. The weeping sisters at their brother's grave; he catches sight of their faces, he looks upon the tomb and — oh, look upon his own face! the tears are flowing there — he sees a multitude around him in the wilderness an hungered and athirst, and it is written he had compassion upon the multitude, because they were as sheep not having a shepherd. What would it be to take all suffering of others upon one sustaining heart, — to see tears, hear sighs, intense wretchedness of any kind, and make it all our own? Could one of us bear it?

Then there was the depth of human ruin into whose abysses his gaze searched. Oh, what had sin wrought! He saw its utter, sad devastations, the effects of the fall, such malice, such hardness of heart, such hatred of truth, such lying, murders, and lusts, such ungrateful and determined hostility to their Redeemer bringing them salvation! What must it have been for him to have to say to them such words as he used to warn and rebuke, "O generation of vipers!" He explored the depth of that great gulf of man's apostasy as no other human eyes ever did before or since.

Then the burden of those ruined ones, we cannot fathom the love that looked out of his eyes, the yearning that made his heart bleed, the restlessness to subdue, win, and deliver. An earnest Christian knows a little of it. His soul is a little fountain of such impulses, but in that soul a great ocean heaved and swelled.

Then his disappointment, the fruitlessness, to so many of his great mission. Oh, what thoughts were his when he sat on Olivet, and apostrophized the city lying there beneath him,—"O Jerusalem!"—Matt. xxiii. 37. And what a tone lingers yet in such words as these: Ye will not come to me that ye might have life"! And then this most desponding utterance, so tender that the tears drop through it yet, "If I had not come and spoken unto them, they had not had sin." But we cannot now go on. We are here to commemorate a Saviour's dying love, and all sorrow to-day may plead unto Jesus.

XVIII.

BALANCE SHEET; OR, TAKING ACCOUNT OF STOCK.

WHAT PROFIT HATH A MAN OF ALL HIS LABOR WHICH HE TAKETH UNDER THE SUN?—Eccl. i. 3.

IT is a wise and needful custom in mercantile life to pause periodically in the current of buying and selling, review the work of our fiscal year, and take account of stock. It were a piece of wilful folly, in neglect of such review, to launch out upon new enterprises, to adventure fresh charges and expenditures, or to dream and drift drowsily onward, careless whether the past had added to or diminished our resources. Of such a reckless and blind confidence there could come, sooner or later, only bankruptcy and ruin. We need to ask what we have gained, what we have lost, how the sum total of capital and effects at the year's close compares with that at the year's beginning; whether our trusted investments are productive; what there is to add to, what there is to subtract from, our whole wealth.

Equally wise and wholesome is it for us, in the revolutions of our natural and moral life, to have our points of self-reckoning, to arrest thereat the swift-gliding stream of our planning, toiling, and hoping; to call up the past for its honest report; to raise the question, What have we gained, what have we lost, in the true wealth of our being? and with careful arithmetic work out our balance sheet of character and spiritual standing before setting forward on the new reaches of our way.

The chimes that toll the death of the old year, and then, changing their tone, ring out joybells for the birth of the new, strike for us a fitting hour for such a faithful reckoning.

We do not need an argument to prove that no man's life stands still. There is inevitably growth and progress with every man in some direction. God's is the only nature without advance or change. Each influence that tries its powers upon us produces some positive effect. If it be yielded to, it governs the pulses of the hour, perhaps of all the future. If it be resisted, its visit is still memorable, as strengthening the forces that have overmastered it and establishing their supremacy. Every day brings up such influences to levy their pressure upon us. These silent visits will have their record in perhaps the imperceptible but real changes of our convictions, our principles, and our purposes, the gradually fading or deepening hues of the coloring of our thoughts and our days. The long procession of such visits that succeed one another through the days of a single year must inevitably affect the man, if not his demonstrations; the worker, if not at once his work. These influences will be of every variety. They will be ordinary and special. They will come from men, from books, from nature, from Providence, from the depths of our own soul, from God's word and spirit. They will make up in their aggregate the whole story of our experience; and this experience will either sharpen our wits or dull them, quicken or stupefy our sensibilities, bring us increments of knowledge and power, or squander and waste the hours and the occasions that ought to have helped our stores of wisdom, and our stability in goodness and virtue.

Let us ask, then, to-day, on this first Sabbath morning of the opening year, looking back before we look forward, and with honest desire to ascertain all that the past can reveal to us, what results of the old year's record must we set down on the side of loss? What may we carry to the side of gain? What "profit have we had of all our labor which we have taken under the sun"?

First, then, on the side of loss, there is an actual diminution of our capital in Time. We embarked on life's career with this capital at its maximum. At what number we could then write the units of its sum total, we knew not then, we never have known since. But God is merciful beyond the appreciation of most minds in this among other tokens of his tender regard for our comfort, that he lays not on human hearts the fear of daily dying. He permits his creatures to rise up and lie down, to go forth to their work and their labor until the evening, without this cold conviction pulsing through their souls, and uttering itself in doleful tones whenever their lips open, "I shall die perhaps to-day. I shall wake no more perhaps with another morning." He has abundantly taught in his word and in his pavilion that human life is frail, that it is short at the longest, that it is as a vapor that appeareth for a little time, then vanisheth away; that its continuance is uncertain. We see the heavy sheaves gathered in, — manhood in its prime laid low, youth drooping in its summer, childhood's blossom and the red bud of infancy nipped by untimely frosts. But God so sustains our hearts that the arm of industry is not paralyzed; hope rises with us every morning and runs at our side, or glides on before us all the day. We send out our ships on far voyages; we sow and wait for future harvests; we invest when years are to roll forward their salient changes before our dividends shall make us rich. Undoubtedly we forget too often life's frailty; the heart is overbold and courageous; we need to have it said to us at least daily, as to the Macedonian of old, "Philip, thou art mortal;" but what comfort and tranquillity in laboring and in gathering the fruits of God's goodness and human toil, notwithstanding the sentence that arches us all, "Dust thou art, and unto dust shalt thou return"! God has permitted it to be written that our eyes may see it, and our spirits know the buoyancy of this narrated hope, "The days of our years are threescore years and ten." I think it is not his pleasure that every man should enter upon his day's work saying to his heart, "I shall die to-day;" but still, as though he might, the man who is always ready can toil in perpetual hope and perpetual tranquillity.

But whatever our capital at the start, in respect to the years ordained for us, we have lost another unit of that loan from God. One year less to expend upon all our earthly schemes; one year less in which to toil for our families, learn the lessons and fulfil the high ends of life; one year less in which to prepare for the life to come; one year less between us and that last chime of the clock wound up to men only with the beating of our heart between us and the grave, and that which is after death, the judgment. And if the completion of each year suggests this thought, the completion of a decade of years makes it more solemn and impressive. Seven such decades touches the utmost bound. You and I have lived two of those seven, three of them, four of them (the plural "we" becomes less comprehensive as we advance) five of them, six perhaps, and cutting in upon the seventh. Look back, not far, to youth, childhood. How near those bright, lawless days! Only yesterday! Measure forward an equal reach, and where are we? Sleeping beneath a green ridge, with a white slab at its head lettered with our name, and that little Latin word "*Obit*," departed, completing the sentence.

But when I raise the question of lost time, I mean much more than the obvious and universal fact that our years drop off one by one, and that another has now gone, taken from the side of the capital yet unexpended to be added to that which is spent. Have there been no days of this year otherwise lost, — lost because unimproved? Have we been frugal of time? Have we been lavish of moments? Have we idled away no swift, underlying intervals between rising and the morning meal? After that meal, and before our industry put on its harness, in loitering along while the working hours shone bright overhead, in drowsy animal indolence through the shades of evening, in sleep beyond the ministries of needful refreshment and recuperation? Nay, is it not possible that our busiest moments, our intensest activities, are those that ought in a faithful reckoning to be carried to the side of loss? Strokes of labor, hours of work given to pride, worldly grasping, self-indulgence, any issues of flesh and sense, any ends that terminate upon the life that now is, — are not these lost to us? Shall we count them finally among our gains? Have they helped our land riches? Have they not robbed us of so much that might have been, if otherwise devoted, grandly productive? All that has been squandered on the needs or the desires and lusts of the present with no other, no higher thoughts or ends has gone hopelessly against us, — lost days, however crowded with diligence, however gladdened by successes; for life is one whole, not a little payment here in time; it has one story of progress and character and destiny, unrolling from the here into the hereafter. Every truly faithful work must take hold of life as a whole, as imperishable and immortal, and the question of gain or loss must be settled by those balances that can be carried forward to the eternal enriching, or that are placed only momentarily on the side of profit to disappear in the tremendous offset of a whole probation wasted.

So that diligence, strong nerved and careful and gainful, is not the true redemption of time. Many a man who pauses in his routine of work to aid in the direct nurture and happiness of his home is saving time; to cheer the comfortless, to guide the perplexed, to hear the sad stories of temptation and remorse, and administer to such forlorn spirits is saving time; to sit down at the board and in the evening circle with wife and children, imparting knowledge and diffusing light and joy, is saving time.

I dwell no longer on this point. Let us look to it, each of us, and give it the place in our reckoning which we judge belongs to it.

With some of us, again, I suppose there has been an actual loss from the capital of strength and vigor. Perhaps we cannot perceive it. We had better ask our friends. Perhaps, again, we know it better than they, are aware of signs not visible or palpable to them, — the foot not quite so light, nor the step so elastic; the form not so perpendicularly upright, or, if so, not so sure a match against weight and pressure; the muscles failing a little in hardiness and roundness, the sinews relaxing, the hair changing its hue by single threads of a new coloring, the power to do and to endure drained of something of its fulness and volume. We weary sooner than we did. We like easy appliances to which we were ever indifferent. We shrink a little from sharp encounters with difficulties which once only put us upon our mettle. We turn over some of our hastening and hurrying to our boys, to younger men. Is it so? Put it down, then, on the side where it goes.

Have there been special opportunities, conjunctions of favoring circumstances for doing some particular work, which have come and gone unimproved, to return no more, — a kindness to be shown, declined; help to render in a dark day refused, and the day not past by; a soul to warn and succor in its crisis; a providence to improve and impress in the family; a co-operation to render in Christian enterprises that were calling earnestly for volunteers; a good for our own souls possible to some consecration of a day or an hour to that end; a word to speak for truth and right and humanity and God when men's ears were open? What account must we make to-day of these precious hours of the year, its most inestimable opportunities, the real and most momentous connections it had in God's purposes with our life, the ends for which God gave it? Reckon them in our lost opportunities, our forfeited occasions of doing and getting good? "Oh, how often we wish backward!"

Has there been any loss of purity and delicacy and conscientiousness? Have the finer sensibilities and the more delicate and retiring sentiments of our soul been toyed with, wantoned with, handled and sullied, made coarse and common, so that our thoughts and feelings are less select and sensitive, less kept within doors and out of the glare and soot of street exposure. Have we become world-hardened and world-soiled, so that we laugh where we used to blush, and can permit a jest where once a light word gave us a wound? Let us look and get the exact state of the balance here, and put the item in where it belongs.

What have we done with special acts of discipline intended for special effects upon us? We needed humbling, we failed in submission, we were afflicted with chronic discontent, we were fluttering with perpetual levity and vanity, we were deep in the solemnest, gravest, and intensest worldliness. God saw and meant us a special mercy, and sent a chastening and helpful providence, a little sharp lesson in his own heavenly tuition, to show us our need and help us to realize a blessed amendment. How have we received these offers and ministries of help? Did they produce their desired and destined effect, or did we overlook their real intent, disappoint their aim, and lose their most invaluable aid? Set them down, if so, so much to our loss.

Has there been with any of us a loss of hope and trust and good courage for truth and right? Have we been ready to give up the proverb that honesty is the best policy? Have we come to feel that it is vain to contend for righteousness and humanity and justice? Have we been so bereft of confidence in God as almost to doubt whether he was on the side of a manful fight for principle and piety? Have the dark clouds that lie with thunderous blackness on our country's horizon caused us to bate one jot of hope or effort for the incoming of the day when involuntary servitude shall float away among the relics of the grim and iron ages reaching along the past of human history? Do we feel as though expediency, as against right and principle and love, were the doctrine of the hour? For ourselves in our own private personal story has so sable a night hung over us that we doubted whether God could bring the day, almost whether there were any sun that shone anywhere? Has the strain upon faith been too long, too severe, patience drawn out to its last nerve of endurance, and the soul settling into the gloom of hopeless insubmission? This loss of confidence in the great Ruler and Father was a dreadful loss. Is it an item in any soul's experience? If so, let it go in. Give it a place on the balance sheet.

Possibly there has been with some soul a loss of character and moral standing. The hour of temptation came. It found you alone, unaided, forlorn, in deep need. No friendly companion to shield and strengthen you. The whisper of evil was delusive, so plausible, no evil intended, the snare so subtle, the wiles so hidden, the meshes so soft and silken, that you were hopelessly entangled before you dreamed of captivity, and now your soul wrestles with mighty fears, with gloomy memories, with black remorse, with environments of blank ruin that stare at you as with Gorgon face, turning your heart to stone. Oh, sad loss! but always in this life when loss is seen and known, if it be any loss short of the soul itself, there is hope, because there is mercy in God. It is a woful history, an experience such as you never dreamed of writing for yourself; but put it down; it belongs to the record of this year gone. It may be a stepping-stone to great riches, but in itself it is a terrible loss. It must stand now on that side of the account.

There may have been another loss, of which there is always danger, concerning which none of us perhaps can ever know with certainty, — the loss of the soul. I do not mean with some who have entered eternity. I mean with some of us who are to-day living men. If the records of a human life teach anything clearly, it is that that life is full of crises; that on these critical points turn the issues of punishment for the present and the future; that on some one of these critical moments the destiny of the soul is settled, and that frequently before, perhaps long before, that soul enters upon eternal scenes. Thus the wave of some great providence, of some special blessing, or some sharp affliction, or some visit of the Holy Ghost, or some melting urgency of truth, lifts the soul nearer to God and to duty and to a newness of life than ever before. It was the grand swell that was appointed as its hour of greatest hope and opportunity. Unimproved, settling back into the old color and the old track of life, it is by and by seen, — seen perhaps in the hour of dying, seen clearly in the light of eternity, that there and then that soul came the nearest to salvation that it ever came, that never again was the prize of a blessed immortality so within its grasp, so nearly possessed. Every year some such history must be enacted. There are some here who ought, with trembling hand and pale cheek, to write down on the side of their losses, the words "my soul," and put an interrogation point beyond.

Oh, it is a solemn reckoning we are holding! It partakes of the character of the final judgment, only here, blessed be God! for every loss but one there is possible yet an infinite gain that shall well-nigh utterly extinguish it.

With many the year has been full of gain all along. With all of us a year of God's kindly, nourishing, paternal care. Put that down to gain, — four seasons of his prodigal mercies, day and night ministering bounty, seed-time and harvest smiling each in turn as with the radiance of the divine countenance.

There is the gain of so much and so many of life's finished work and tasks. There is the gain of so much service for God and man, the service itself, not its successes, counting as gain for character and reward. There are special lessons of truth and heavenly wisdom which God has taught us, and which we could not barter for a solid orb of gold, — precious secrets of spiritual living that used to be mysteries, and are now a part of our daily magic of overcoming. There are fruits of discipline, in patience and contentment and resignation, and sweet submissiveness and serenity of spirit, worth more than any language can tell or any currency measure. There are new spiritual traits nurtured within us and upon us which we have so long coveted and almost despaired of, and concerning which we now sing with broken heart, — broken in tender joy, — "Oh, to grace how great a debtor!"

There are new views of Bible truths, — God's deductions, rich promises, and positive precepts which clear up many doubts, guide us out of long wandering in weary paths and brighten all our sky as with sunbeams.

There is a vantage ground for future conflicts and victories shown us, in which our feet have become divinely established, and on which we may wait with celestial allies the assaults of the great adversary.

There are sweet daily mercies that have fallen for us every morning as the manna fell for Israel on the face of the desert, and the taste of which was as wafers mixed with honey.

Oh, how these gains foot up! What song of gratitude can fully utter our hearts' recognition of this long column of God's contributions to our growing riches? Even amid sorrows we count still our profits, — friends departing, chairs and chambers left vacant, the earth opening her arms and taking to the rest of her bosom those whom our arms were clasping and would fain have detained; but so God came nearer to our circle than ever before; we felt his blessed presence and comforting; we saw how faith could triumph over nature's fainting, and looking up when the last sigh went outward from fading lips, we saw the heavens opened and caught a glimpse of white-robed spirits entering into joy and rest.

So stand the accounts with us to-day, a monition from the past for the future, a sober arrest for thought and life on this transition point. Yes, pause here yet one moment longer. All our losses — ALL, let us hope — God may blot out now with the gift of his most generous pardon, the overflowing wealth of his favor and love.

Oh, leave no such fearful balance against you, my friends, as those items foot up which we have dwelt upon; drag not such a debt forward into the burdened future. Come to the great Proprietor, that these peculations upon his estate intrusted to you may be graciously and pitifully blotted out, and your way lie onward for all coming labors and ventures with the everlasting gain of his friendship.

XIX.

ALL-SUFFICIENCY OF CHRIST.

FAREWELL SERMON DELIVERED IN PARK STREET CHURCH, FEBRUARY 4, 1866.

. . . BUILT UPON THE FOUNDATION OF THE APOSTLES AND PROPHETS, JESUS CHRIST HIMSELF BEING THE CHIEF CORNER-STONE. — Eph. ii. 20.

THE firmness and security of a building depend not so much upon what we can see of the structure as upon the parts which are mainly hidden and unseen. As we approach from a distance, the pile may look fair and stately, with broad front and lofty walls and crowning turret and tower, and we may be ready to pronounce it massive and strong. But we cannot know whether it be so in truth until we have come nearer, and have examined that lowlier and less visible part upon which the superstructure rests. The strength of the edifice is not in lofty wall or decorated porch or crowning dome, but in the foundation. When all the materials are piled aloft, when the tempest rocks it and the earthquake heaves, it stands only if the foundation be solid and unyielding.

And the foundation, too, is distinguished into parts, both for its honor and its security, its glory and crown. The corner-stones take the chief burden of the superincumbent mass. To them the foundation lines are clamped and joined. In their steadiness the whole is unshaken. Among these, one is "Chief," the Head Stone of the corner, the Key of that compacted strength, of costliest material and most careful workmanship, to whose setting in its place is gathered whatsoever can do it grace and reverence, to whose keeping are confided the treasured memorials which are to be preserved unto coming ages and generations.

The scriptural Church as a whole, and so with each particular church, both as a vital part and as a representative of the whole, is described as a building, a living temple fitly framed together, resting on a certain definite foundation with one chief corner-stone.

That foundation is nothing laid by the hand of man, or found within the compass of man's nature and capacity. It is what God revealed to prophets and apostles, what he gave them to know and to build upon, the truth and the life which they experience and to which they bear witness, themselves as witnesses to the words and works of their Lord. And the Head of the corner is that Stone elect and precious, which the pride of the builders rejected, but on which God has built his Church so firm that "the gates of hell shall not prevail against it." That rock is Christ. In him the foundations meet in unity and strength. In him the whole building is compacted. No forces of nature, not all the powers on earth or beneath, can overturn a structure so founded.

We have, then, from our Scripture this cheering and comforting truth,—the all-sufficiency of Christ for his Church.

There will be in our communion at this time so much that belongs simply to the occasion, to be said, that we must pass briefly and rapidly over points that were worthily dwelt upon with largest treatment.

And I remark, in the first place, that we find enough in Christ for the doctrine of the Church. The Church must have a doctrine. It will live only as it holds living truth. Its conquests are victories over minds. It gains and holds its subjects not by the terrors and constraints of power, the sword in one hand, the keys of destiny here and hereafter in the other. It has to persuade men, to secure the convictions of their souls, to show them something to believe, on which the longing and inquiring heart can rest. And it brings forth this grand compendium of its teaching, — "God manifest in the flesh, justified in the spirit, seen of angels, preached unto the Gentiles, believed on in the world, received up into glory." Here are height and length and breadth and depth. "It is a broad land of wealth unknown." There is no narrowness here to disappoint and fret the exploring mind. There are background and foreground to this truth. Touch it at whatever point, come upon it in whatever aspect, and you are led off either way into the Infinite. It is not a little round of human working, or of earthly moralities in which the preacher of this doctrine treads. He need not be compassionated of the reformers and the philosophers because he is shut up to the doctrine of Christ. If he determine not to know anything, as a religious teacher, but Jesus Christ and him crucified, he is no captive in a cell that denies him range of feet and thought. The universe of

God's nature, God's government, and God's providence, the eternity of God's purposes, the everlasting principles of justice and right compacted in law, the wonders of redemptive mercy and vicarious love, the marshalling of human histories in all their annals of blood and crime and heroic achievement, their dark shades and their light shades, their progressive civilizations, their painful experiments, their sciences and philosophies and acts as tributary to the reign of Christ, — this is the limitless field, the sphere without walls or cope, in which the preacher of Christ and his salvation ranges at will. Here is enough to stimulate the mind, to gird every power for strenuous wrestling, to feed it, to expand it, to hold it in awe, and to satisfy it that God has worthily broken silence to make a revelation of his will vocal to the race.

Here, again, in the doctrine of Christ is sufficient for the attraction of those outside the Church. God loving his human children astray and lost, guilty and condemned, and coming among them in the incarnation, moved by that great love to take their sicknesses, sorrows, and sins upon him, and through his sacrificial death in the flesh to reconcile them unto himself and restore them to the heirship of heaven and immortality, is a story men will stop to hear. There is an earnest element under all the light frivolities of human consciousness. There is a deep voice in the heart to whose pleading nothing less than the atonement wrought by the Lamb of God can make answer. There are dark solitudes of human experience in which each man walks alone repeating after the false disciple, that traitor Judas, "I HAVE

SINNED." It does not meet such an experience to call to this man to listen to a song, all whose strains are borrowed from nature's minstrelsy, the notes of birds, the chant of streams, the "deep, profound, eternal bass" of oceans; or to lead him up before some exquisite picture in which the loveliness of human nature is painted; or to exhort him in pleasant words to be just and true and gentle as a man and a brother among his fellow-men. This treatment does not go deep enough, — I mean deep enough powerfully to attract and hold the interest of men. But this great tragedy of the cross has power in it. It comes to deal in earnest with earnest matters. It is full of dramatic life and force. It does not attempt the adjustment of sinful man's relation to a holy God with smooth words and surface manipulations. It goes to the root of the difficulty. It cuts through the fair bloom of the surface to the hidden diseased core. It is downright radical, and thorough in its treatment of human hopes and fears. Every voice from this doctrine commands attention. If sick men or wounded men call in a physician or surgeon, they want to be healed. They want thorough, effectual treatment. Pleasant drinks and opiates are not an equivalent for health and soundness. And men's religious wants are not met, their souls are not at rest, they are not satisfied with hearing, till they hear of a slain Lamb that taketh away the sins of the world. It is found that an earnest gospel gathers men to its proclamation. The words of Christ are verified, "I, if I be lifted up, lifted on the cross, lifted in human teaching as the object of attraction before the world, will draw all men unto me. The pulpit that preaches Christ crucified need not run out into literature, or social life, or current providences, or the sweep of reform movements, or advertise quaint and whimsical themes, to supplement the charm of that gospel. The dying of Jesus for human salvation touches the world's heart. Publish these glad tidings, and the feet of men run together to catch that message.

Again, Christ is sufficient for the pastoral care of his Church. He shepherdizes each flock and guards every fold of his people. He is the good Shepherd, ever faithful, constant, and vigilant, and giveth his life for the sheep. He leads them out into green pastures and beside still waters. He taketh the lambs in his arms and carrieth them in his bosom. It is he who appoints under shepherds to go in and out with the flock, to guide and feed and defend them. But he does not himself retire. The under shepherds are responsible to him. He furnishes and strengthens them for their calling. They are a living bond between him and the souls for whom they watch. They hold their office from him. They derive all their authority from him. They have so much authority as his spirit and his truth dwelling in them and communicated through them confer upon them. It is his voice, and not theirs, which the sheep are to hear from their lips. If they are unfaithful, he does not cease to care for the flock whom they mislead or neglect. If they die or remove, he resumes all their functions. The flock is not left shepherdless. Forever he leads them and feeds them and keeps them. He never changes his place.

He never breaks the tie that binds him to them. Loving once, he loves unto the end. They are never bereaved of him. Whoever goes, he remains. Whatever post is vacant, whatever office work resigned, he may always be found. To all that call upon him he is ever near.

Is not this sufficient for the comfort of believers? It is natural that they should look for the words of Christ and the consolations of Christ to those whom Christ has set over them for this very ministry; that they should feel in their times of doubt, of sickness and pain, of sorrow and anguish, that they must have this representative of Christ to stand by their side, to bend above the pillow, to bow low with their prostrate forms and breathe the salutations of Jesus. And it is natural that they should feel that if this messenger of their Lord be not their helper in such hours of trial, their burdens will weigh heavily, and their hearts seek relief in vain. Who will come to their chamber when the strong fever is on them and lay on their brow a gentle touch, as though his hand had brought from Jesus' palm some virtue of soothing? Who will meet the look of their upturned eye searching for some promise that invites the unworthy to be at peace, and answer it as though Jesus replied, "I do not condemn thee, go and sin no more"? Who will have the first burdened confession of the penitent wishing to be led to the hand that distributes pardons? Who will open tender arms for their babes at the font of baptism? Who will bless the bridal hour when their sons and daughters stand at the altar of wedded love? Who will listen to the ever varying tale of their personal and domestic history, now with smiles and now with tears, with looks that give and words that speak love and sympathy in all that can befall them as pilgrims through earth? Who will hold their hand and repeat words of promise and strength and pleasant voices out of heaven when their heads droop in the last faintness and the scenes of time grow dim to their failing sight?

He whom they have known and loved so well and chosen for all these sweet and sacred offices may have gone to be a dweller with another people, and will fill no more any of these wonted relations to their life. Yes, but Christ abides. He is sufficient for all these wants of the heart, these vicissitudes of an earthly experience. He comes to the solitary mourner, whispering, "I will never leave thee nor forsake thee." He stretches out his arms toward the babes of the nursery and pleads, "Suffer little children, and forbid them not to come unto me." He calls all the weary and heavy-laden to his presence to find rest at his feet. If there be no human face bending above the sick, the sad, the fearful, the self-condemned, will they not look with clearer eye and straighter glance into the face of Jesus? Is there any sting of bitterness he cannot remove, any sorrow he cannot comfort, any burden he cannot lighten, any ministry of strength and growth and fruitfulness he cannot fulfil? Is he not sufficient for all the pastoral care of his people? Will not that even be a happy hour to many of them when they cease from communion with his messenger and come nearer to himself, with neither man nor angel between?

And if our thought were not of individuals and families, but of the whole brotherhood, in all that concerns their prosperity; if any of you ask, with troubled foreboding, what will be the future of this church and people; who will throng its porches and fill its interior spaces; who will adhere to it now and who will desert it; who will break unto us the bread of life and draw water for us from the wells of salvation; who will help us to meet with just sentiment, earnest purpose, and vigorous action the great practical living questions of the day, to which the gospel is to be applied, and the Christian life to be adjusted; whose hand will lift our banner and carry it in the fore front of the host of God in their onset upon the kingdom of darkness and of evil, — oh, let every heart rest on the solid rock of this assurance, Christ is sufficient for all this need of coming days; he will not see his flock perish of hunger or thirst; he will not leave them defenceless in the presence of ravening wolves; the honor of his name is bound up with the honor of yours; both are inscribed together on the folds of the flag, and he will not suffer that banner to trail in dust and shame. He loves this church. He will take care of its future. It is built on him. It cannot be overturned. Let none of you say or think or dream that its prosperity has culminated, its power to bless the world has passed the meridian, for you do thus dishonor the "strength of Israel," and show that you confide more in man's weaknesses than in almighty love and grace.

Christ is sufficient for his Church as a bond of union among its members. For a deep and abiding harmony in Christian fellowship there must be an overcoming of the natural selfish tempers of the heart. Each must be able to look on the other, and through whatever variety of feature and of expression, see a likeness that speaks of brother's blood, and publishes the fact of a common family tie, a household unity. This common likeness must be, more or less distinct, — a likeness unto Christ. Only in partaking of the spirit of Christ can the wilfulness and wantonness of our corrupt natures be so corrected as to blend in self-forgetful amity. To keep Christ's ordinances, to obey his commands, to commemorate his life and death, to help one another grow by transformation unto his image, and to bring strangers to love and serve him as his children and friends, is the ideal of Christian association under Church covenants. Of such a union Christ is at once the object and the strength.

Is it not in him, my brethren, that you are one? Is not he the crystallizing centre of this household of ours? Is it not his body and blood that have made the sweetness of our sacramental feasts? Is it not his presence that has made our place of weekly prayer as the vestibule of heaven? Is it not his truth that has held you to its Sabbath utterance in these thronged aisles? Is he not the head and heart and soul of which we are the body and members visible? Has your fellowship been merely in the strength of your attachment to a man? Will you say this with your lips and publish it as your withdrawing feet pass outward from this family home? Will you let the world discover that this is the seal of a Christian covenant? Will you set up a man as rival of Christ, and put the human above the divine as a bond of the fellowship of believers? If this is our household relationship, the tie has not been severed any too soon. It had better never have been formed. If this be all, it is no matter how quickly we fall apart as a rope of sand, nor how widely we scatter to be henceforth indistinguishable on all the surface of the earth and unknown in heaven.

But it is not so. It is in the love of Christ and in the service of Christ you have been joined. It is in the likeness of Christ you see eye to eye. This bond you will not dishonor. This bond is indestructible. While this remains first in your regard, you cannot grow cold toward one another or wish to part. Proclaim it by word and deed that you are one in no temporary surface agreement, no passing touch and clasp of a human hand, but one forever and indissolubly in Christ.

As I think of my personal relations to you, and of the many years in which we have walked together, in the fellowship of the gospel "from the first day until now," there is one expression of the heart of Paul toward his brethren of Philippi, which perpetually recurs to me: "I thank my God upon every remembrance of you." Happy church concerning which the chief apostle could bear such a testimony! How must that line have been read and heard as they came together at the tidings that Paul had written to them out of his captivity at Rome! Happy Paul who could so write, not in the mere forms of hollow courtesy, but as the honest voice of his truth-loving soul! In all his past with those beloved brethren in whatsoever demonstration of theirs toward him, there was no "root of bitterness," nothing that rankled, nothing to be forgiven or forgotten; "every remembrance" was so sweet and pleasant to him as to be a matter of joyful thanksgiving to God.

It is my exceeding felicity that I can borrow this witness of the apostle and give it public utterance to-day, without qualification or reserve concerning this beloved church and people. If there were anything in all your treatment of me that called for the charity of oblivion, I hope I should be equal to such generosity. But I find here no occasion for the grace of magnanimity.

There is no incompatibility of any sort that makes it needful that we should part. It seems to me that we could dwell together in unity and harmony through time and eternity. If there are any of you who cannot echo this sentiment, you have left me in utter ignorance of such dissent.

It is a voice from across the continent that persuades my reluctant feet away from you, the voice of God in the shout of a new-rising empire beyond the mountains and on the Pacific coast.

Our Republic is to be continental. Our eastern wall and our western are to be washed by Atlantic and Pacific waves. There must be no risk, which we can avert, of such a strain across the ridge of the Rocky Mountains that the country shall by its own weight break and fall apart. We must secure the bridal of that occidental realm with our own by bonds that cannot be riven. Lives that are deep-rooted here must stretch out their pendant boughs and take root there, and make and keep the nation one by clasping fibres which cannot wither or die.

Our American Zion must be continental also. We can hold no inch for nationality's sake which we would not hold more eagerly for Christ. Wherever the Old Flag goes and receives fealty, there must the banner of the cross be planted too. We cannot content ourselves with a Christian civilization at the East, and see with unconcern all its sweet charities and gentle decencies struggling with barbarism on those new shores. The hunt for gold pushed fiercely forward by rough and adventurous men, carrying with them no homes, no society, no Sabbath, no civil order, no code of law, and making that rude materialism their idolatry, of course has tended to barbarism. There was need of a vigilance committee, there was need of purer and cleaner elements of civil and social life, there was need of the watch-towers of religion, and clear-voiced prophets to proclaim from their summits the divineness of government and justice, and all the softening and restraining influences of a gospel of peace and love. There was need that a Sabbath should be carried over, and that the lawlessness of wild spirits flushed with gold and strong drink, and making of that day a carnival of greed and rioting, should hear its calm, holy voices, and be led back from their frenzy to decency and sobriety.

There has been, in such reforming and refining influences, great and good progress. But the struggle is still going on. "Come over and help!" is the cry on every Western breeze. There is abundance of energy there, acuteness, daring, and resolute force. But the sweeter and gentler graces of life are crowded in such rude contact quite into the background. They must be reinforced and held in countenance and made all-penetrating and pervasive by the entering in of a more demonstrative Christian culture until the whole lump of this vigorous society is leavened. Men who carry that culture with them, who have it as the atmosphere of their homes, and the breath of their own life, who can stand up amid all deteriorating and roughening influences without being dragged down by them, and lift other men to their fairer level, — men who will go in with the charm of refined Christian households, and the sweet contagion of a godly and gentle life, as well as with the messages of an elevating and sanctifying gospel, are yet needed, — oh, in what numbers! — to enter into this unfinished strife and help goodness and purity and charity to their full triumphs.

There is power there, alert and girded, ambitious of large success and great achievements, — power unmatched, perhaps, in sharpness of intellect, boldness of will, and keen ambition in any other community of our land, young or old; but as to the work it shall accomplish, the institutions it shall build, the future of which it shall be the architect, not so certain as it would be and ought to be either of its direction or inspiration.

The great tides of strong life surge to and fro waiting the orbed influences of heaven, ready enough to follow any masterful leadership, though it head toward error and evil. How readily those tides, now so easily turned, might gather a motion and momentum which the reforming work of years could not check, and the happy future of that new land be postponed for half a century of hard and costly reformation!

Now a great multitude of voices there, full, clear, and earnest, are asking, "What next?" in their march toward the inheritance of coming days. Who shall stand among them to answer such questions and to lift an index hand, kept parallel with the divine counsels, and point forward?

How shall the longing be met on that distant shore that turns ever back to this, giving it, as tidings come from it, as steamers sail for it, as the heart revisits it amid the business of the day and the dreams of the night, no geographical name, but only that one, dear, all-comprehending word, "Home"? Who will carry New England out thither, import it into the midst of them, its honest Yankee faces, its holy chimes of Sunday morning, its law-abiding habits, its plea for order and organic growths, its soft light of evenings at the fireside, and the gentle ministries of wives and children crossing inward and outward the sunny threshold of domestic life?

Who will join to the breadth of all this outflowing Christian nurture the divine passion for saving souls, and go down into all dark and slimy depths to bring up and polish these living gems for the diadem of our Lord? There are churches of Christ already there, and many an earnest and true ambassador of the Master setting forth his kingly claims. But these fortresses of truth and salvation are lonely and distant one from another. They do not stand so thickly, as here at home, that hill-top can call to hill-top, and vale answer back to vale. They are few, and the field is broad and the work mighty, and the pressure great, and fateful decisions imminent.

It is one of these burdened churches that has been pleading with you and with me for this year past, and we could not choose but hear its voice. It did not seem at first as though that voice ought to prevail with us. And it sought many another audience, and plead with many another representative of New England life and Christianity. But it searched and plead in vain. And out yonder the great issues that hold all our hopes for Christ, country, and humanity on that deep western border were swiftly forming and ripening, and the solicitudes of men who carried these great spiritual burdens on their souls were ever more and more weighty and oppressive. Could no one be found to man this particular post and make it strong in the eventful conflict? And when that voice, all the more importunate because none would listen to it, fell again upon my ear, calling in the name of Christ and the future of Christian America, "Come!" it seemed to me that I heard in it diviner accents than before, and that its counterpart called to me out of heaven, "Go!"

Yes, it were easy to go if there were no detaining bands. As I set my face toward the sunset, the ties of the present tug at me, the memories of the past come back upon me, — ties sweet and strong, memories tender, pleasant, priceless.

"I thank my God upon every remembrance of you."

I remember your first welcome to me here when I had the grief of that original parting in my soul as I was torn from my first love, and a great doubt whether I had followed a divine leading in coming weak and young to this ancient and honored church, to be its banner-bearer in coming years. Ah, many of those who shared in that welcome are not, for God has taken them. I see in the densest crowd their vacant places. I look wistfully for their absent faces, my early friends and helpers. I miss the touch of their hands and the greetings of their warm words. But some of you remain of those whom I first looked upon here as my people, companions, and lovers of many years; whose faces have never been turned away from me; whose homes and whose hearts have always been open to me; who have borne with me so long and yet have not wearied of me; to whom I have looked for cheer and help and strength, and never looked in vain. Your remembrance—remembrance of the living and of the dead—I have on my heart to-day, both for tenderness and gratitude.

I recall our early hopes and fears as we began our work of serving the kingdom of Christ in building up this church, and all our later efforts and burdens in the prosecution of that work unto the present time. How much better has God been to us as a co-worker and rewarder than our expectations or our faith! How often has he visited us with the refreshing influences of his quickening and reviving Spirit! Scarce a season has passed that we have not enjoyed something of such a visitation. Scarce a communion Sabbath has come and gone without adding some to our fellowship. In all, nine hundred and fifteen have been joined to us since our fellowship in these labors and cares commenced, of whom four hundred and fourteen were newly gathered from the world. What glad, burdened, tearful, rejoicing, intense days we have lived through those harvest times! How pleasant to remember them now and to lay up their memories for the refreshing of our immortality! This church has believed in revivals, has prayed for revivals, has labored for revivals, and refused to be comforted unless revivals came. I do not mean that is singular among our churches in this respect. It would have been singular had it repudiated such pentecosts. Be, still and ever, true to this past! But seek to have the home work always deep and thorough; to have every heart in the church broken and contrite, and newly baptized with the comfort and power of the Holy Ghost. We may have restricted the fruitfulness of our harvest days by being eager to run out upon demonstrative labor, to subsidize all agencies and activities in forward movements, before the burden of our own sinfulness and the burden of souls had brought ourselves low enough into the dust of humility and penitence. Set a watch here for coming days. Be not less active, but strive for a deeper personal experience of the condemning and saving truths of the gospel in your own souls as your best and indispensable preparation for the rescue of other souls. There is no rebuke or reproach in this counsel. Our summers of grace are a precious part of my thankful heritage out of the past.

I look here upon many now in the bloom of youth, who were laid in my arms as a parent's offering to God in that rite which seals his covenant with believers and their seed. The seal was affixed long ago; the years have gone by, each testifying to God's faithfulness, each calling upon you to take the vows of that covenant upon your own willing heart and consecrate yourselves to be the Lord's.

No other and later pastor can ever have such right as I have to ask you whether you have truly entered into that covenant relation with God, and are walking with him in love, reverence, and obedience every day, seeking unto him, serving him, and kept by him along every youthful path? Is it so? When shall it be so? I am a witness for Christ, my babes of years ago. You belong to him. Give him his own.

I see those whom I have joined at the bridal altar. There is more soberness, but not less peace, upon your faces than on those bright evenings gone, when of twain you were made one. I have a grateful remembrance of being so associated with your domestic history and joys. It is, I think, always my prayer in such official duty that the new home may be a Christian home, that the family altar may be built in it even on the bridal eve, and that morning and evening incense may be kindled thereon daily. I may question you, therefore, intimately and tenderly, as none other might in my place, whether the voice of household prayer and praise is indeed heard in your dwelling? Oh, build the altar, if it be not built! If it have been built, keep its sacrifice ever burning.

I search here amid the crowd for those who are so often overshadowed in the home and in the Sabbath congregation by full-grown adult life, the little ones of our families. It has always seemed to me that that were a most neglectful and incomplete shepherd care that should forget the lambs of the flock, and most unlike the heart of Christ. I have felt that you had a right to share in the pastoral ministrations, not only as they sought you within the household circle, or joined themselves to the conduct of the Sabbath-school, but as they uttered the messages of Jesus from the pulpit on the Lord's day, I have had no more inspiring or rewarding audiences than when your earnest eyes and bright faces have been turned toward me in the house of God, to listen to his word. And in how many friendly and festive scenes have we mingled, when we were all young together, our faces putting off their gravity, our feet their staid decorum, light hearts sitting visibly on smiling lips, and every harp string of our souls swept by the fingers of joy! Oh, my lambs, I have gathered you in my arms, I have carried you on my heart, I stretch my arms out for you still! My heart shall never lay off that pleasant burden. I shall remember you and write to you from afar. But you must be Jesus' lambs as well, more than you are mine. His arms are always stretched out to receive you. His heart is longing for you. Make him your Shepherd, his embrace your safe and happy fold.

Some of you here to-day — I might count you perhaps by hundreds — are my spiritual children. I saw your first tear of penitence fall, heard your first burdened inquiry, "What shall I do to be saved?" kneeled with you in your first prayer of consecration, and caught the earliest sweetness of your new song of praise. There is a tie between us that can never be sundered. Eternity will only hallow and strengthen it. That connection with your present and your immortal future I would not part with at any price earth could offer. I can never be robbed of it. None that come after me can take it from me. I would not stand, you would not let me stand, between you and Jesus. If I led you right, I led you to him. He must be nearest and dearest. He must increase, and I must decrease. But I shall stand with you at his side here and now, yonder and hereafter, and say to him, "I and the children thou hast given me." Oh that I could add to these the names of some not yet written here on the scroll of the disciplehood! My dear friends whom I have so often invited to come to Christ, let me call you once more to make him your Saviour and portion. How have I failed of commending him to your love and trust? There is no earthly favor for myself which you would suffer me to ask of you in vain. But when I plead for Jesus, I cannot win you. Must that close the record of my ministry in its effect upon you? Is our parting of to-day ominous of an eternal separation? Shall we meet but once more, perhaps, before the great white throne, and then pass from each other's presence forever? I linger yet a moment even as I grasp your hand in parting to draw you toward that long-waiting divine Friend, who is ready to enter into everlasting covenant with you. This day of our weeping together would be to me the happiest of all these years, if I might have now the assurance that I have not preached Christ to you in vain.

Pleasant among the thankful remembrances of this hour are the kindnesses, I have received from you all, through these seventeen years. It would be a long story and many pages that should recite them every one. It would count up every smiling salutation, every hearty hand-shake, every token simple and costly of love and remembrance, sympathy with me and mine in the times of trial, tender vigils with my sick, tears that seemed to fall as warm and fast as my own over my beloved dead, care for my bodily health and comfort, long leaves of absence when I was weary, permission to visit the "Summer Isles," to go abroad amid Old World wonders, even to the sacred hills trod once by the feet of the Lord, the city he loved, the stream in whose margin he and John stood together for his baptism, and the generous providence that has kept my board spread and my house bright and warm through all these summers and winters until now. To bring back this generous past of your ministry to me and those dearer to me than life would be to live over again day by day the experience which has made each season of the past, since that wintry day that plighted our vows, a festival of your love and care.

I have written ineffaceably on the record of my heart your ready and fervent response when the dark days of our country's trial came, when many minds were perplexed and many souls fearful, and some were faltering and lukewarm; and the call was sounded here for all loyal hearts to be true and steadfast, and for our young men to go forth armed to the defence of the capital and the flag. The young men stood up. They buckled on the sword. They took hold of the rifle. Old men blessed them. Fathers and mothers said "Go! we have nothing dearer we can give." Fond sisters gave both tearfully and cheerfully the parting kiss. Young wives unclasped their arms from about the necks of young husbands. And they went forth, our fairest, our noblest, our bravest.

And you who went not remained to pray (there were none but loyal prayers here), remained to give your nimblest industry to the soldier's comfort, to forward all bountiful supplies for the sick and the wounded and the prisoner; you lent your pastor for a campaign of nine months; you kept good courage and unfaltering loyalty and a spirit of large self-sacrifice and triumphant hope to the last. And the young men, our elect hundred, have come back to share the ovations of a rescued and grateful country, bringing with them many and honorable scars, shattered limbs, and dismembered frames, leaving behind many a sod stained with the best blood in their veins, — leaving behind, alas, some of their gallant comrades whose dust sleeps in safety and honor beneath the victorious flag, whose names are written in our hearts and on our country's long scroll of heroes, — names which no distant and coming generation on our soil will willingly let die. Oh, had you been recreant in this great crisis of our nation and of humanity's long struggle, you and I should have parted long ere this. But I thank God that the record of this church for loyalty, patriotism, and valor at home and in the high places of the field is without blot or stain.

Our co-working here in this vineyard of the Lord will cease from to-day. The official tie is severed. But that is all. Every other bond holds. One who goes out from the home of his kindred to far-off lands does not cease, because of such distance, from the household relation. He is a son, a brother, a kinsman, just as truly and with just as near a tie of blood and love as before. Nothing shall dismiss us from one another's confidence, affection, and memory. When you think of me or hear of me on that other shore of our common country, let your hearts answer, He is ours. And forever, no matter how time or distance or other and new relations may protest, I shall call you mine. Such mutual ownership has no statute of limitation. It never expires.

This is no plea against what you owe to my successor in office. Your hearts are large enough to hold us both. He is on his way to you. God has already chosen him for you. Pray for him. Let every unseen step of his toward this place be paved by your intercessions. Withhold no cordiality of welcome from him. Say not, one of you in the deepest solitude of your soul, I will never love him as I have loved. Transfer all your kindness and fealty. He may not be the choice of you all. Be generous and forbearing, in such case, and let your majority draw after it and carry with it unanimity.

Be to him all that you have been to me. He cannot wish for more. You could not render more.

Sustain him as you have sustained the ministry that yields this place back to you to-day. Gather here as you have gathered on the Sabbath-day whether the sun shone or the storm raged. Go to your meeting for prayer. Oh, keep that room below thronged with your praying hearts, vocal with your songs of Christian communion. "It is your life," the life of your individual piety, the life of this church as a power for good. Remember the concert eve. Be true to Christ in his longing for the outlying nations. Keep the missionary flame burning bright on these altars and in your souls evermore.

Welcome the calls, the incessant calls, of a world-wide charity. I have few pleasanter recollections than those which are associated with the almost weekly summons to you from this pulpit to contribute of your substance to relieve the wants of men's bodies and souls. I presume I have often been urgent and importunate in such appeals. My memories of them may possibly be pleasanter than yours. But I do not believe you would recall one such appeal and put the seal of silence upon it. I do not believe you regret one offering which you have laid, under such stress, at the feet of your Lord. Be as you have been, an open-handed church, eyes to the blind, feet to the lame, a mother to the orphan, causing the widow's heart to sing for joy, and gathering the grateful memorials of the ends of the earth.

Cling together. Oh, let none fall out of the ranks now, unless by order of the Commander-in-Chief. Do you know what one word is the deepest reproach and the guiltiest shame a soldier can wear on the eve of battle? Will any of you take upon you, when the pinch comes to this church, the name of "Deserters"? Lock arms and stand firm. Are you friends for bright days and not for dark days? They are dark days that try the soul and show what our friendships are. Stand by one another till another hand lift the banner at your head and bear it forward.

Give me your blessing and your prayers! You will not say nay to that request. But if you say yes, you must do the same for that church and people to whom I go. How am I to be blessed if they are not blessed in me?

You must love them and pray for them. Have they forfeited their claim to this because their need is greater than yours? There is no other church in the land to which you will stand in so tender a relation. Take them on your hearts from this day and bear them perpetually before God for his richest favor, and such praying will be doubly blest, the suppliant and the subject sitting together beneath heaven's wide-open window.

Every step forward is into the unknown. God may accept me that it is in my heart to build for him on that Western shore. But he may not let me build. The Atlantic waves are first to be crossed. I may never cross them. The Pacific crests lift themselves between. Their white interdict may bar my way. Instead of that distant Golden Gate, my feet may pause earlier at the gate of pearl. Danger, disappointment, sickness, death, these may be the near heritage to which I seem in such haste to be gone. Say not in such issue, "He would have done well to have stayed." That would not thus be made certain. The willing mind is what God accepts. The results that lie beyond make no proper part of his estimate, or of ours, of the value of obedience.

And so we take leave of one another. It does not seem real to me yet. Is this my last Sabbath with you? Am I preaching my last sermon here? When another Sabbath dawns, will its rising sun come up for me out of the sea, and its setting sun go down into the sea? And are none of my Sabbaths any more to lead my feet hither? And yet it will be a short leave. God may permit us some greetings again by the way. He will soon bring us together never to part.

I leave with you the labors of seventeen years, still, if God will, to bear fruit among you. I leave my manifold imperfections and frailties to your charity, that they may be forgiven. I leave for your occasional watch one little grave in the shades of Auburn, where my first-born sleeps. I leave my memory to be cherished and guarded by you, if you will accept the trust. I leave my love, my thanks, my prayers. . My feet may go and bear my body forth, but I leave my heart behind.

www.ingramcontent.com/pod-product-compliance
Lightning Source LLC
Chambersburg PA
CBHW022043230426
43672CB00008B/1055